PIANO / VOCAL / GUITAR

THE BEST FOLK/POP SONGS EVER

ISBN 978-1-4950-0259-5

HAL•LEONARD®
CORPORATION
7777 W. BLUEMOUND RD. P.O. BOX 13819 MILWAUKEE, WI 53213

Visit Hal Leonard Online at
www.halleonard.com

ABRAHAM, MARTIN AND JOHN

Words and Music by
RICHARD HOLLER

peo - ple, but it seems the good die young. _ But I just looked a -

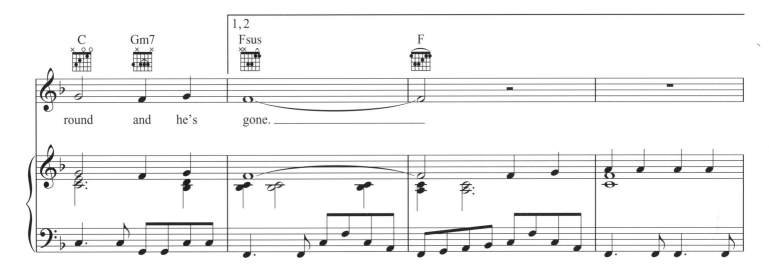

1, 2

round and he's gone. _____

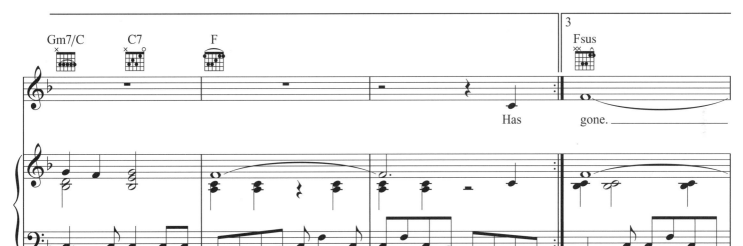

3

Has gone. _____

Did - n't you love ___ the things they ___

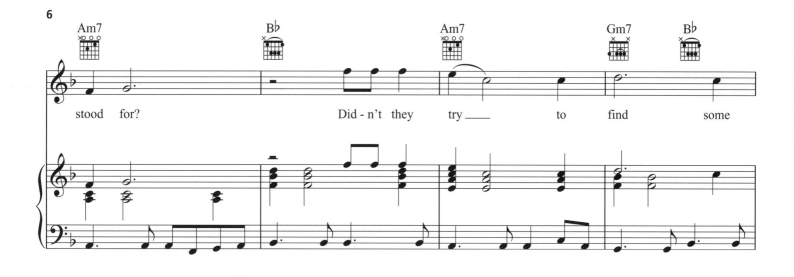

stood for? Did - n't they try ____ to find some

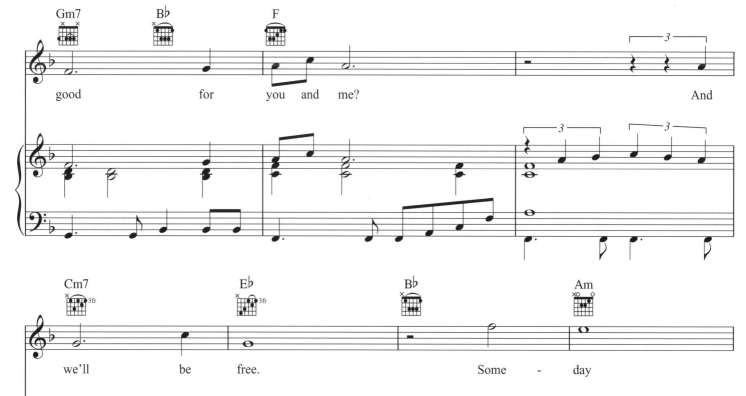

good for you and me? And

we'll be free. Some - day

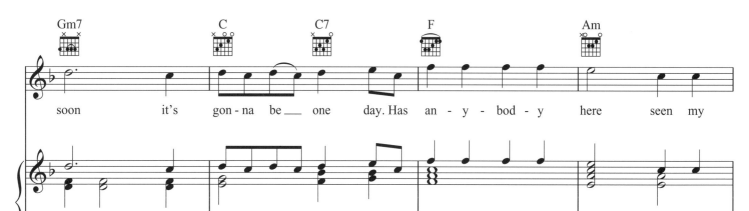

soon it's gon - na be ____ one day. Has an - y - bod - y here seen my

old friend Bob-by? Can you tell me where he's

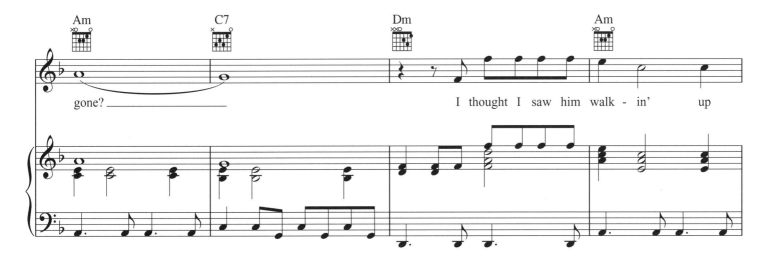

gone? _____ I thought I saw him walk-in' up

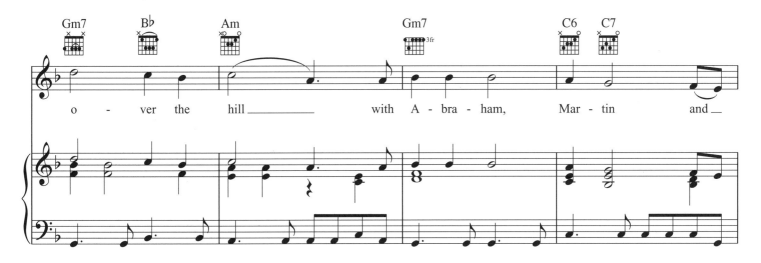

o - ver the hill _____ with A - bra - ham, Mar - tin and _

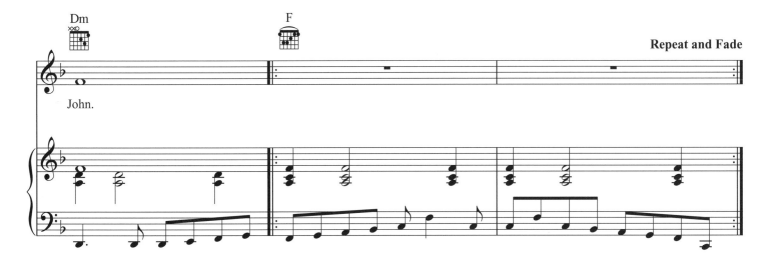

Repeat and Fade

John.

AFTERNOON DELIGHT

Words and Music by
BILL DANOFF

In a moderately slow Country 2

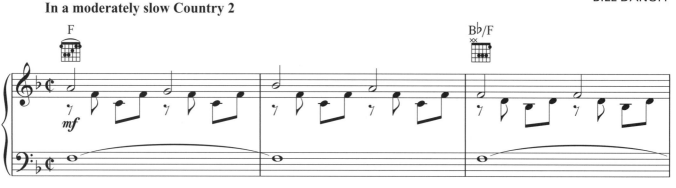

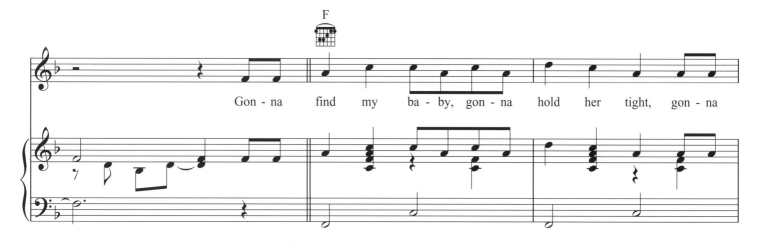

Gon - na find my ba - by, gon - na hold her tight, gon - na

grab some af - ter - noon _____ de - light. _____ My mot - to's al - ways been "When it's

right, it's right." Why wait un - til the mid - dle of a cold, dark night

when ev - 'ry - thing's a lit - tle clear - er in the light of day _____

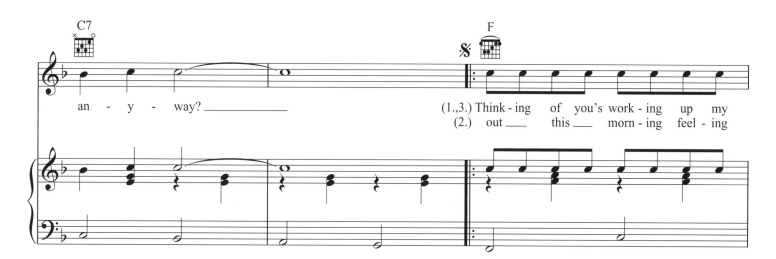

_____ and _____ we know the night is al - ways gon - na be here

an - y - way? _____ (1.,3.) Think - ing of you's work - ing up my
(2.) out ___ this ___ morn - ing feel - ing

ap - pe - tite, look - ing for - ward to a lit - tle af - ter - noon de - light. _ Rub - bing
so po - lite, I al - ways thought a fish could not be caught who did - n't bite. _ But you

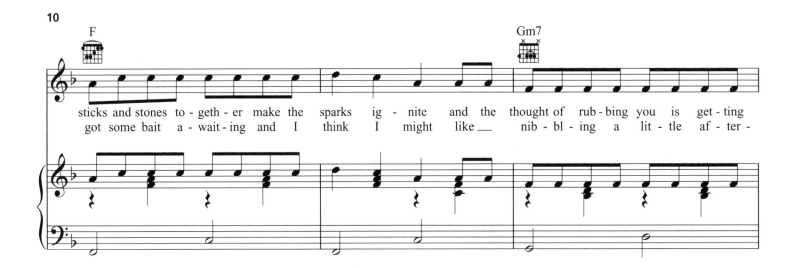

sticks and stones to-geth-er make the sparks ig - nite and the thought of rub-bing you is get - ting
got some bait a-wait-ing and I think I might like ___ nib-bl-ing a lit - tle af - ter -

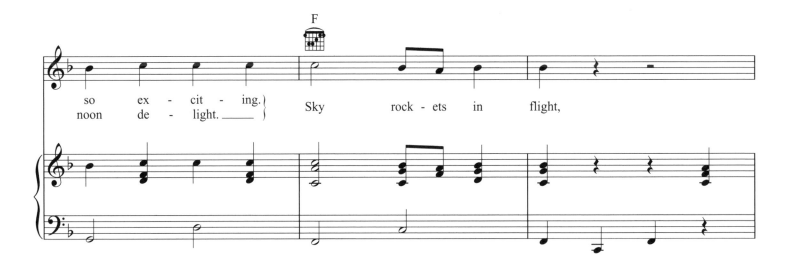

so ex - cit - ing.⎱ Sky rock-ets in flight,
noon de - light. ___ ⎰

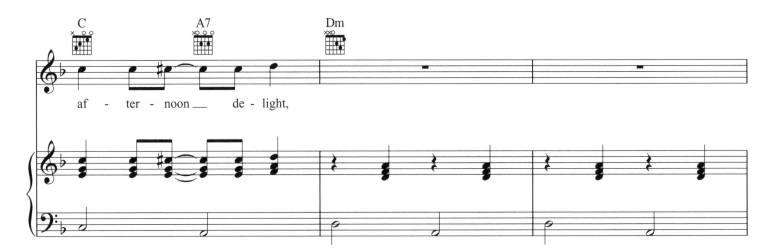

af - ter - noon ___ de - light,

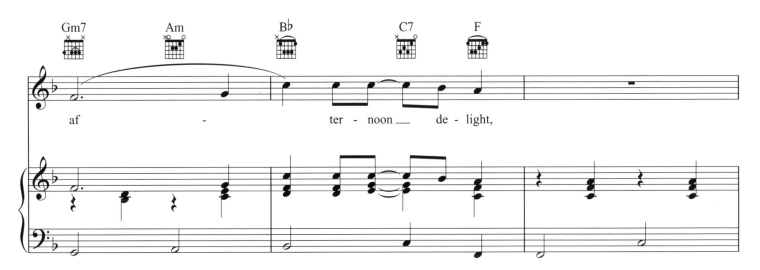

af - ter - noon ___ de - light,

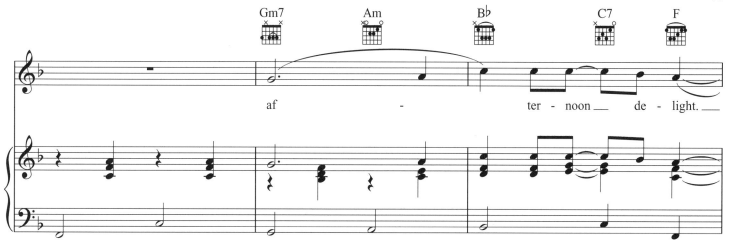

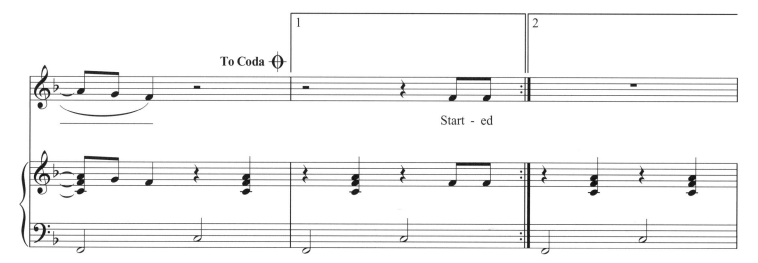

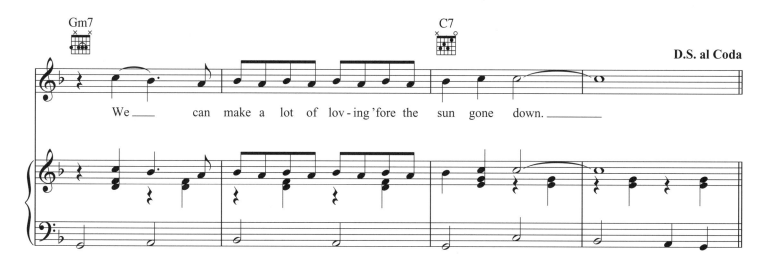

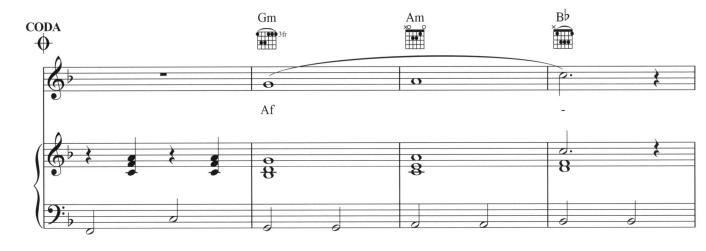

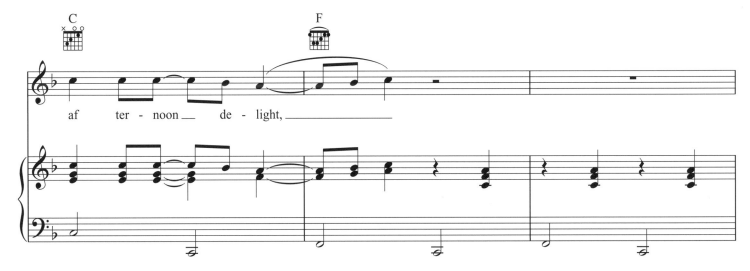

BOTH SIDES NOW

Words and Music by
JONI MITCHELL

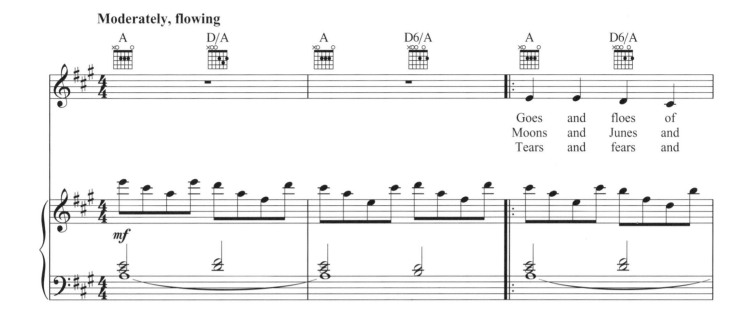

Moderately, flowing

Goes and floes of
Moons and Junes and
Tears and fears and

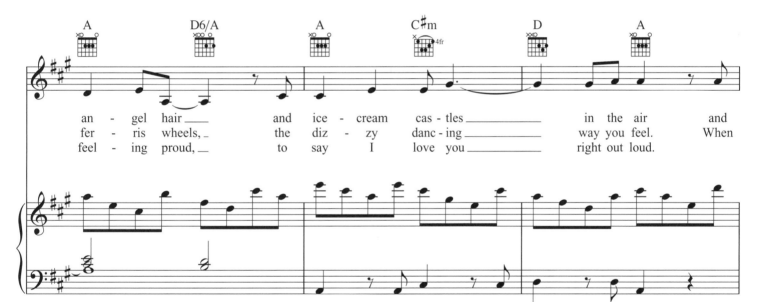

an - gel hair ___ and ice - cream cas - tles ___ in the air and
fer - ris wheels, _ the diz - zy danc - ing ___ way you feel. When
feel - ing proud, _ to say I love you ___ right out loud.

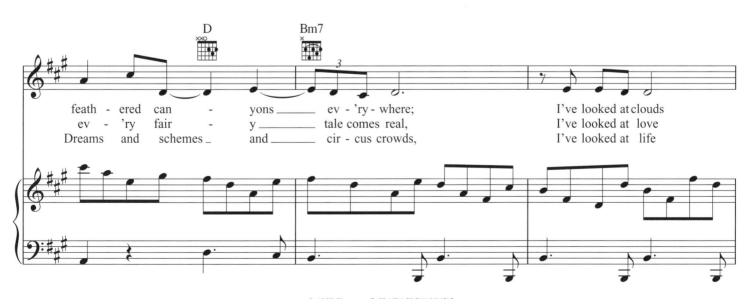

feath - ered can - yons ___ ev - 'ry - where; I've looked at clouds
ev - 'ry fair - y ___ tale comes real, I've looked at love
Dreams and schemes _ and ___ cir - cus crowds, I've looked at life

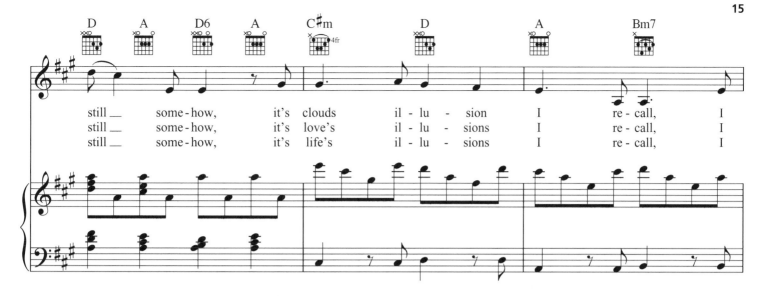

still ___ some-how, it's clouds il - lu - sion I re - call, I
still ___ some-how, it's love's il - lu - sions I re - call, I
still ___ some-how, it's life's il - lu - sions I re - call, I

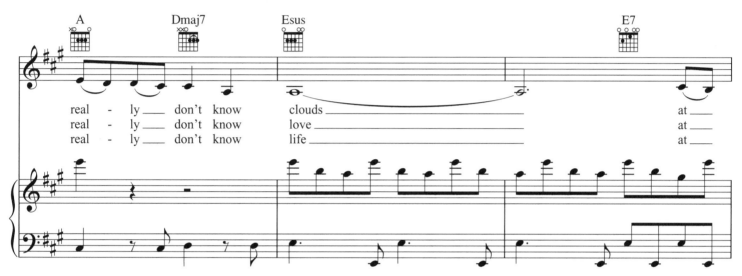

real - ly ___ don't know clouds _____ at ___
real - ly ___ don't know love _____ at ___
real - ly ___ don't know life _____ at ___

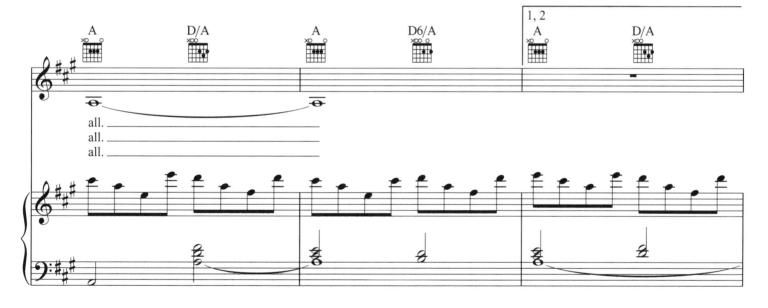

all. _____
all. _____
all. _____

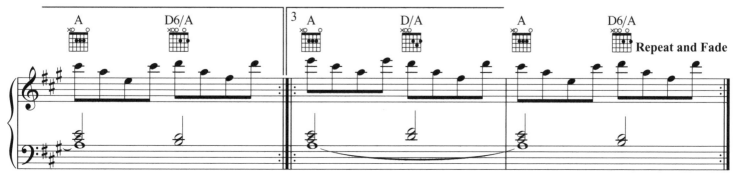

Repeat and Fade

AQUARIUS

from the Broadway Musical Production HAIR

Words by JAMES RADO and GEROME RAGNI
Music by GALT MacDERMOT

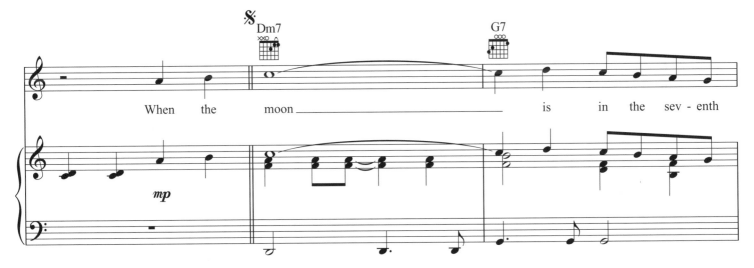

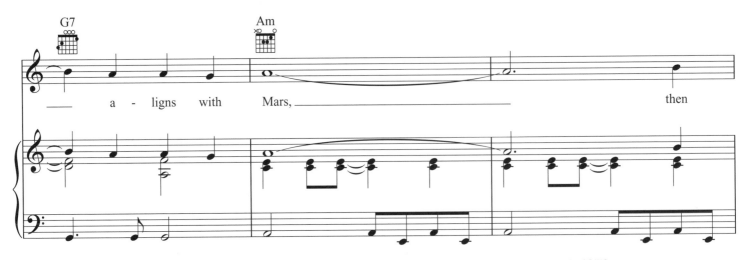

peace _____ will guide ___ the ___ plan - ets, _____

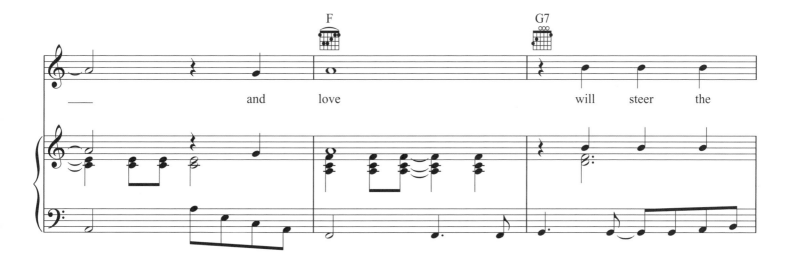

___ and love will steer the

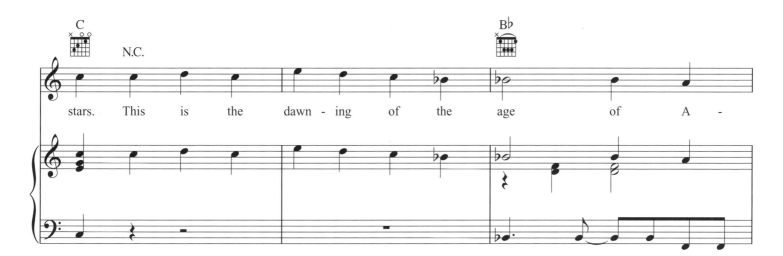

stars. This is the dawn - ing of the age of A -

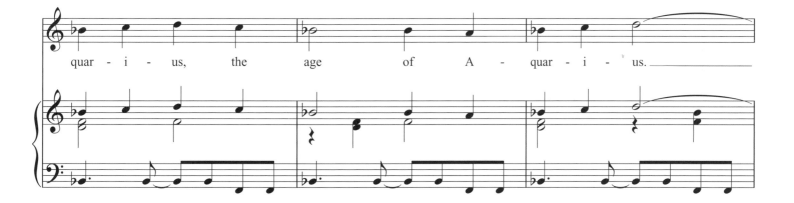

quar - i - us, the age of A - quar - i - us. _____

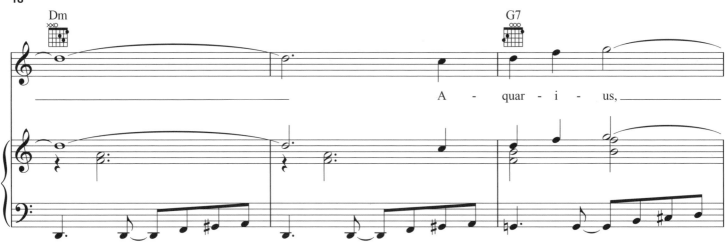

No more false-hoods or de-ri- sions, gold-en liv-ing dreams of vi-sions, mys-tic

crys-tal rev-e-la-tion, and the mind's true lib-er-a- tion. A-

quar-i- us, _____ A-

D.S. al Fine

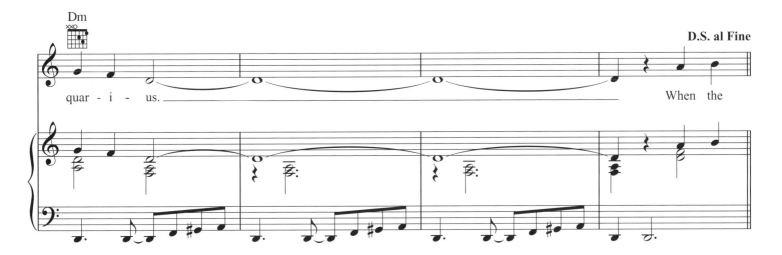

quar-i- us. _____ When the

(It's A)
BEAUTIFUL MORNING

Words and Music by FELIX CAVALIERE
and EDWARD BRIGATI, JR.

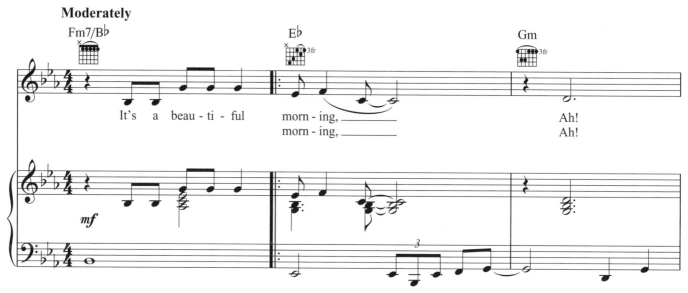

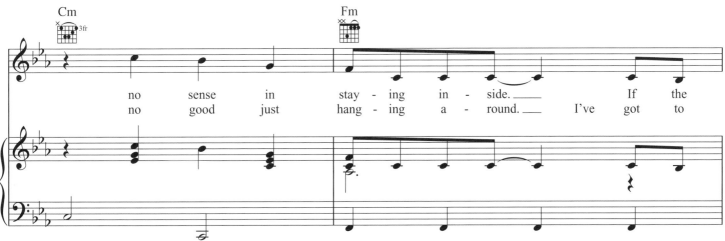

no sense in stay - ing in - side. _____ If the
no good in just hang - ing a - round. _____ I've got to

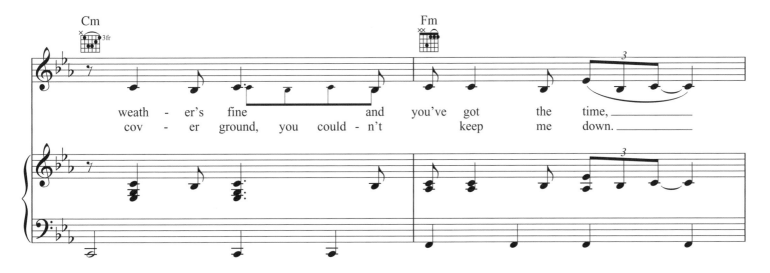

weath - er's fine _____ and you've got the time, _____
cov - er ground, you could - n't keep me down. _____

it's your chance to wake up and plan _____ an - oth - er
It just ain't no good if the sun _____ shines and you're

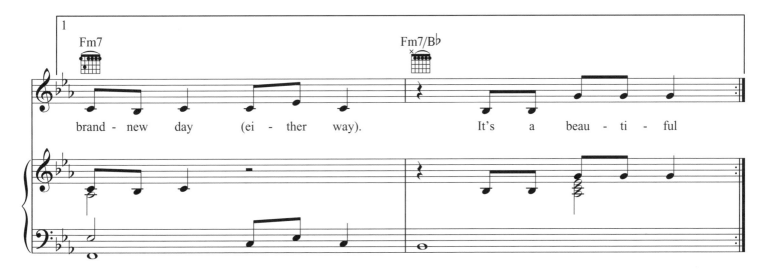

brand - new day (ei - ther way). It's a beau - ti - ful

still in - side (shoot-ing high). Still in - side (shoot-ing high). ____

Still in - side (shoot-ing high). Oh, oh. ____

Ah ____

There will be chil - dren with rob - ins and flow - ers.
Sun - shine ca - ress - es each new wak - ing ho - ur.

Seems to me ____ that peo - ple keep see - ing more and more to - day. (Got - ta say)

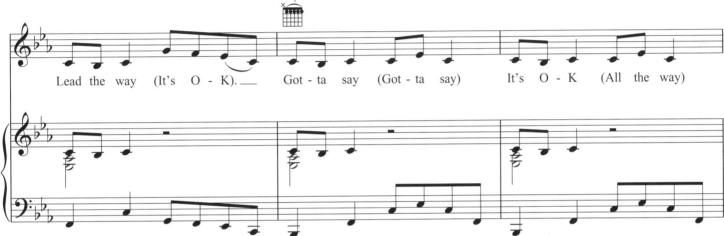

Lead the way (It's O - K). ____ Got - ta say (Got - ta say) It's O - K (All the way)

Got - ta say (Lead the way). Oh, oh. ____

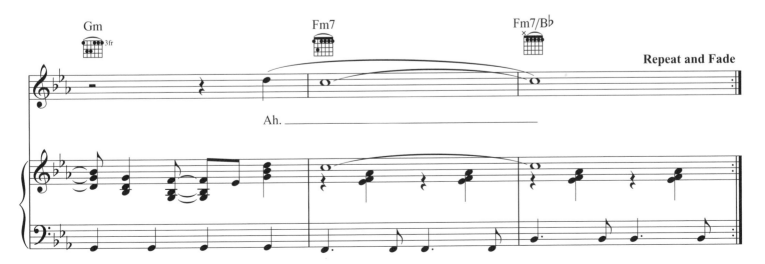

Repeat and Fade

Ah. _____

BEIN' GREEN

Words and Music by
JOE RAPOSO

that. It's not eas-y be-in' green.

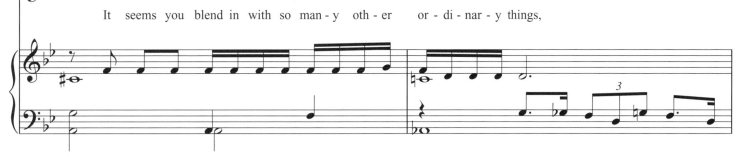

It seems you blend in with so man-y oth-er or-di-nar-y things,

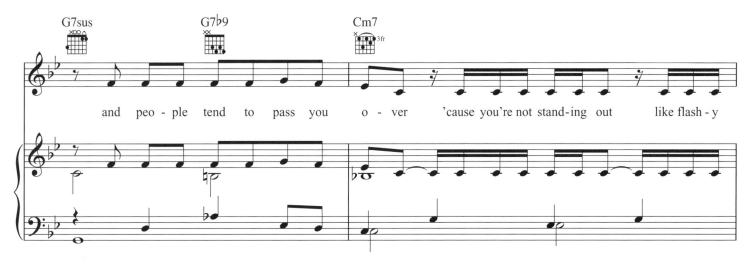

and peo-ple tend to pass you o-ver 'cause you're not stand-ing out like flash-y

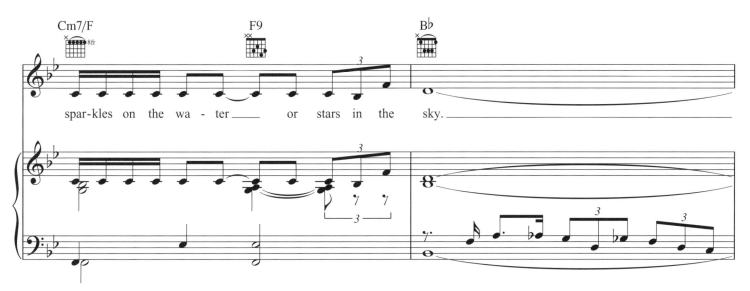

spar-kles on the wa-ter or stars in the sky.

But green is the col-or of spring, and green can be cool and friend-ly-like, and green can be big like an o-cean or im-por-tant like a moun-tain or tall like a tree.

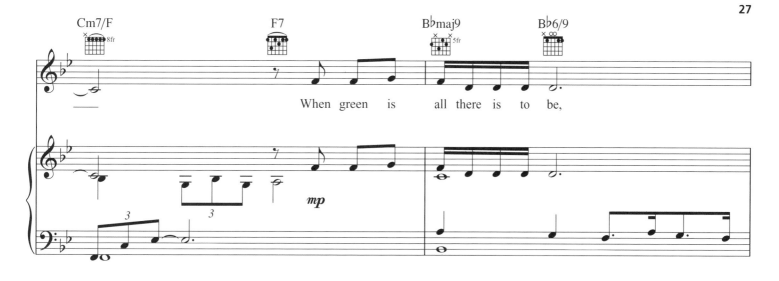

When green is all there is to be,

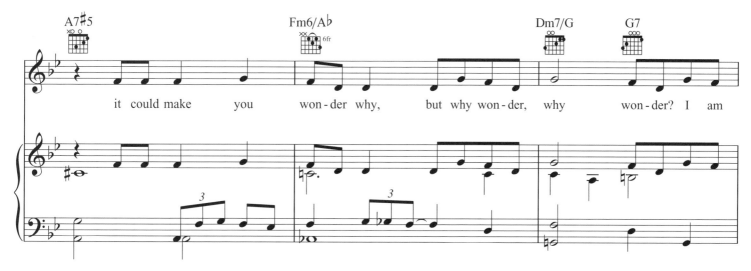

it could make you won-der why, but why won-der, why won-der? I am

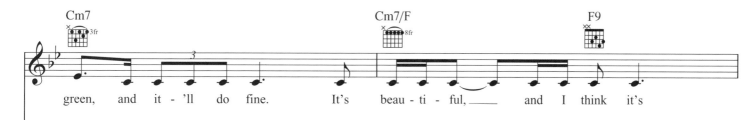

green, and it-'ll do fine. It's beau-ti-ful,_____ and I think it's

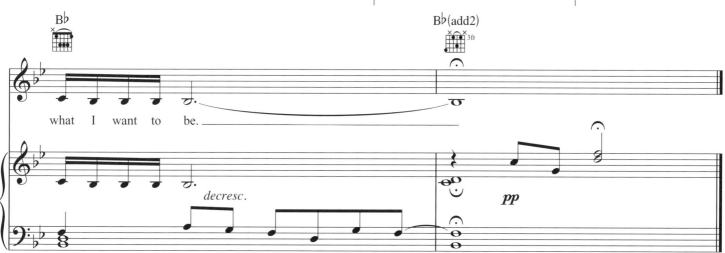

what I want to be._____

decresc.

pp

CALIFORNIA DREAMIN'

Words and Music by JOHN PHILLIPS
and MICHELLE PHILLIPS

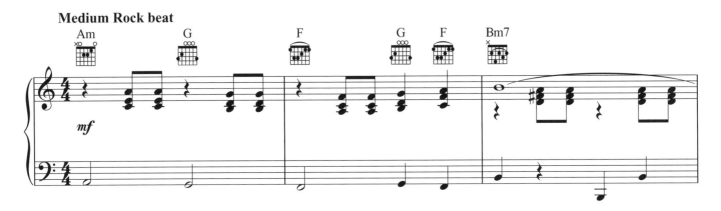

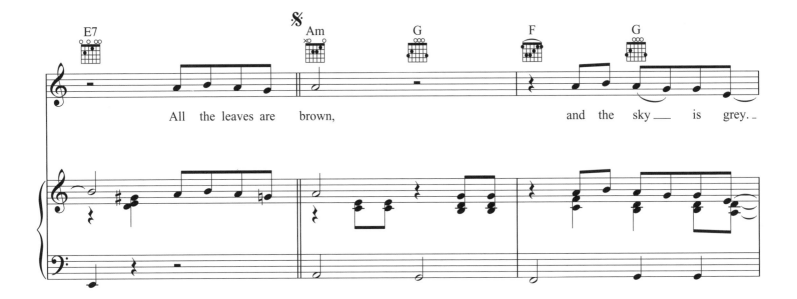

All the leaves are brown, and the sky __ is grey. __

I've been __ for a walk

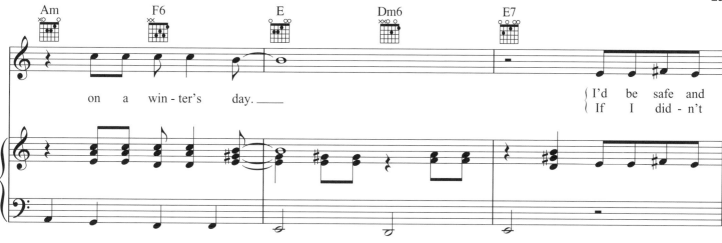

on a win - ter's day. _____

I'd be safe and
If I did - n't

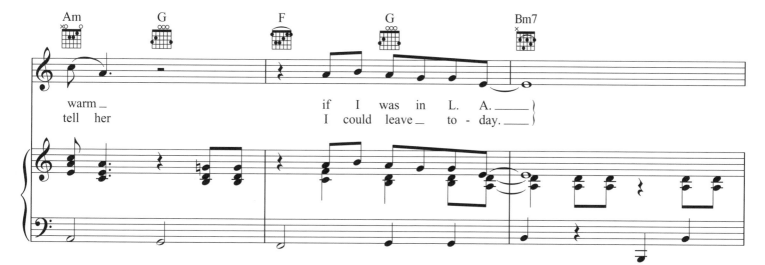

warm _____
tell her

if I was in L. A. _____
I could leave _____ to - day. _____

To Coda

Cal - i - for - nia dream - in'

on such a win - ter's

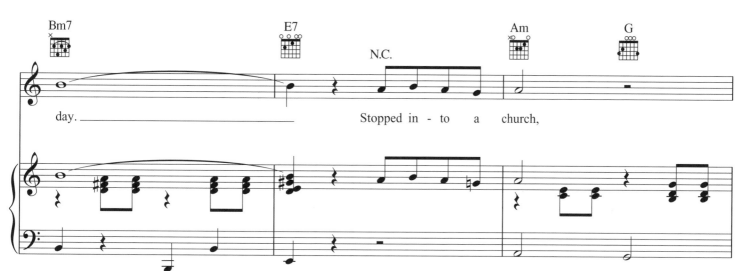

day. _____

N.C.

Stopped in - to a church,

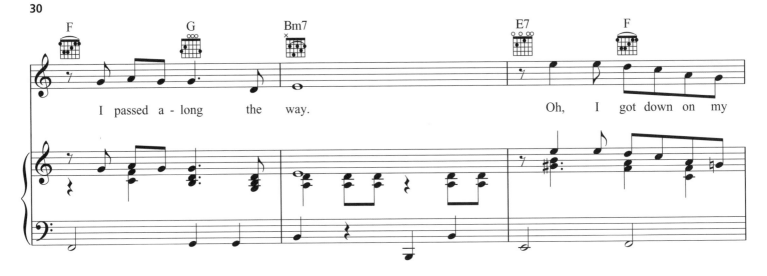

I passed a - long the way. Oh, I got down on my

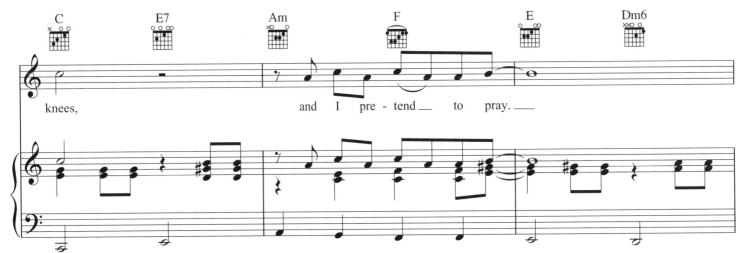

knees, and I pre - tend __ to pray. __

You know the preach - er likes the cold. __ He knows I'm gon - na

stay. Cal - i - for - nia dream - in'

on such a win-ter's day. _____ All the leaves are

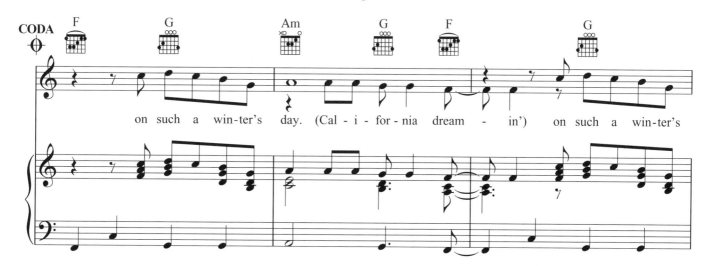

on such a win-ter's day. (Cal - i - for - nia dream - in') on such a win-ter's

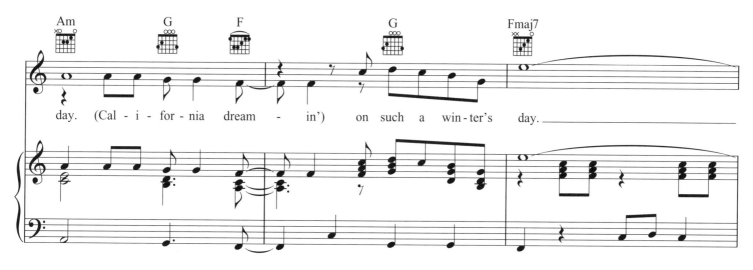

day. (Cal - i - for - nia dream - in') on such a win-ter's day. _____

CAREFREE HIGHWAY

Words and Music by
GORDON LIGHTFOOT

Medium Country Rock beat

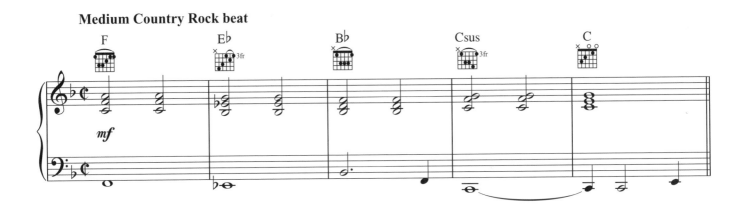

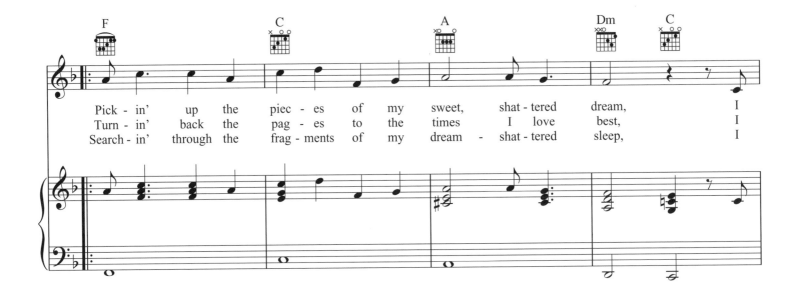

Pick - in' up the piec - es of my sweet, shat - tered dream, I
Turn - in' back the pag - es to the times I love best, I
Search - in' through the frag - ments of my dream - shat - tered sleep, I

won - der how the old folks are to - night.
won - der if she'll ev - er do the same.
won - der if the years have closed her mind.

Her
Now the
Well, I

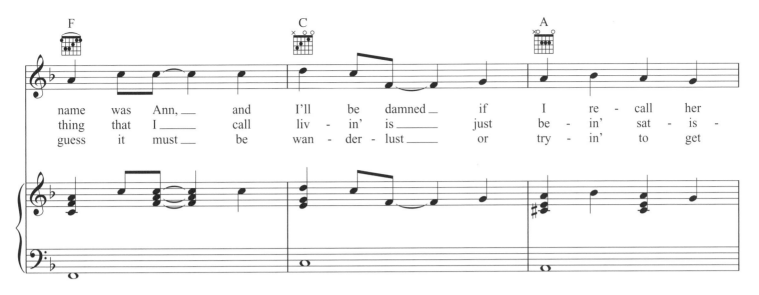

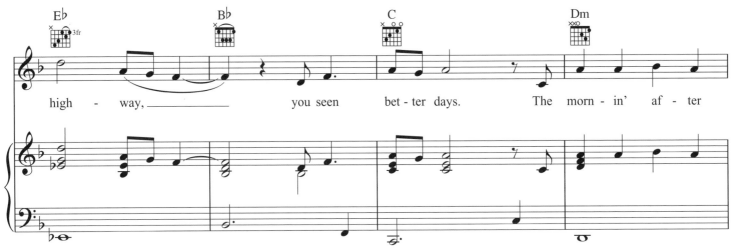

high - way, _____ you seen bet - ter days. The morn - in' af - ter

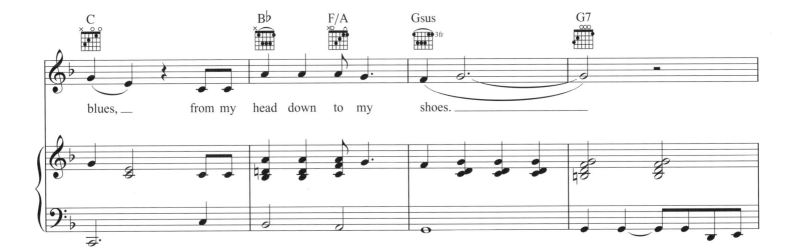

blues, __ from my head down to my shoes. _____

Care - free high - way, _____ let me slip a - way, _____

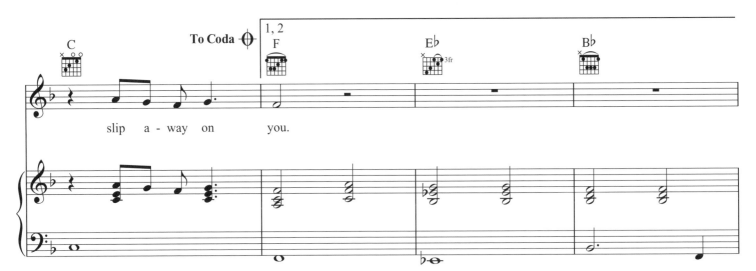

slip a - way on you.

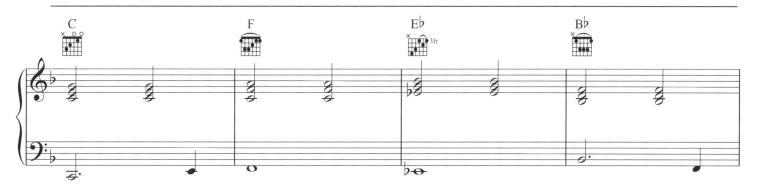

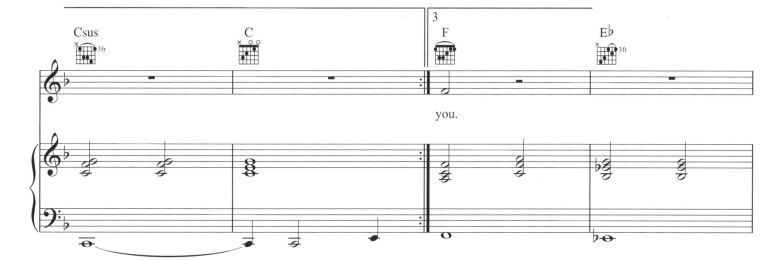

you.

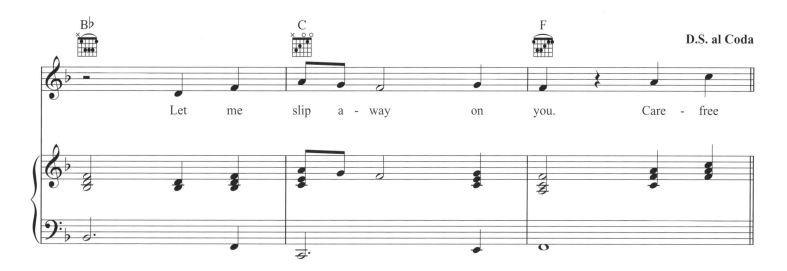

Let me slip a - way on you. Care - free

D.S. al Coda

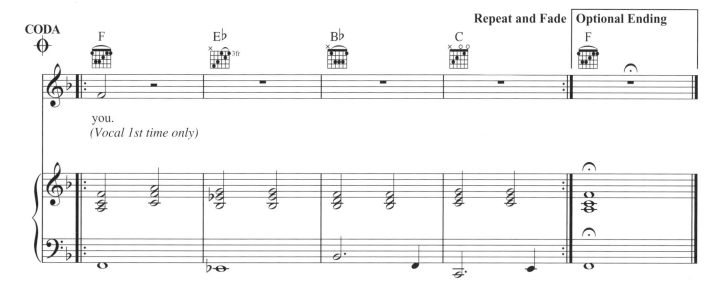

CODA

Repeat and Fade | **Optional Ending**

you.
(Vocal 1st time only)

CARRIE-ANNE

Words and Music by ALLAN CLARKE,
TONY HICKS and GRAHAM NASH

Then you played with old - er boys and pre - fects. What's the at - trac - tion in
You lost your charm as you were ag - ing. Where is your mag - ic ___
When the les - son's o - ver, you'll be with me. Then I'll hear the oth - er ___

what they're do - ing?
dis - ap - pear - ing? } Hey, Car - rie - Anne, _____ what's your game _
peo - ple say - ing:

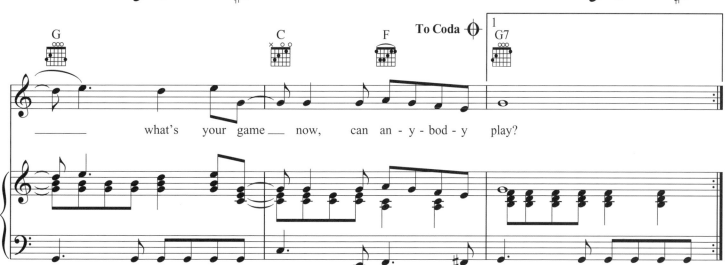

___ now, can an - y - bod - y play? Hey, Car - rie - Anne, _

what's your game _ now, can an - y - bod - y play?

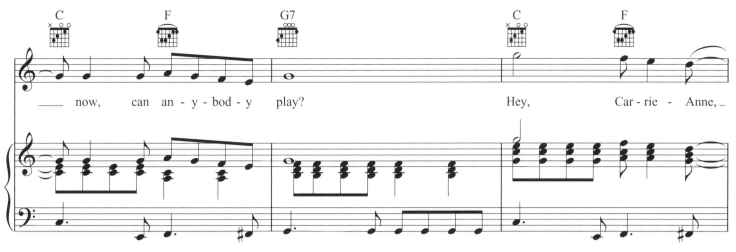

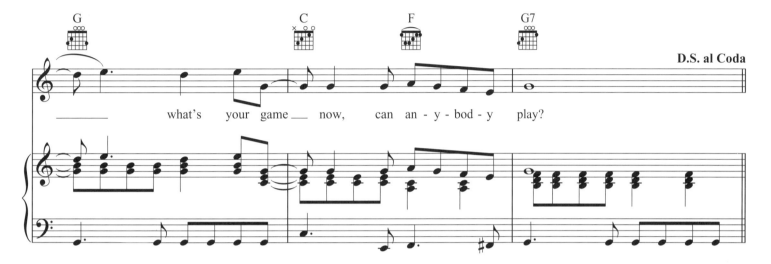

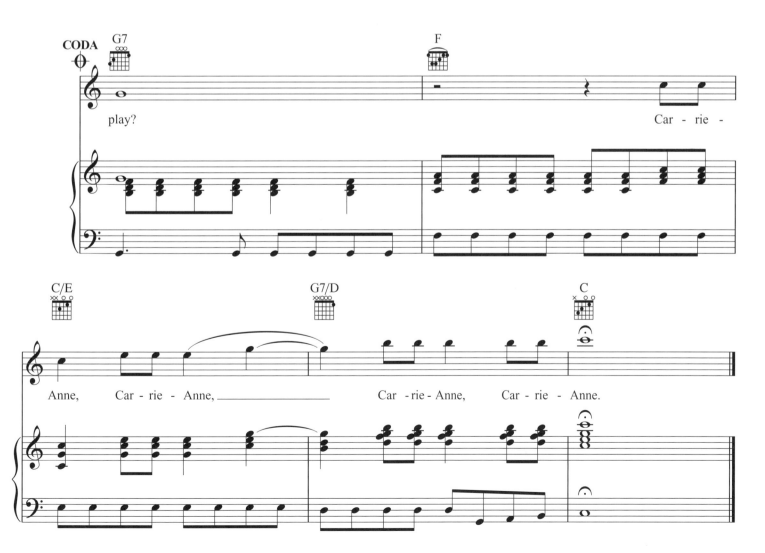

CASEY JONES

Words by ROBERT HUNTER
Music by JERRY GARCIA

DAYDREAM BELIEVER

Words and Music by
JOHN STEWART

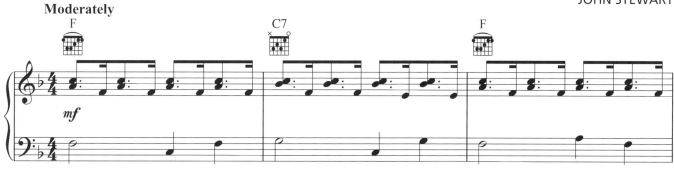

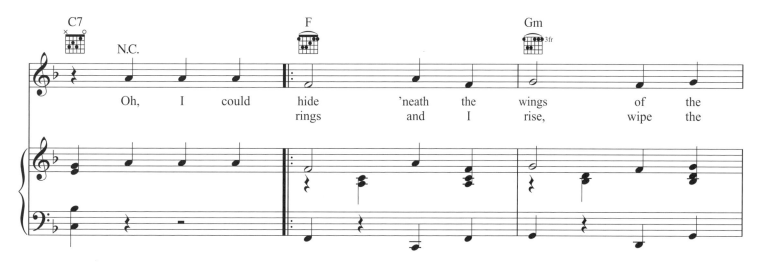

Oh, I could hide 'neath the wings of the
rings and I rise, wipe the

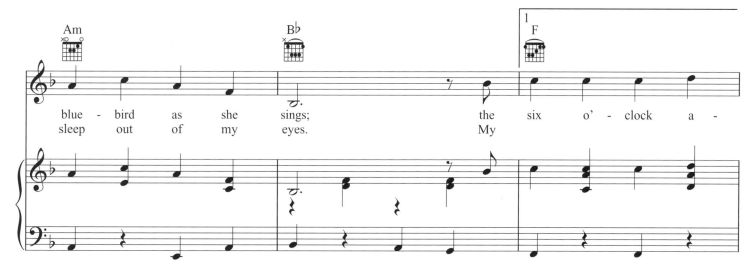

blue-bird as she sings; the six o'-clock a-
sleep out of my eyes. My

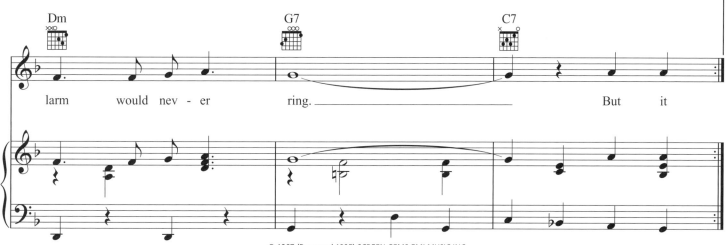

larm would nev-er ring. _____ But it

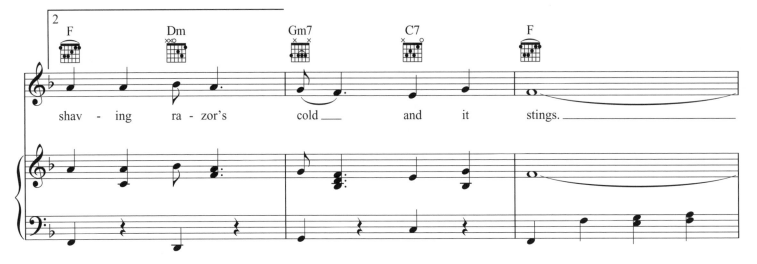

shav - ing ra - zor's cold ___ and it stings. ___

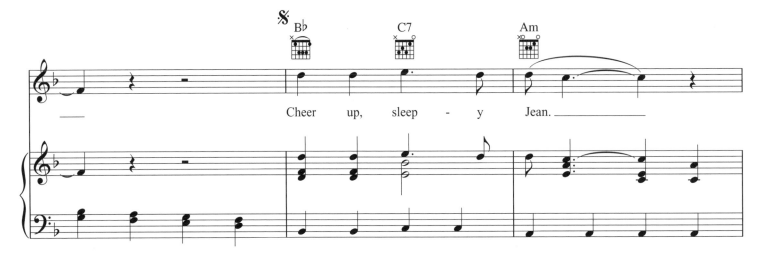

___ Cheer up, sleep - y Jean. ___

Oh, what can it mean to a day - dream be -

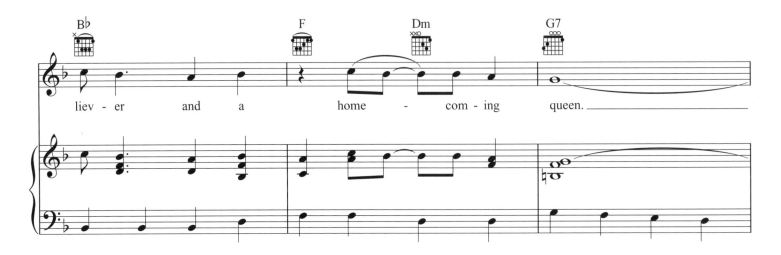

liev - er and a home - com - ing queen. ___

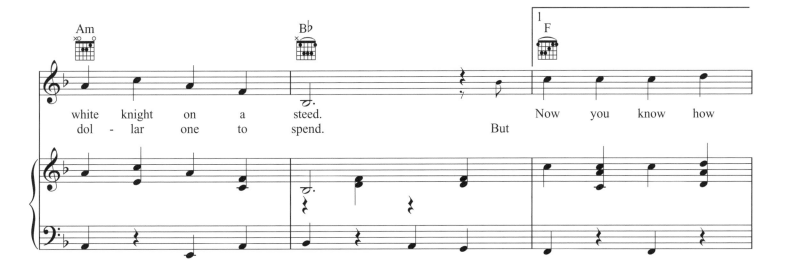

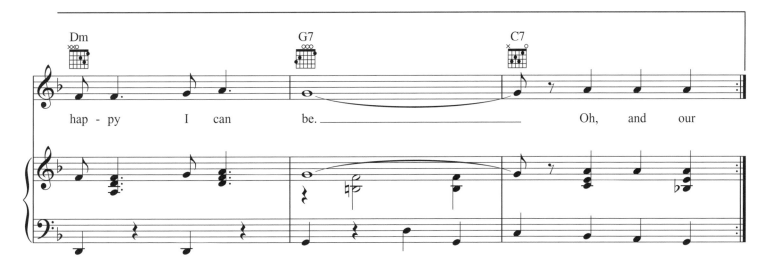

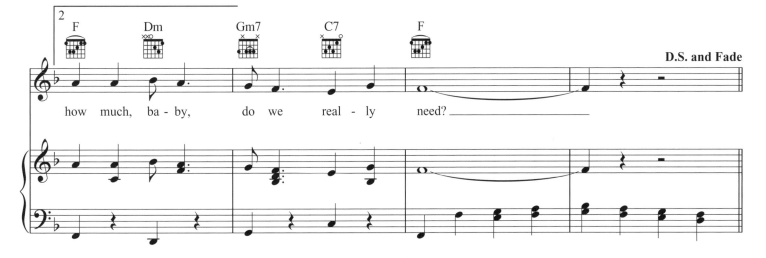

FALLING SLOWLY
from the Motion Picture ONCE

Words and Music by GLEN HANSARD
and MARKETA IRGLOVA

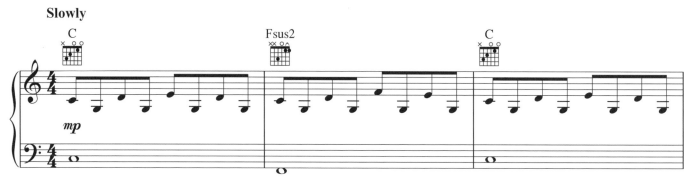

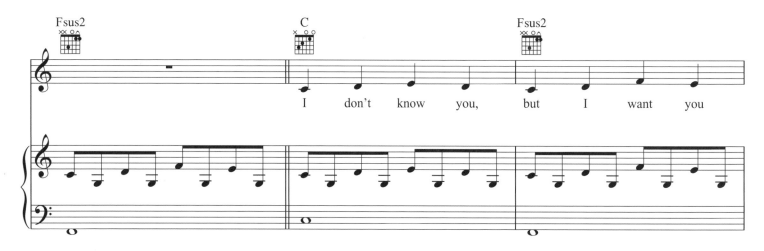

I don't know you, but I want you

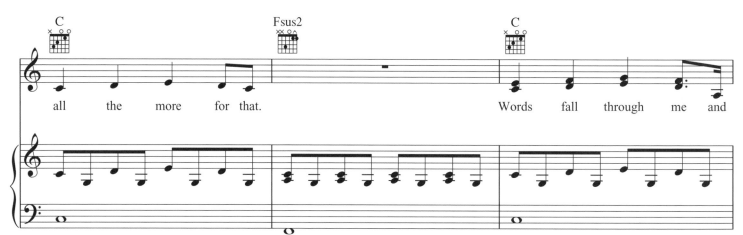

all the more for that. Words fall through me and

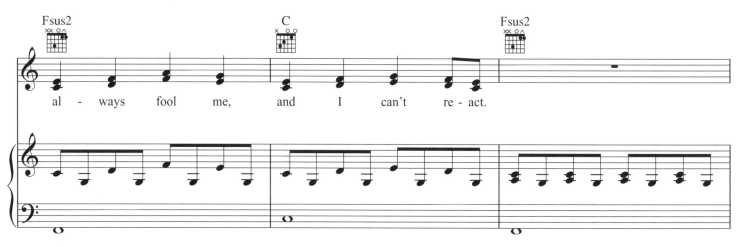

al - ways fool me, and I can't re - act.

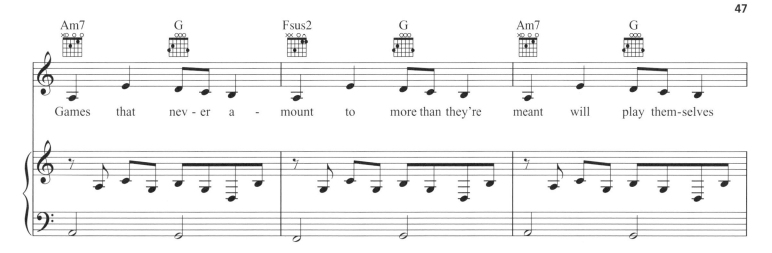

Games that nev - er a - mount to more than they're meant will play them-selves

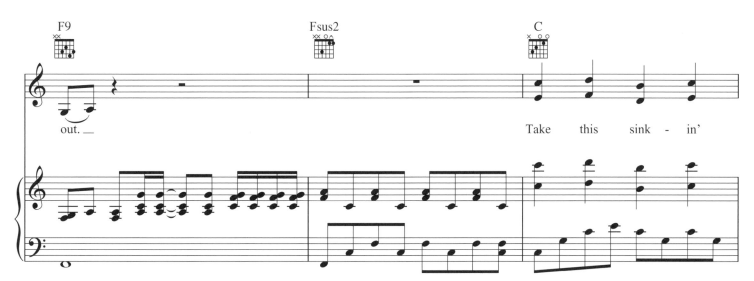

out. ___ Take this sink - in'

boat and point it home; we've still got time. ___

Raise your hope - ful voice; you have a choice; you make it

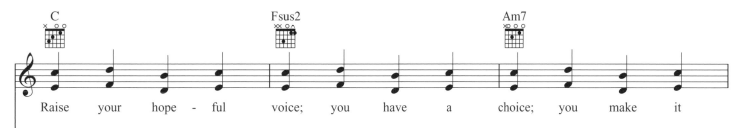

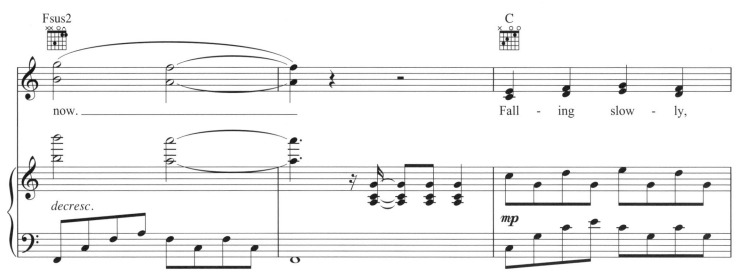

now. _____ Fall - ing slow - ly,

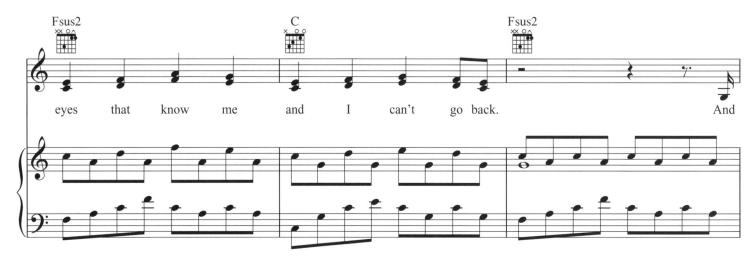

eyes that know me and I can't go back. And

moods that take me and e - rase me, and I'm paint - ed black.

Well, you have suf-fered e - nough and warred with your -

self; it's time that you won. _

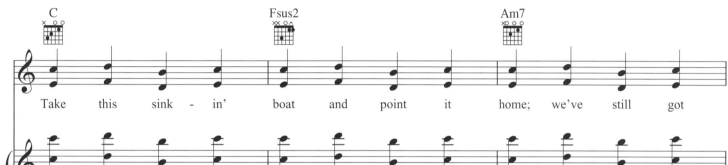

Take this sink - in' boat and point it home; we've still got

time. _____ Raise your hope - ful voice; you have a

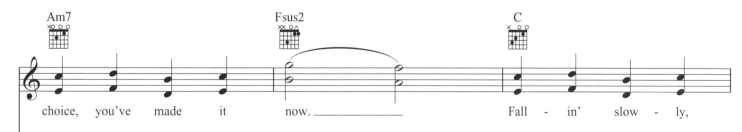

choice, you've made it now. _____ Fall - in' slow - ly,

sing your mel - o - dy; I'll sing it loud. _____

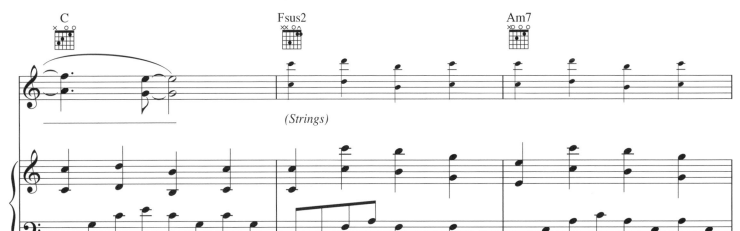

(Strings)

Take it all. ___

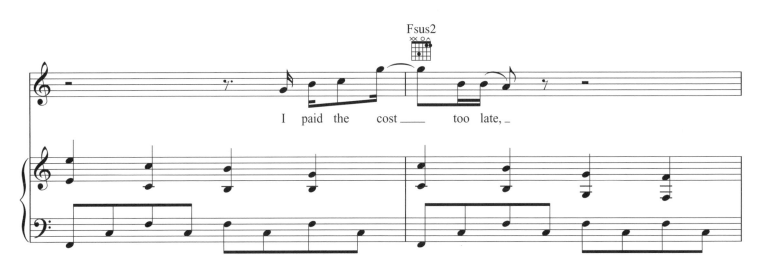

I paid the cost ___ too late, _

now you're gone. ___

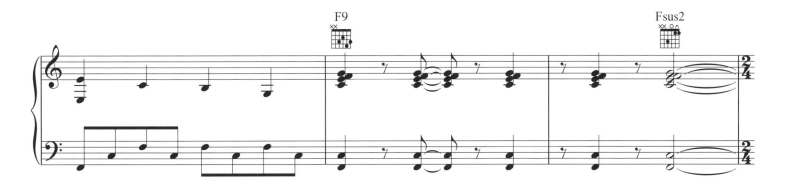

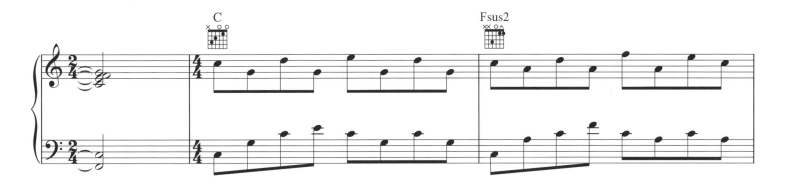

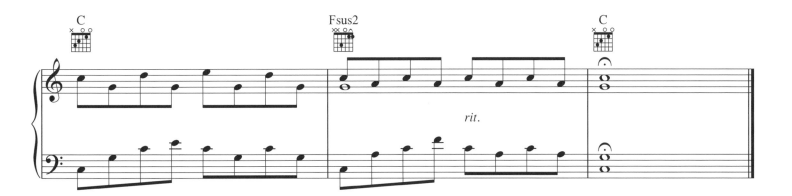

rit.

THE 59TH STREET BRIDGE SONG
(Feelin' Groovy)

Words and Music by
PAUL SIMON

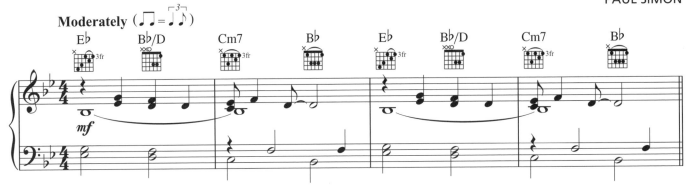

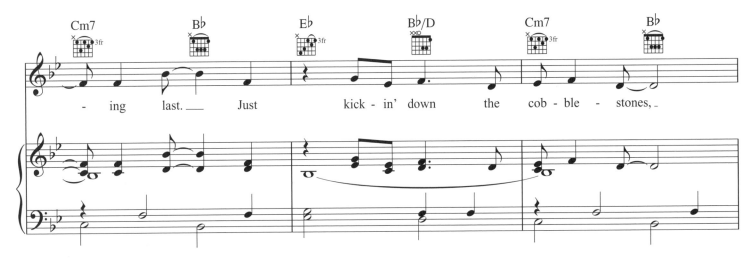

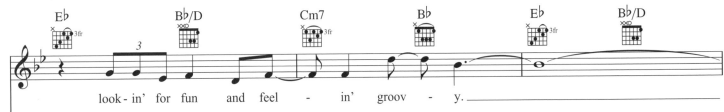

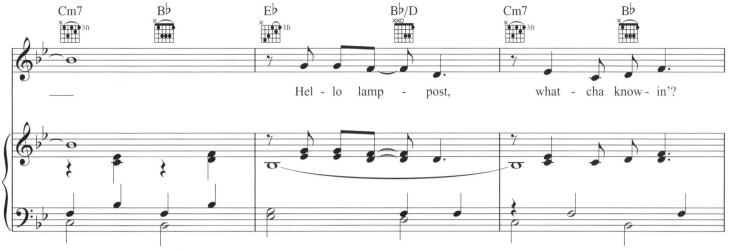

Hel - lo lamp - post, what - cha know - in'?

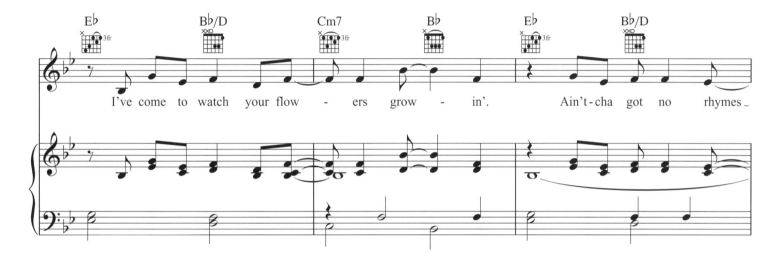

I've come to watch your flow - ers grow - in'. Ain't - cha got no rhymes ___

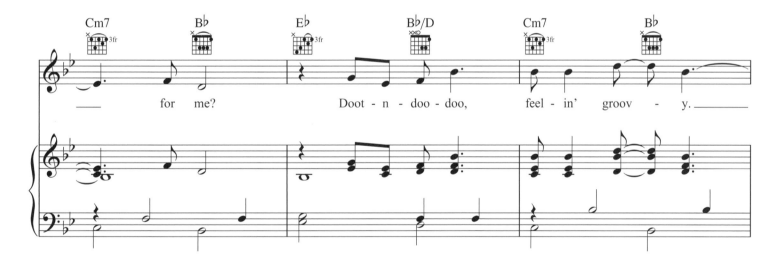

___ for me? Doot - n - doo - doo, feel - in' groov - y. ___

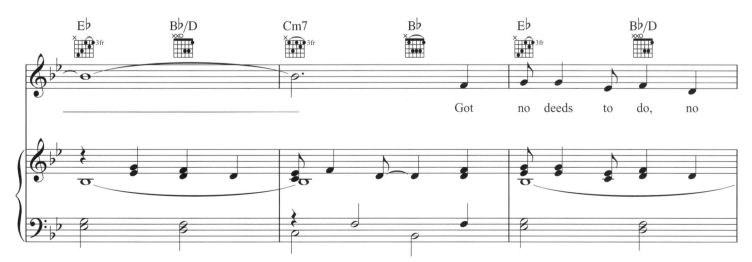

___ Got no deeds to do, no

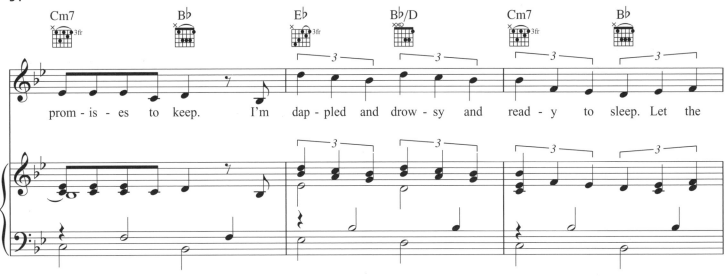

prom-is-es to keep. I'm dap-pled and drow-sy and read-y to sleep. Let the

morn-ing-time drop all its pet-als on me. Life, I love you.

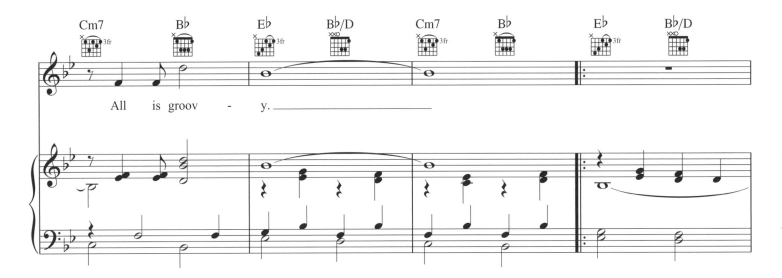

All is groov-y.

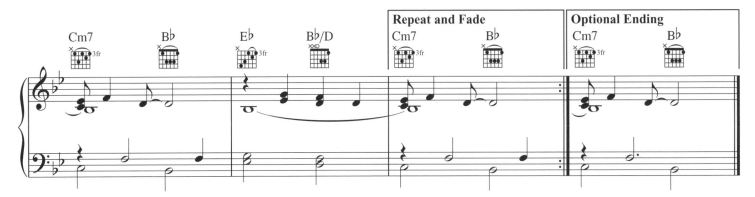

HOMEWARD BOUND

Words and Music by
PAUL SIMON

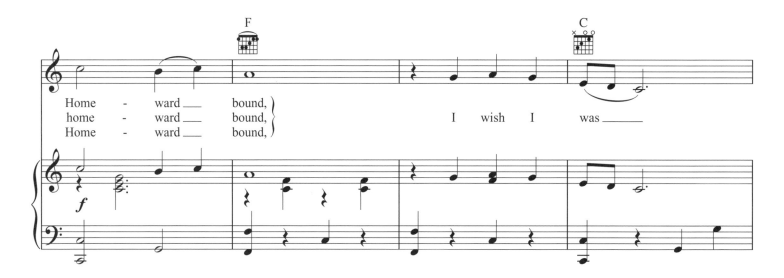

es - cap - ing, home where my mu - sic's play - ing, home where my love

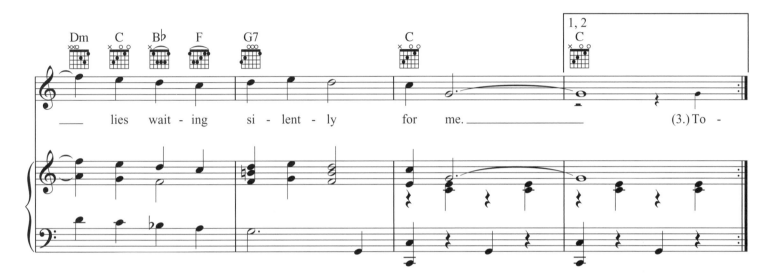

lies wait - ing si - lent - ly for me. _____ (3.) To -

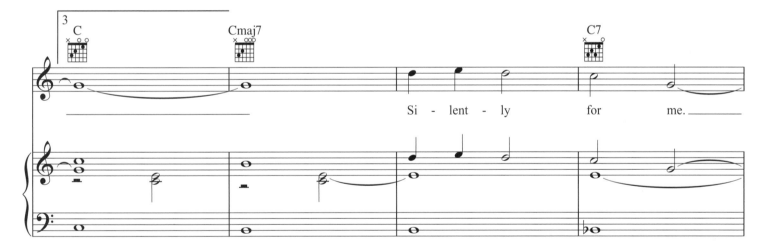

Si - lent - ly for me. _____

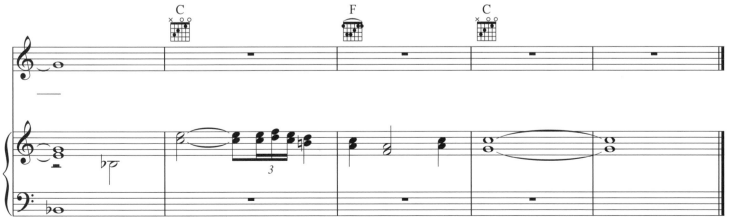

GOOD MORNING STARSHINE

from the Broadway Musical Production HAIR

Words by JAMES RADO and GEROME RAGNI
Music by GALT MacDERMOT

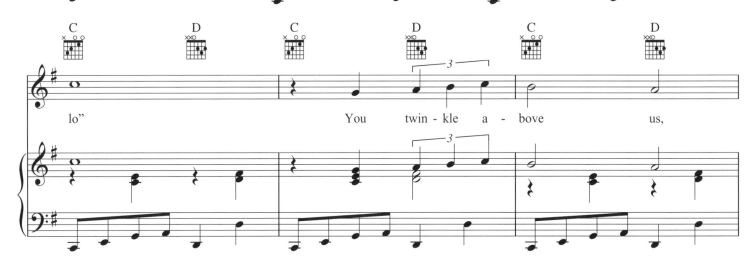

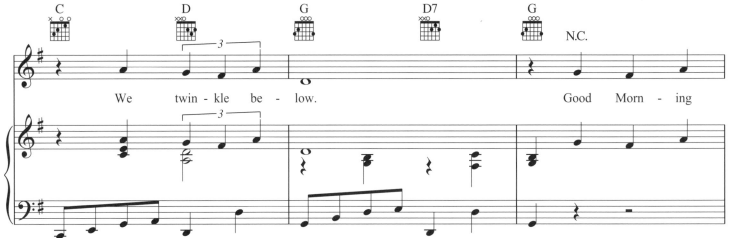

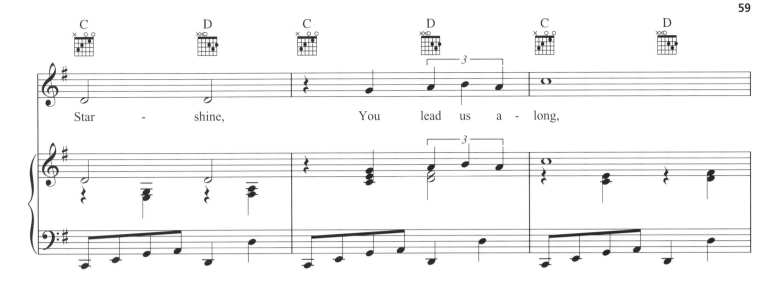

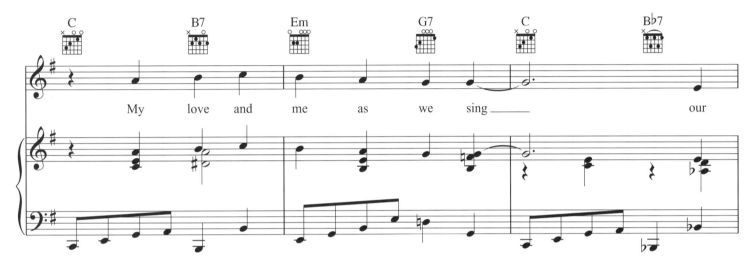

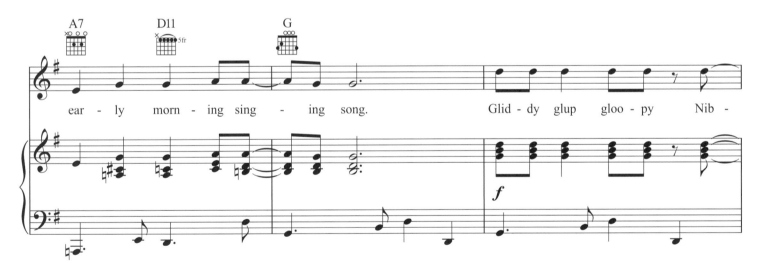

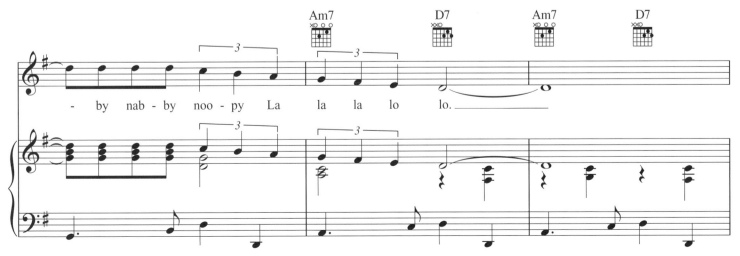

Sab - ba sib - by sab - ba Noo - by ab - ba nab - ba Le le lo lo.

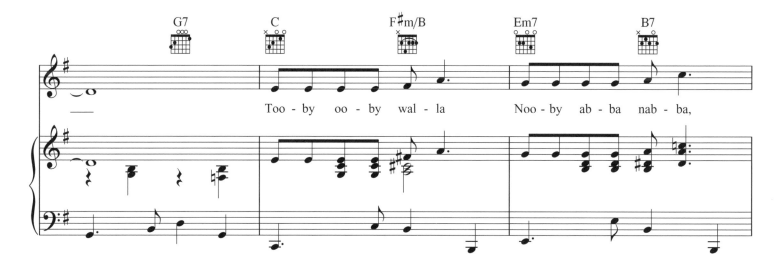

Too - by oo - by wal - la Noo - by ab - ba nab - ba,

Ear - ly morn - ing sing - ing song. Good Morn - ing

Sing - ing a song, Hum - ming a song, Sing - ing a song,

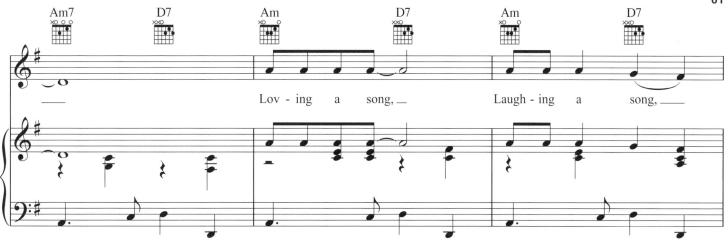

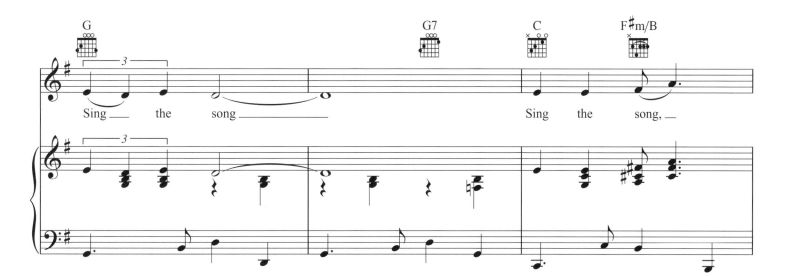

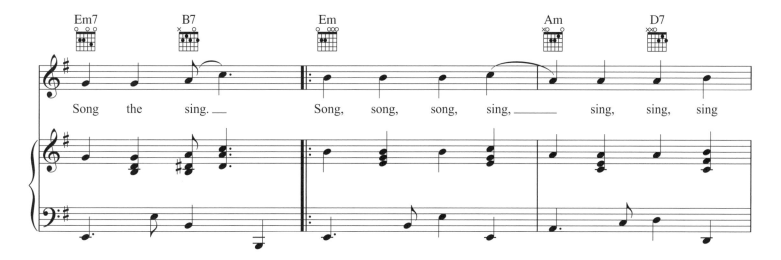

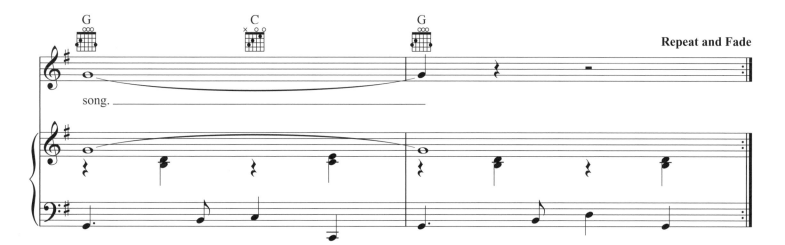

GUANTANAMERA

Musical Adaption by PETE SEEGER and JULIAN ORBON
Lyric Adaption by JULIAN ORBON, based on a poem by JOSE MARTI
Lyric Editor: HECTOR ANGULO
Original Music and Lyrics by JOSE FERNANDEZ DIAZ

Guan-ta-na-me-ra gua-ji-ra Guan-ta-na-me-ra

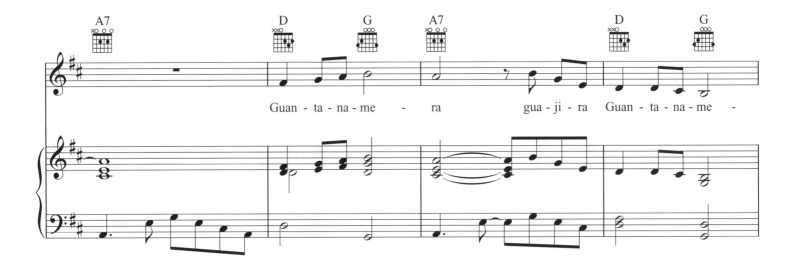

Guan-ta-na-me - ra gua-ji-ra Guan-ta-na-me -

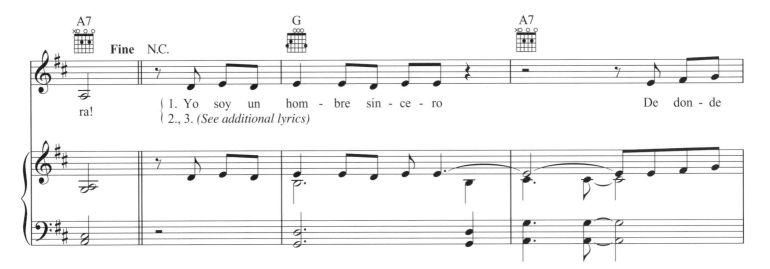

ra! 1. Yo soy un hom-bre sin-ce-ro De don-de
2., 3. (See additional lyrics)

cre - ce la pal - ma   Yo soy un hom - bre sin - ce - ro

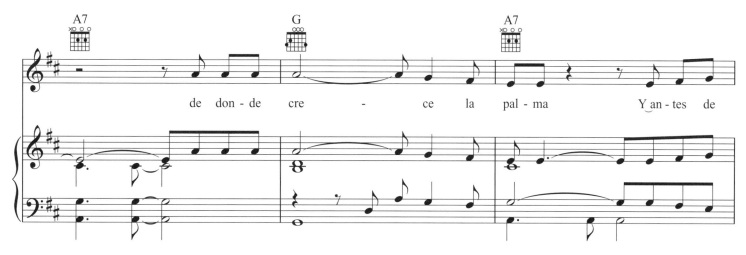

de don - de cre - ce la pal - ma   Y an - tes de

2nd time, D.S. al Fine

mo - rir - me quie - ro   E - char mis ver - sos del al - ma.

Additional Lyrics

(Literal English Translation)

2. Mi verso es de un verde claro
   Y de un carmin encendido
   Mi verso es de un verde claro
   Y de un carmin encendido
   Mi verso es un cierro herido
   Que busca en el monte amparo.
   Chorus

3. Con los pobres de la tierra
   Quiero yo mi suerte echar
   Con los pobres de la tierra
   Quiero yo mi suerte echar
   El arroyo de la sierra
   Me complace mas que el mar.
   Chorus

1. I am a truthful man, from the
   land of palm trees. Before
   dying, I want to share these
   poems of my soul.

2. My poems are light green,
   but they are also flaming
   crimson. My verses are like
   a wounded fawn, seeking
   refuge in the forest.

3. With the poor people of this
   earth, I want to share my fate.
   The little streams of the
   mountains please me more
   than the sea.

HALLELUJAH

Words and Music by
LEONARD COHEN

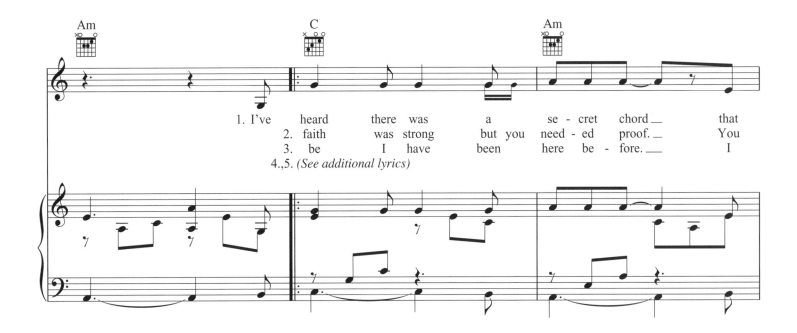

1. I've heard there was a se - cret chord that
2. faith was strong but you need - ed proof. You
3. be I have been here be - fore. I
4.,5. *(See additional lyrics)*

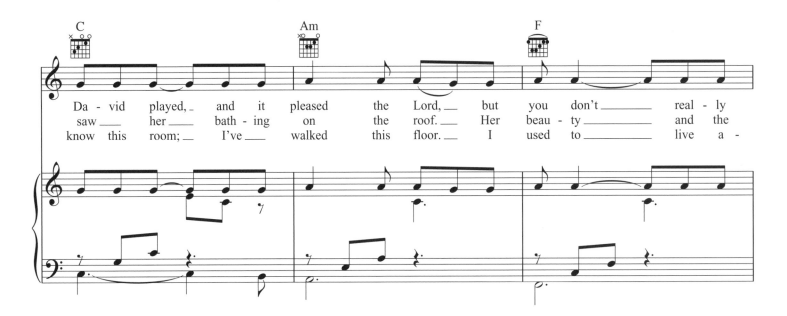

Da - vid played, and it pleased the Lord, but you don't real - ly
saw her bath - ing on the roof. Her beau - ty and the
know this room; I've walked this floor. I used to live a -

care for mu - sic, _____ do you? _____ It
moon - light o - ver - threw you. _____ She
lone be - fore I _____ knew you. _____ I've

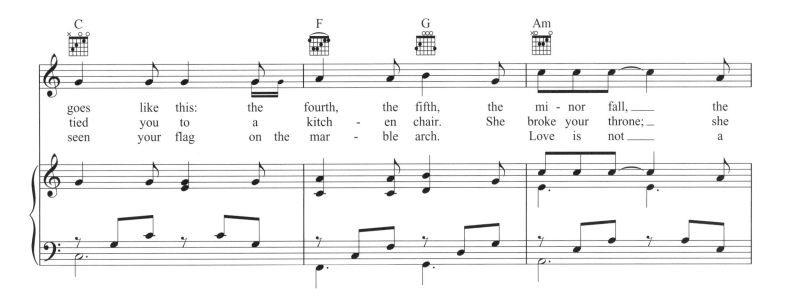

goes like this: the fourth, the fifth, the mi - nor fall, _____ the
tied you to a kitch - en chair. She broke your throne; _____ she
seen your flag on the mar - ble arch. Love is not _____ a

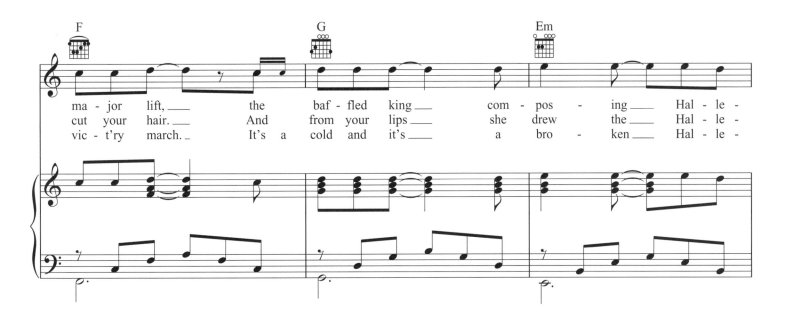

ma - jor lift, _____ the baf - fled king _____ com - pos - ing _____ Hal - le -
cut your hair. _____ And from your lips _____ she drew the _____ Hal - le -
vic - t'ry march. _____ It's a cold and it's _____ a bro - ken _____ Hal - le -

Chorus

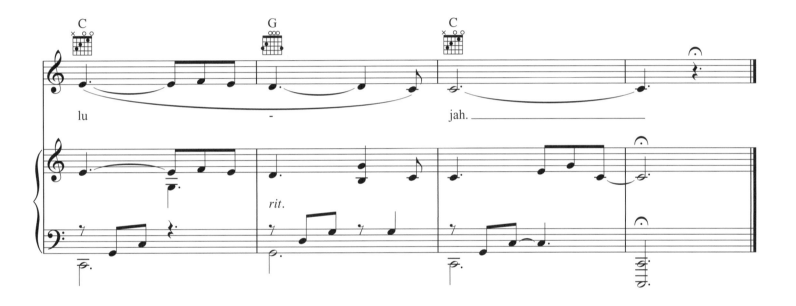

Additional Lyrics

4. There was a time you let me know
   What's real and going on below.
   But now you never show it to me, do you?
   And remember when I moved in you.
   The holy dark was movin', too,
   And every breath we drew was Hallelujah.
   Chorus

5. Maybe there's a God above,
   And all I ever learned from love
   Was how to shoot at someone who outdrew you.
   And it's not a cry you can hear at night.
   It's not somebody who's seen the light.
   It's a cold and it's a broken Hallelujah.
   Chorus

HAPPY TOGETHER

Words and Music by GARRY BONNER
and ALAN GORDON

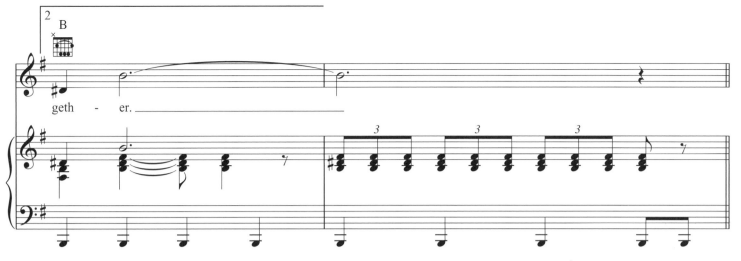

geth - er. _____

I can see me lov - in' no - bod - y but you for all my life. _

When you're with me, ba - by, the skies - 'll be

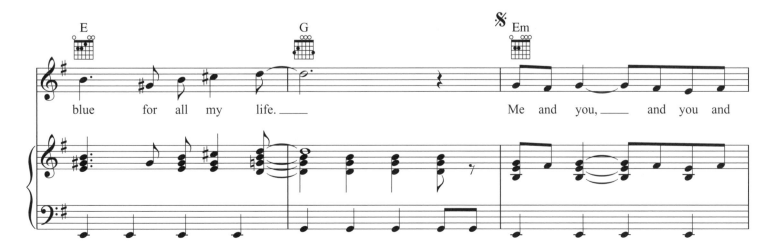

blue for all my life. _____ Me and you, _____ and you and

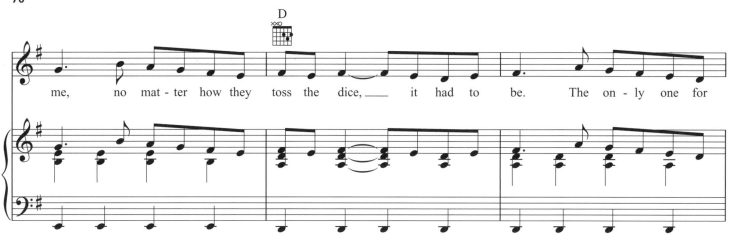

me, no mat-ter how they toss the dice,____ it had to be. The on-ly one for

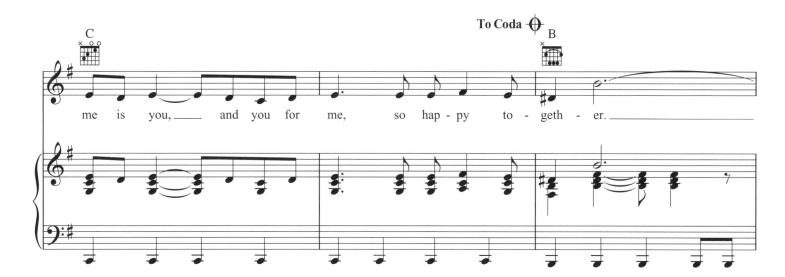

me is you,____ and you for me, so hap-py to-geth-er.____

Ba ba ba ba ba ba

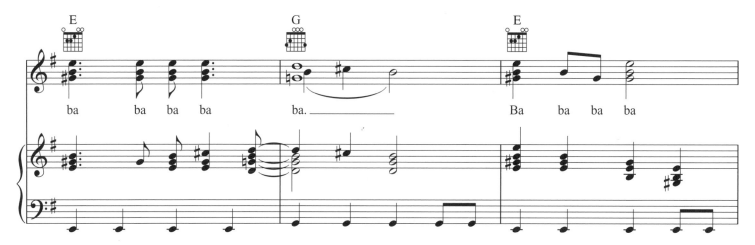

ba ba ba ba ba.____ Ba ba ba ba

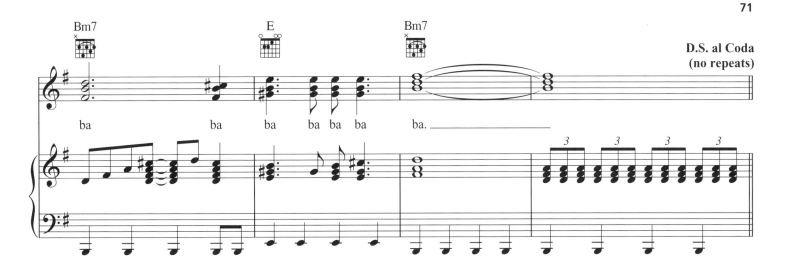

D.S. al Coda
(no repeats)

ba ba ba ba ba ba ba.____

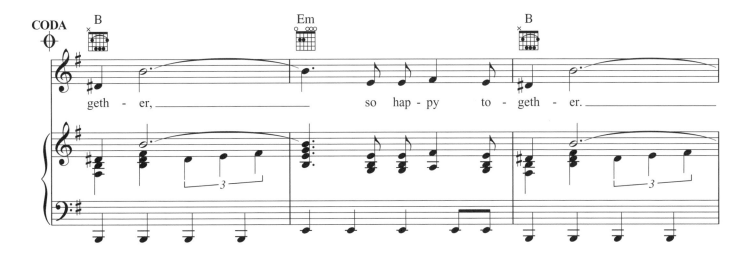

CODA

geth - er,_____ so hap - py to - geth - er._____

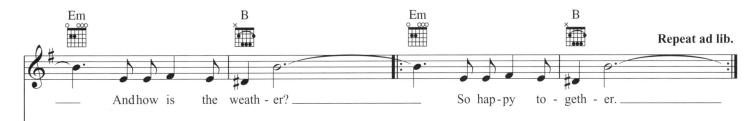

Repeat ad lib.

And how is the weath - er?_____ So hap - py to - geth - er._____

____ So hap - py to - geth - er._____

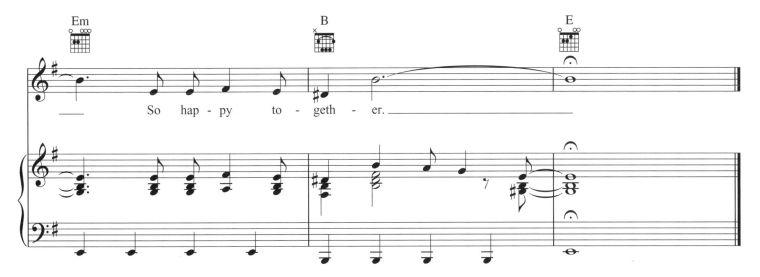

HE AIN'T HEAVY, HE'S MY BROTHER

Words and Music by BOB RUSSELL
and BOBBY SCOTT

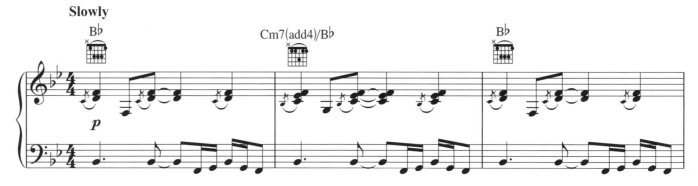

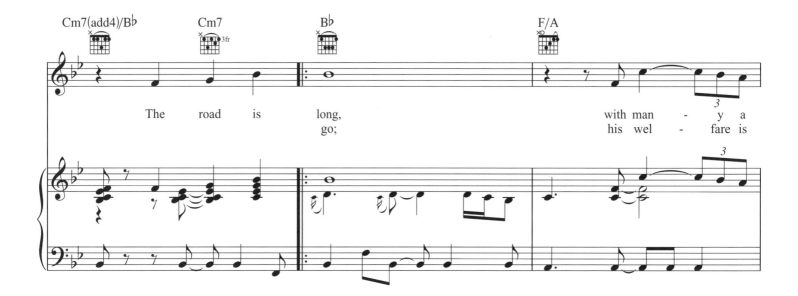

The road is long, with man - y a
go; his wel - fare is

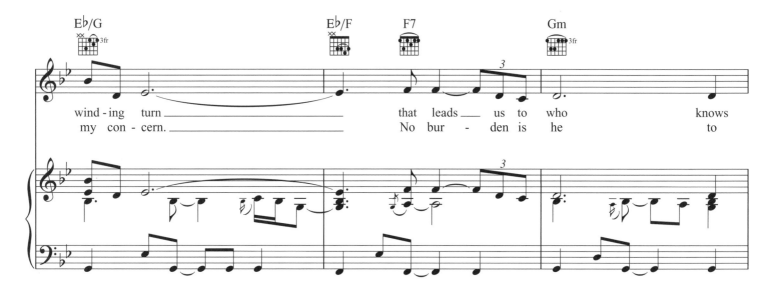

wind - ing turn _____ that leads ___ us to who knows
my con - cern. _____ No bur - den is he to

I'D LIKE TO TEACH THE WORLD TO SING

Words and Music by BILL BACKER,
ROQUEL DAVIS, ROGER COOK
and ROGER GREENAWAY

like to teach __ the world __ to sing __ in per - fect har - mo - ny, __

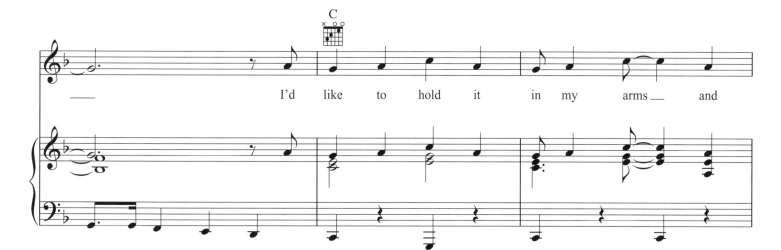

__ I'd like to hold it in my arms __ and

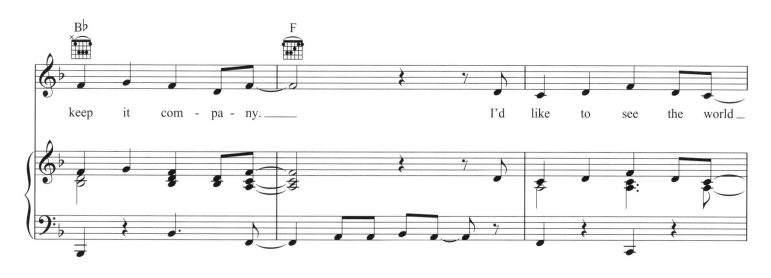

keep it com - pa - ny. _____ I'd like to see the world __

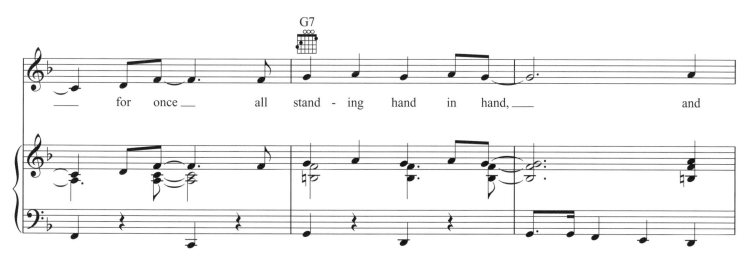

__ for once __ all stand - ing hand in hand, _____ and

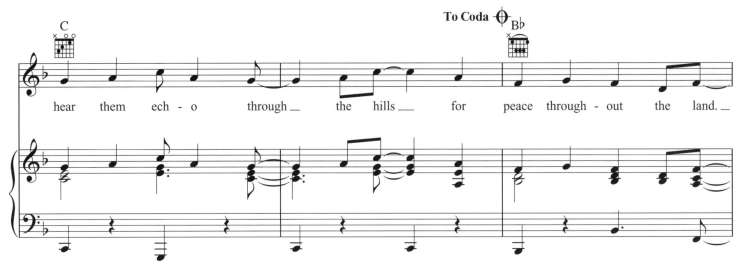

hear them ech-o through __ the hills __ for peace through-out the land. __

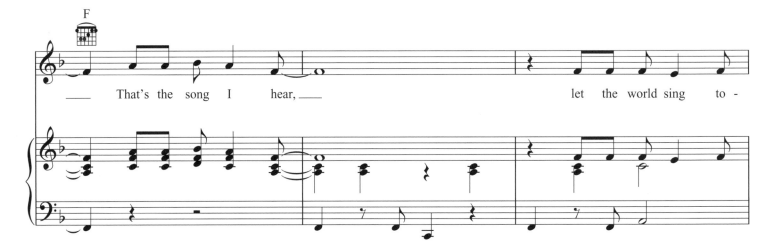

__ That's the song I hear, __ let the world sing to-

day. _____ A song of peace that

ech-oes on __ and nev-er goes a-way. __

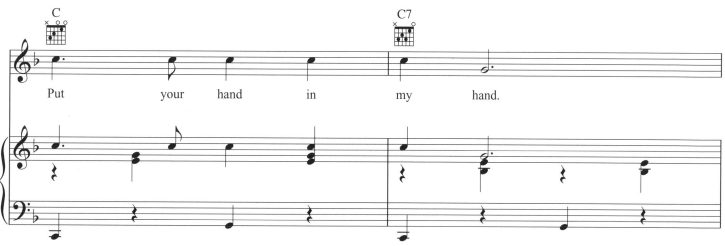

Put your hand in my hand.

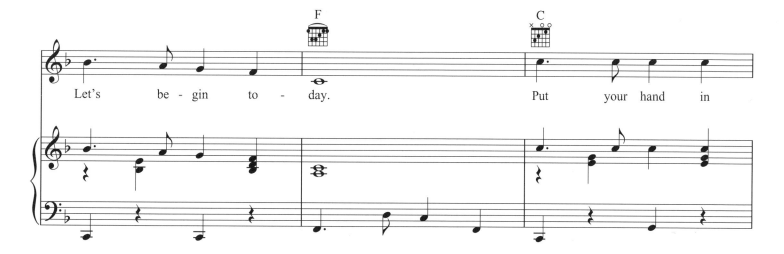

Let's be - gin to - day. Put your hand in

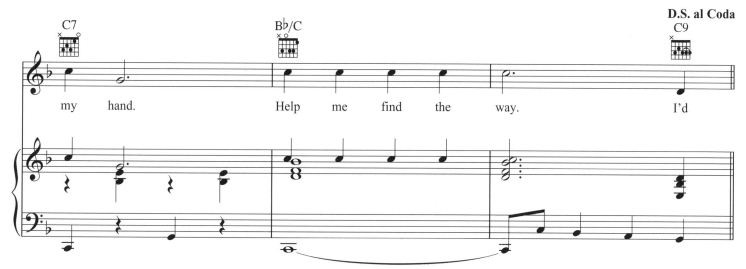

my hand. Help me find the way. I'd

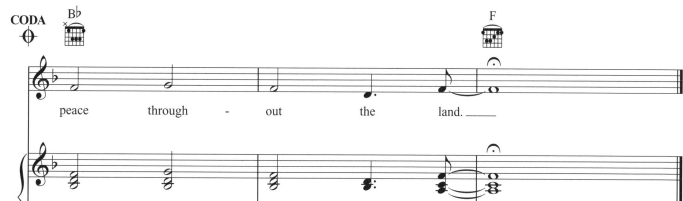

peace through - out the land. ___

IF I HAD A HAMMER
(The Hammer Song)

Words and Music by LEE HAYS
and PETE SEEGER

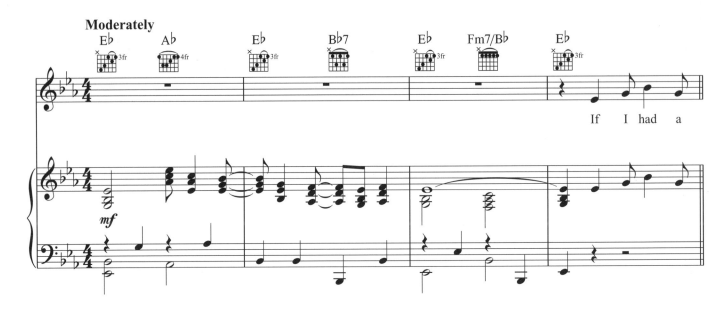

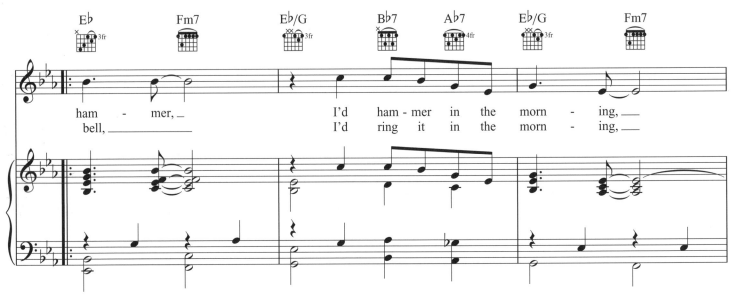

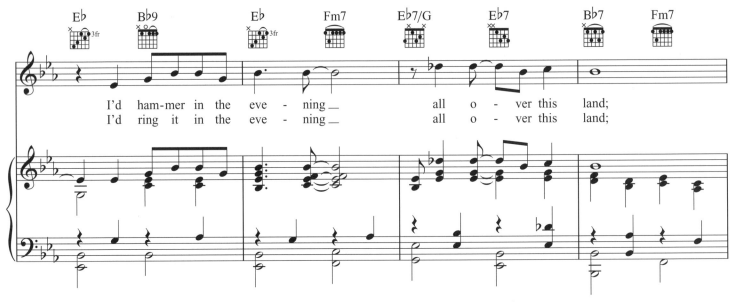

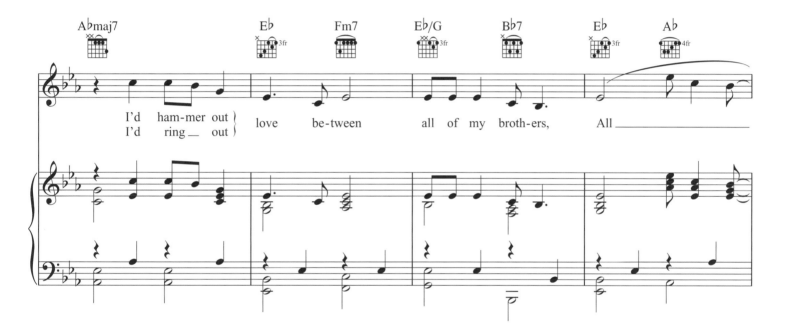

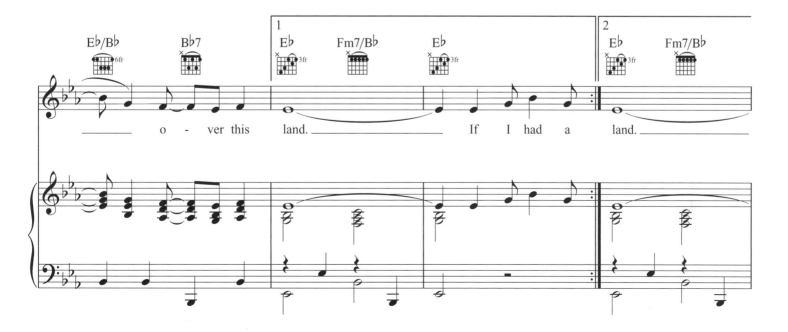

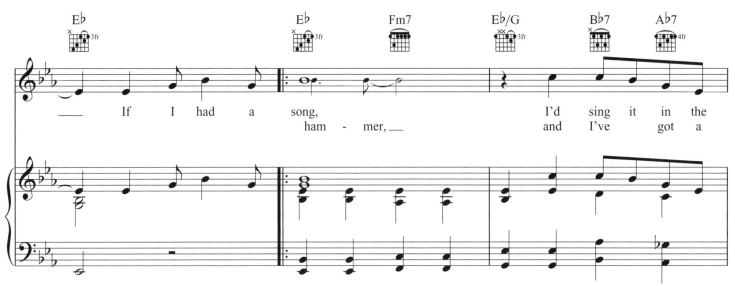

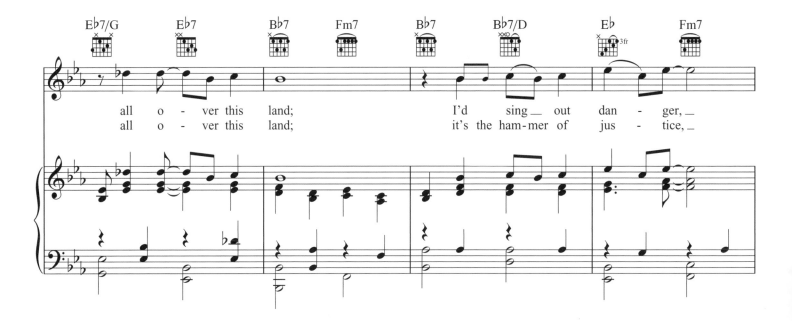

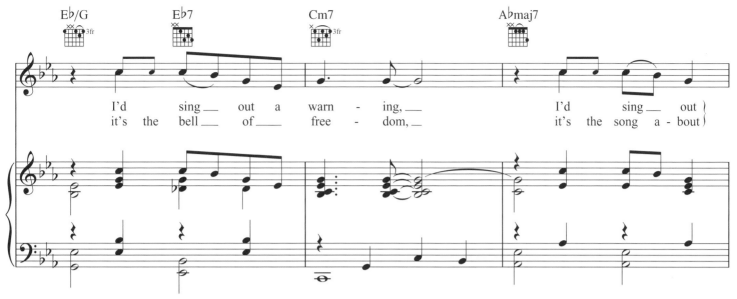

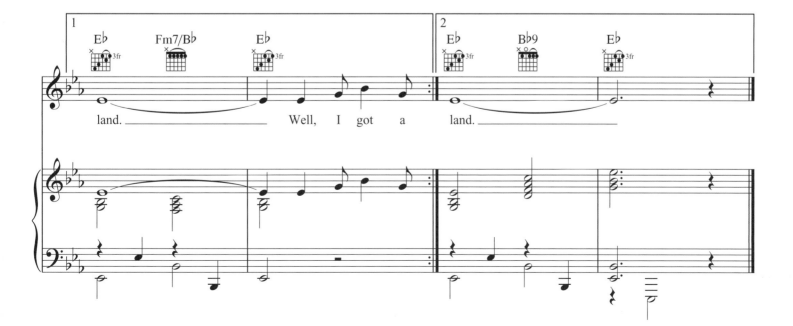

IF I WERE A CARPENTER

Words and Music by
TIM HARDIN

If I ___ were a car - pen - ter, ___
If I ___ worked my hands in wood, __

and you were a la - dy,   would you mar - ry me
would you still ___ love me?   An - swer me, ___ babe,

INTO THE MYSTIC

Words and Music by
VAN MORRISON

Moderately

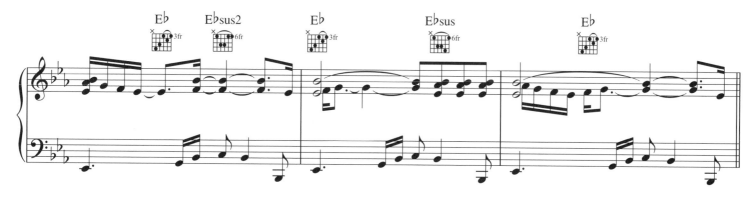

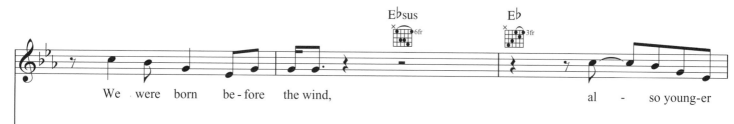

We were born be - fore the wind, al - so young - er

than the sun, ___ ere the bon - ny boat was

wan - na rock your ___ gyp - sy soul, ___

just like ___ way back in the days of old.

{And mag - nif - i - cent - ly we will flow}
{And to - geth - er we will flow ___ }
in - to the

mys - tic.

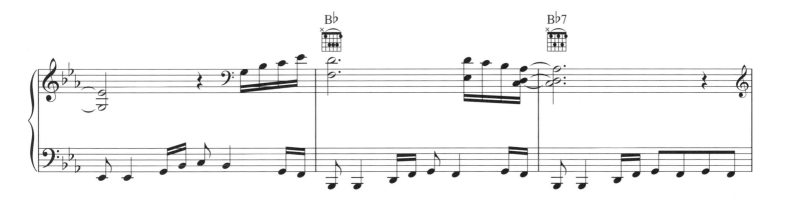

Too late to stop now. _____

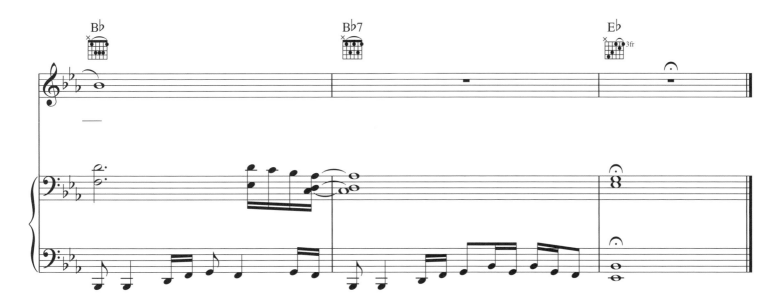

JAMAICA FAREWELL

Words and Music by
IRVING BURGIE

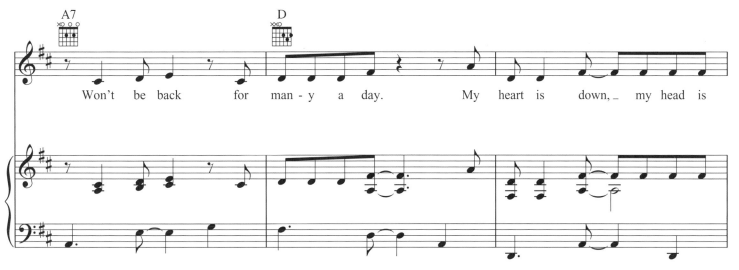

Won't be back for man-y a day. My heart is down,_ my head is

To Coda

turn-ing a-round,_ I had to leave a lit-tle girl in King-ston town._

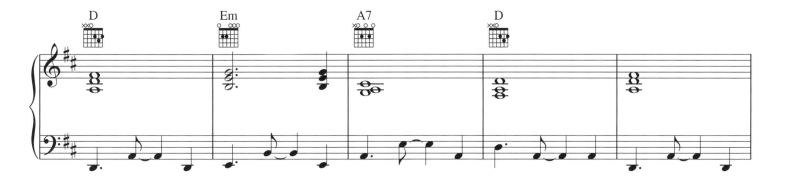

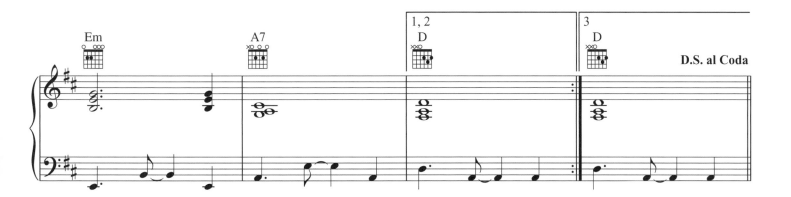

D.S. al Coda

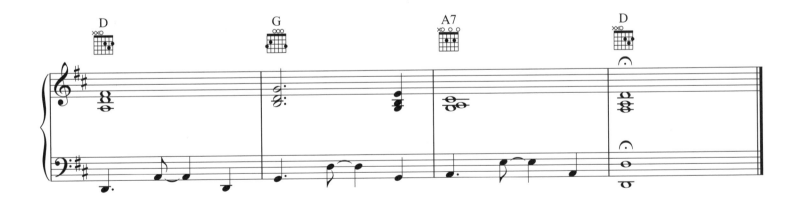

Additional Lyrics

3. Down at the market you can hear
   Ladies cry out while on their heads they bear
   Ackie, rice; salt fish are nice,
   And the rum is fine any time of year.
   Chorus

KOKOMO
from the Motion Picture COCKTAIL

Music and Lyrics by JOHN PHILLIPS,
TERRY MELCHER, MIKE LOVE
and SCOTT McKENZIE

Moderately bright

A-ru-ba, Ja-mai-ca, oo ___ I wan-na take ya. Ber-

mu-da, Ba-ha-ma, come ___ on, pret-ty ma-ma. Key Lar-go, Mon-te-go, ba-

-by, why don't we go, Ja-mai-ca. Off the Flor-i-da Keys ___

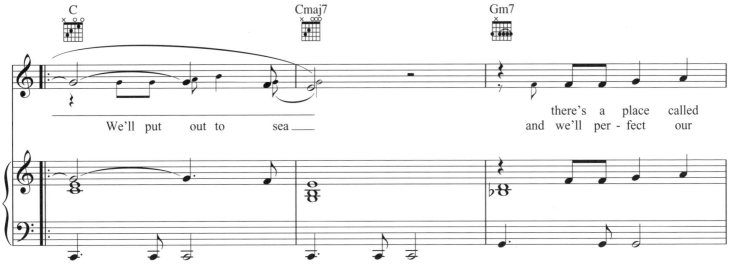

We'll put out to sea ___
and we'll per-fect our
there's a place called

Ko-ko-mo. ___
chem-is-try. ___
That's where you want to go ___ to get a-
By and by we'll de-fy ___ a lit-tle bit of

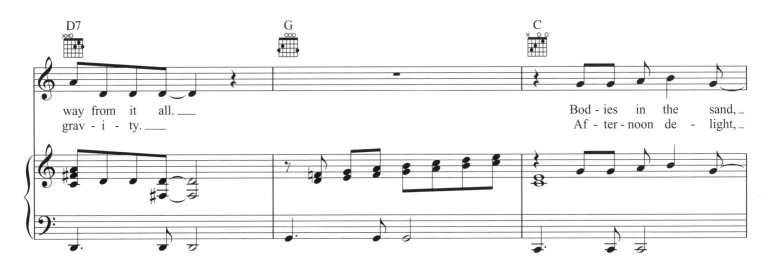

way from it all. ___
grav-i-ty. ___
Bod-ies in the sand, ___
Af-ter-noon de-light, ___

___
trop-i-cal drink melt-ing in your hand. ___
cock-tails and moon-lit nights. ___

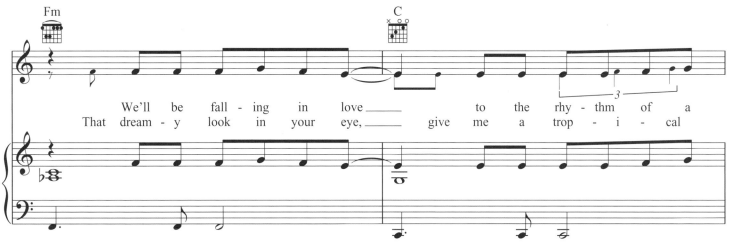

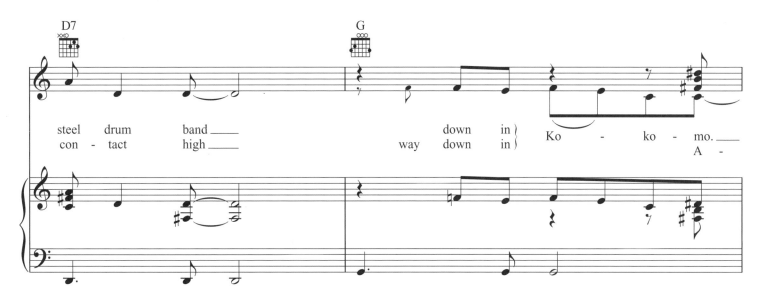

We'll be fall-ing in love ___ to the rhy-thm of a
That dream-y look in your eye, ___ give me a trop-i-cal

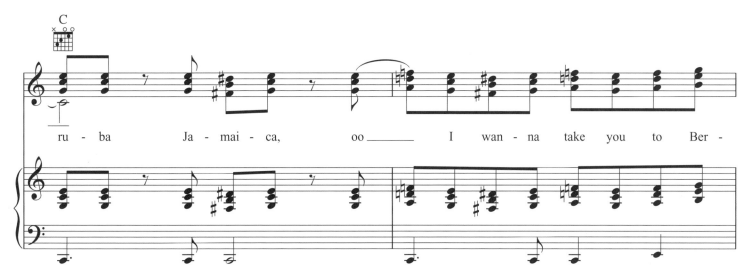

steel drum band ___ down in Ko-ko-mo.
con-tact high ___ way down in A-

ru-ba Ja-mai-ca, oo ___ I wan-na take you to Ber-

mu-da, Ba-ha-ma. Come ___ on, pret-ty ma-ma. Key

Lar - go, Mon - te - go, ba - by, why don't we go?
Oo _____ I wan - na take you down to

Ko - ko - mo. _____ We'll get there fast _____ and then we'll

take it slow. _____ That's where we wan - na go, _____

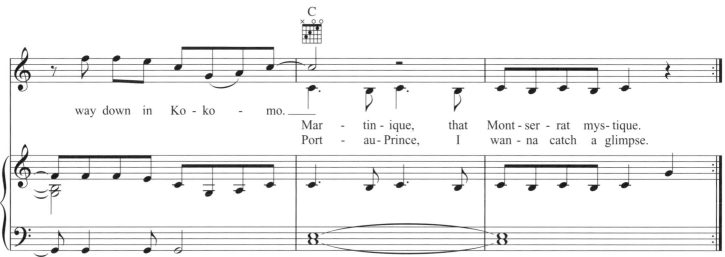

way down in Ko - ko - mo. _____ Mar - tin - ique, that Mont - ser - rat mys - tique.
Port - au - Prince, I wan - na catch a glimpse.

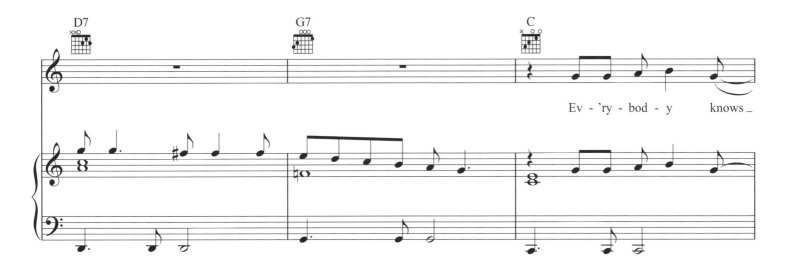

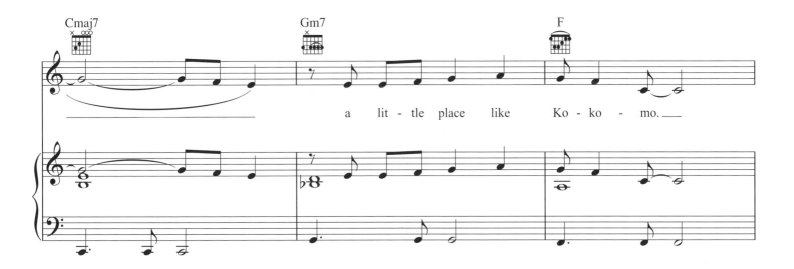

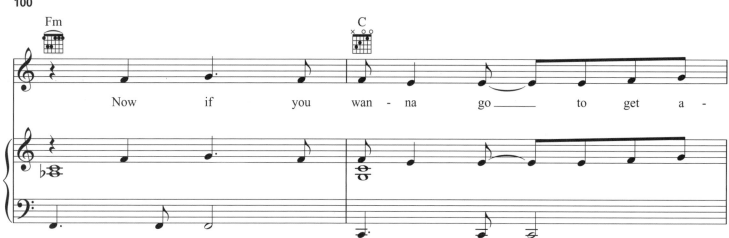

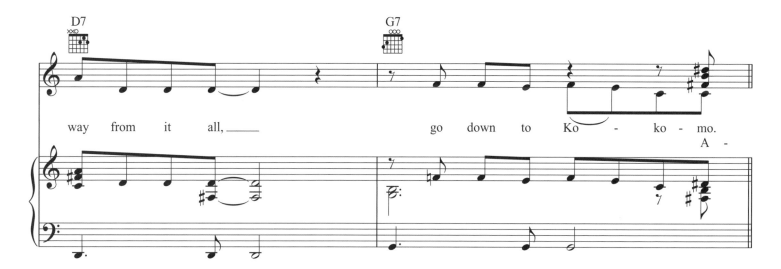

Now if you wan-na go _____ to get a - way from it all, _____ go down to Ko - ko - mo.

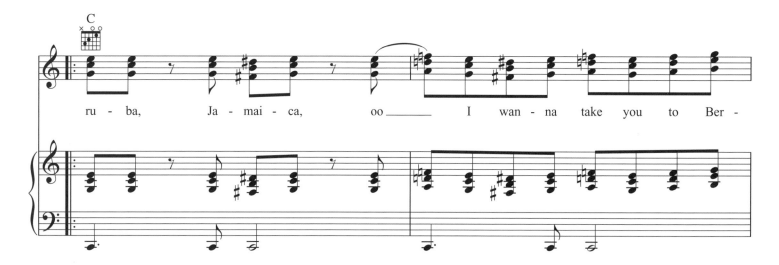

A - ru - ba, Ja - mai - ca, oo _____ I wan-na take you to Ber -

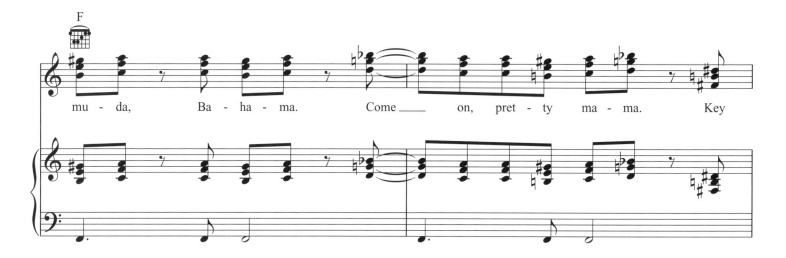

mu - da, Ba - ha - ma. Come _____ on, pret - ty ma - ma. Key

Lar - go, Mon - te - go, ba - by, why don't we go?
Oo _____ I wan - na take you down to

Ko - ko - mo. _____ We'll get there fast _____ and then we'll

take it slow. _____ That's where _____ we _____

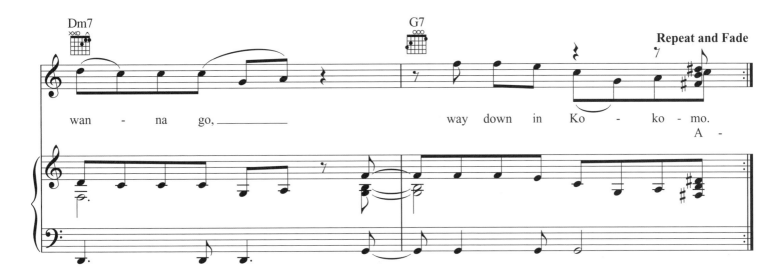

wan - na go, _____ way down in Ko - ko - mo.

A -

LEMON TREE

Words and Music by
WILL HOLT

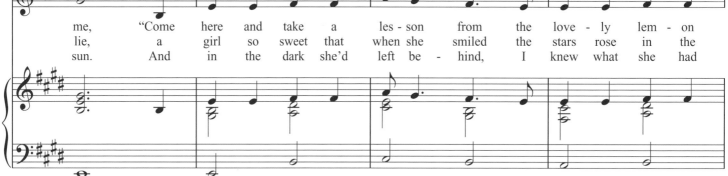

When I was just a lad of ten my fa-ther said to
day be-neath the lem-on tree my love and I did
day she left with-out a word; she took a-way the

me, "Come here and take a les-son from the love-ly lem-on
lie, a girl so sweet that when she smiled the stars rose in the
sun. And in the dark she'd left be-hind, I knew what she had

tree. Don't put your faith in love, my boy!" my fa-ther said to
sky. We passed that sum-mer lost in love __ be-neath the lem-on
done. She'd left me for an-oth-er, it's __ a com-mon tale but

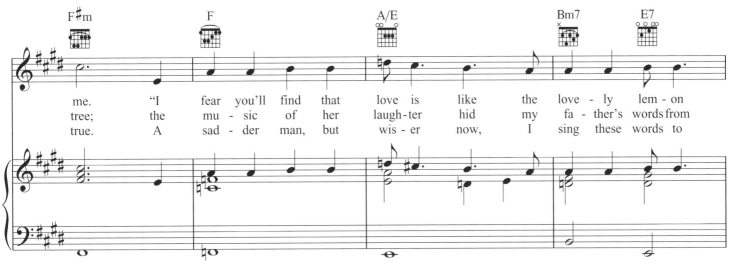

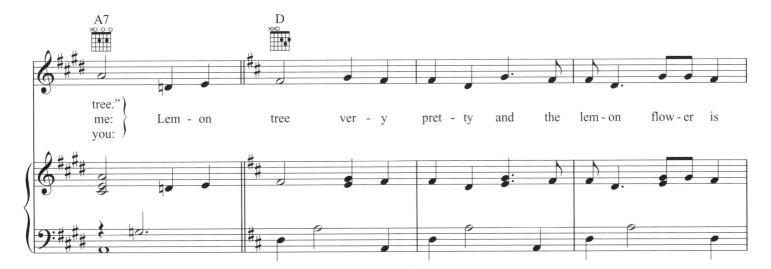

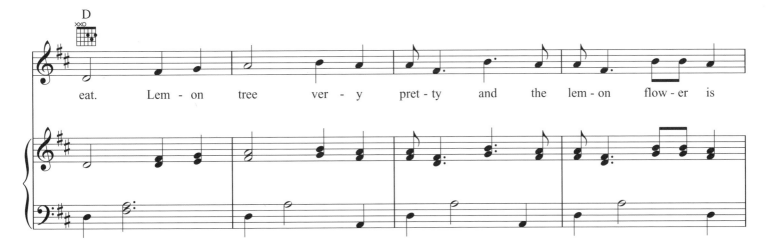

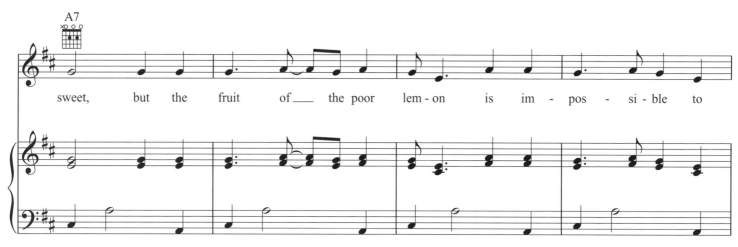

sweet, but the fruit of ___ the poor lem-on is im - pos - si - ble to

eat.   One   eat.   Lem - on   tree, _____

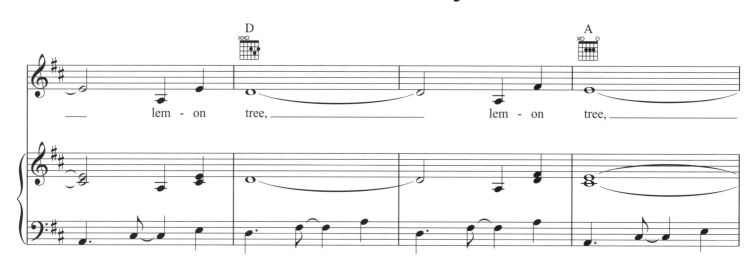

__ lem - on   tree, _____   lem - on   tree, ____

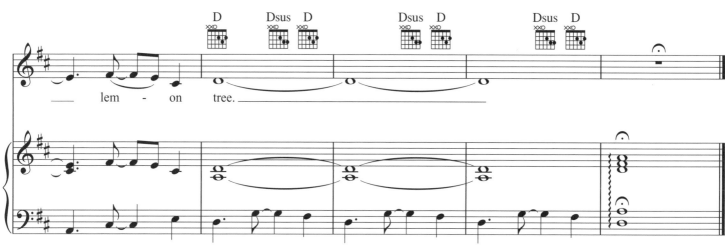

__ lem - on   tree.

LIKE A ROLLING STONE

Words and Music by
BOB DYLAN

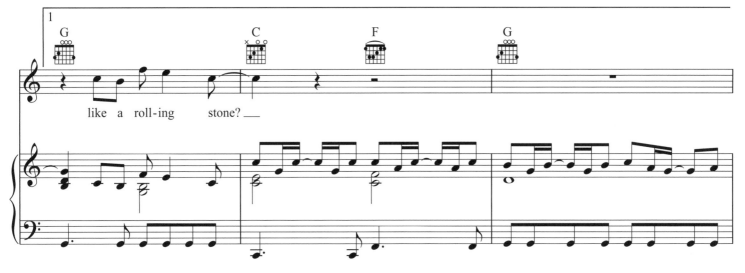

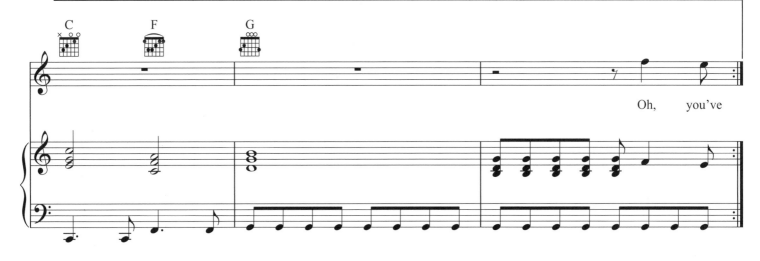

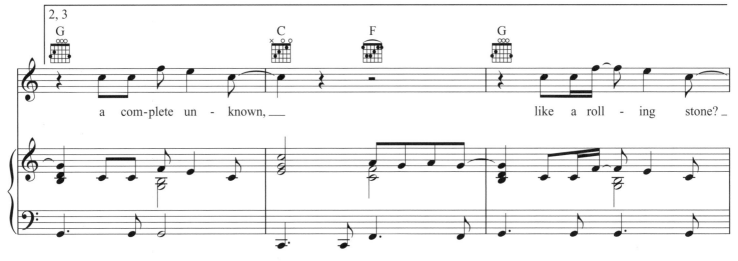

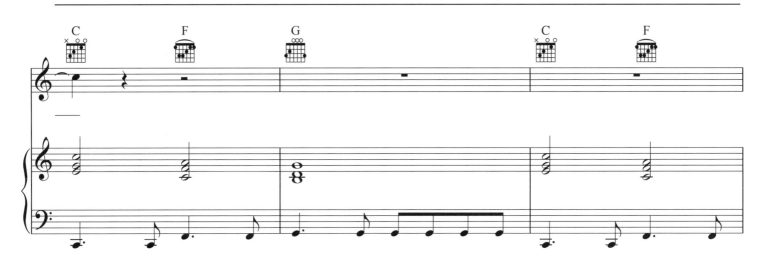

Additional Lyrics

4. Princess on a steeple and all the pretty people
   They're all drinkin', thinkin' that they got it made.
   Exchanging all precious gifts,
   But you better take your diamond ring,
   You better pawn it, babe.
   You used to be so amused
   At Napoleon in rags and the language that he used.
   Go to him now, he calls you, you can't refuse.
   When you ain't got nothin', you got nothin' to lose.
   You're invisible now, you got no secrets to conceal.
   Chorus

LYIN' EYES

Words and Music by DON HENLEY
and GLENN FREY

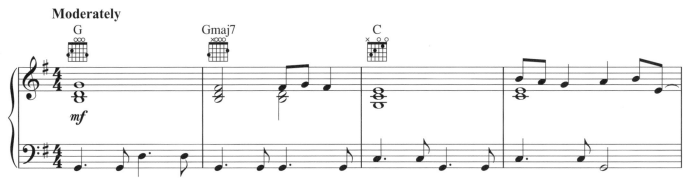

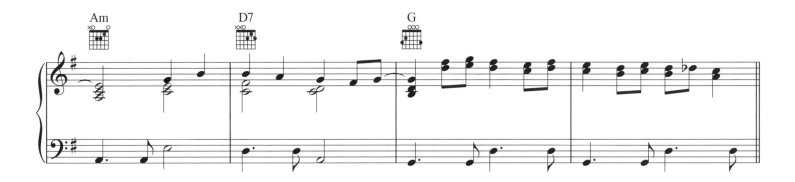

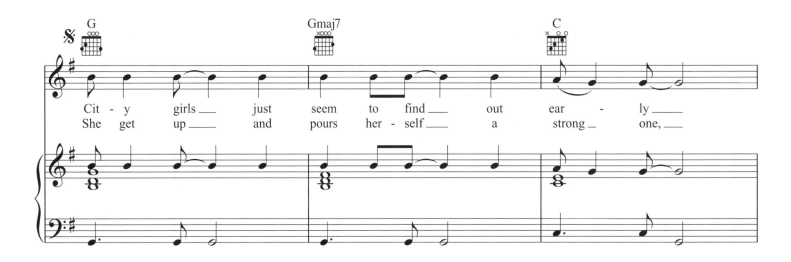

City girls just seem to find __ out ear - ly __
She get up __ and pours her - self __ a strong __ one, __

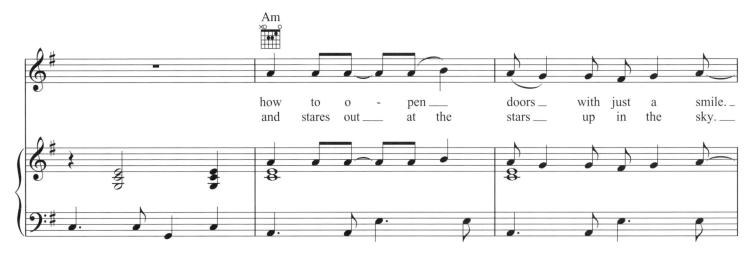

how to o - pen __ doors __ with just a smile.
and stares out __ at the stars __ up in the sky. __

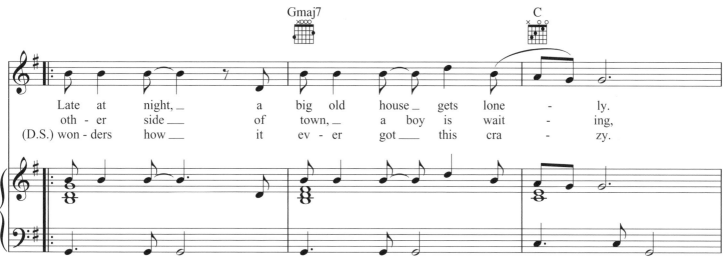

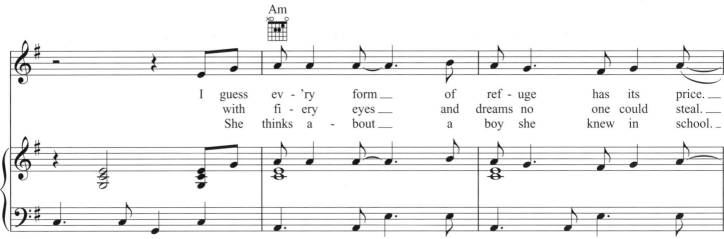

I guess ev-'ry form __ of ref-uge has its price. __
with fi-ery eyes __ and dreams no one could steal. __
She thinks a-bout __ a boy she knew in school. __

___ And it breaks her heart __ to
___ She drives __ on through to the
___ Did she get tired, __ or

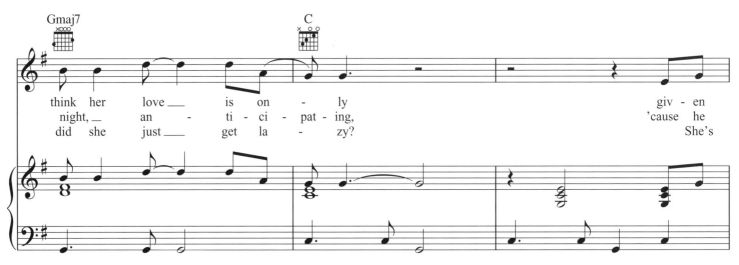

think her love __ is on-ly
night, __ an-ti-ci-pat-ing,
did she just __ get la-zy?

giv-en
'cause he
She's

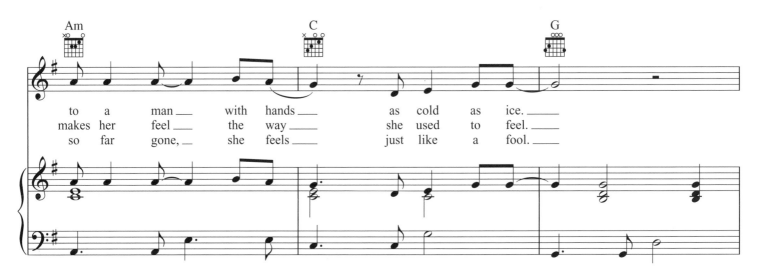

to a man __ with hands __ as cold as ice. __
makes her feel __ the way __ she used to feel. __
so far gone, __ she feels __ just like a fool. __

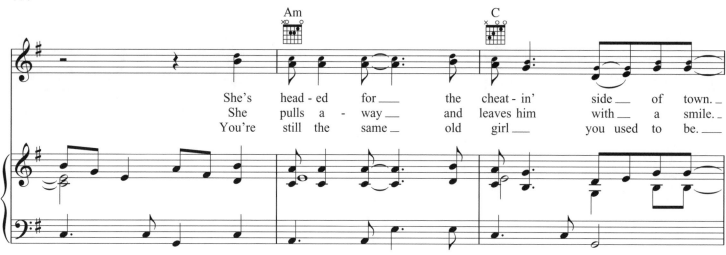

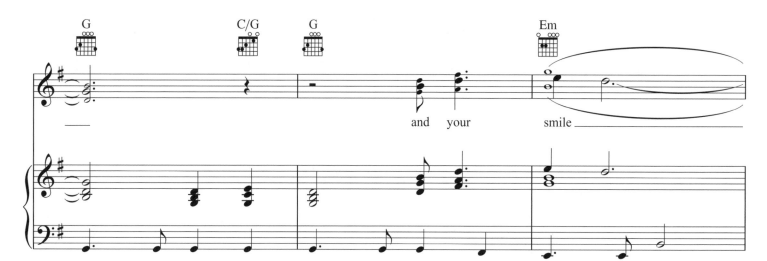

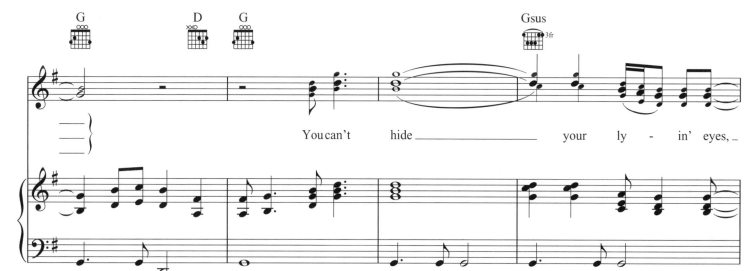

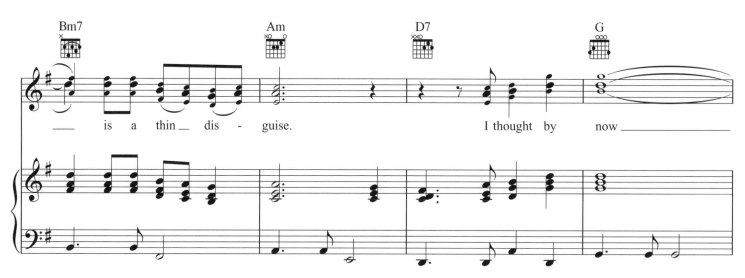

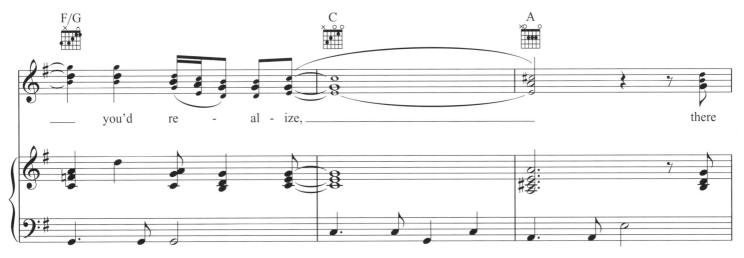

you'd re - al - ize, _____ there

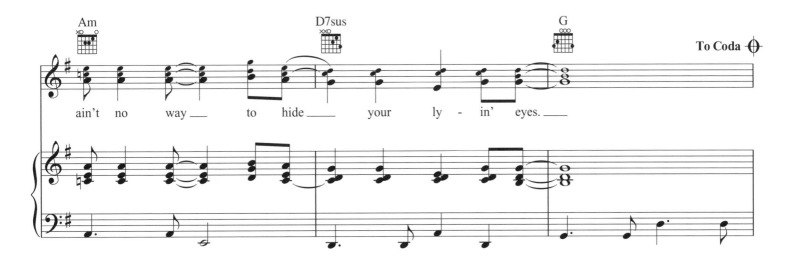

ain't no way ___ to hide ___ your ly - in' eyes. ___

To Coda ⊕

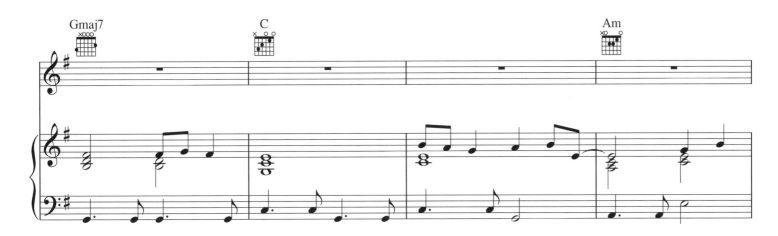

On the

D.S. al Coda

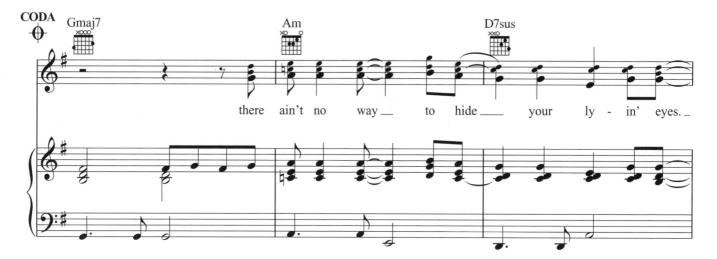

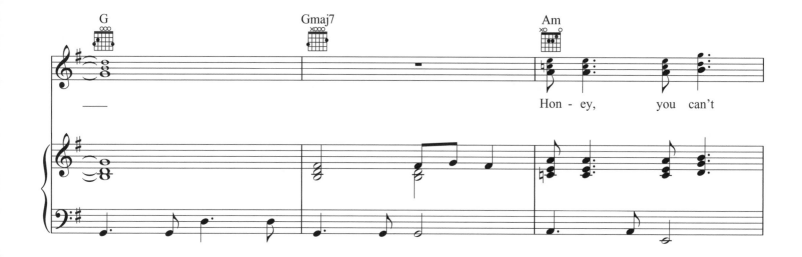

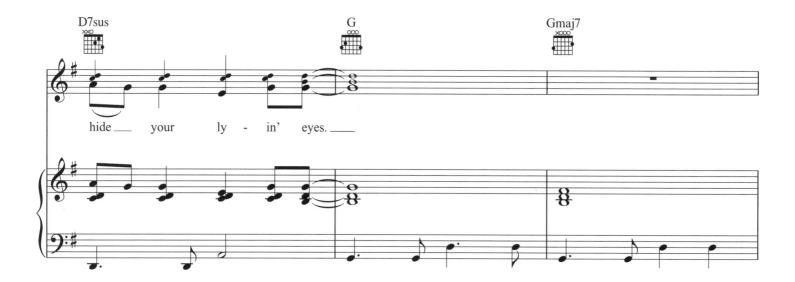

MRS. ROBINSON

Words and Music by
PAUL SIMON

Moderately bright

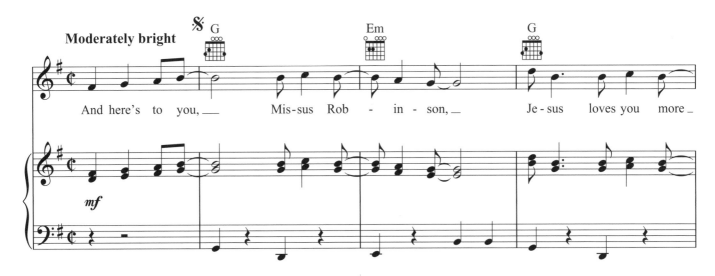

And here's to you, __ Mis-sus Rob - in - son, __ Je - sus loves you more __

__ than you __ will know. _____ (Wo, wo, wo.) __

God bless you, please, Mis-sus Rob - in - son, __ Heav-en holds __ a place __

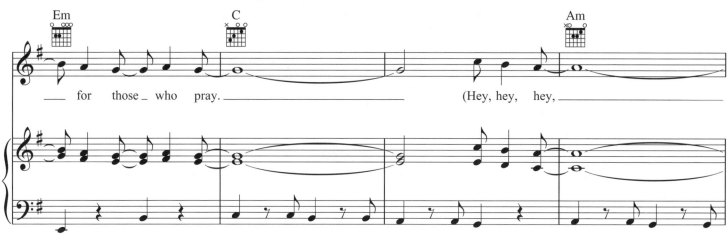

for those who pray. (Hey, hey, hey,

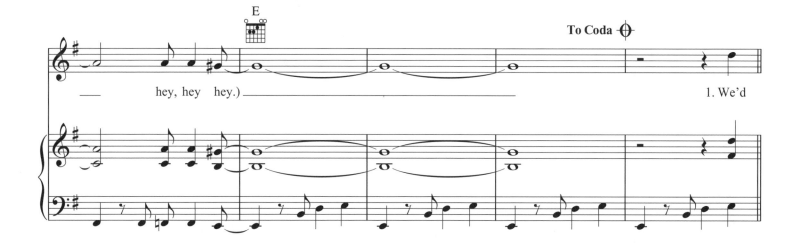

To Coda

hey, hey hey.) 1. We'd

like to know a lit - tle bit about you for our files,

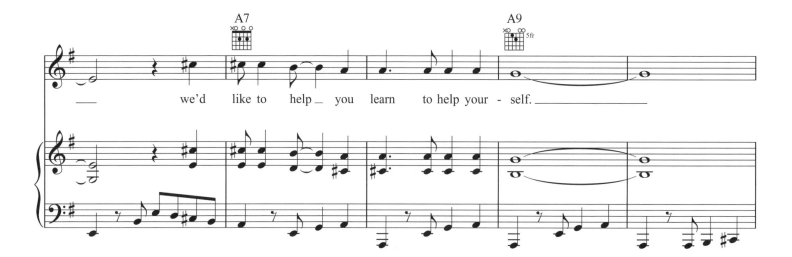

we'd like to help you learn to help your - self.

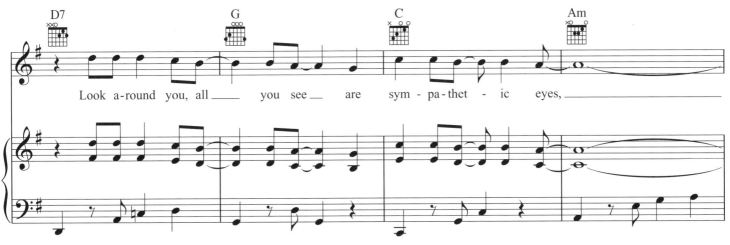

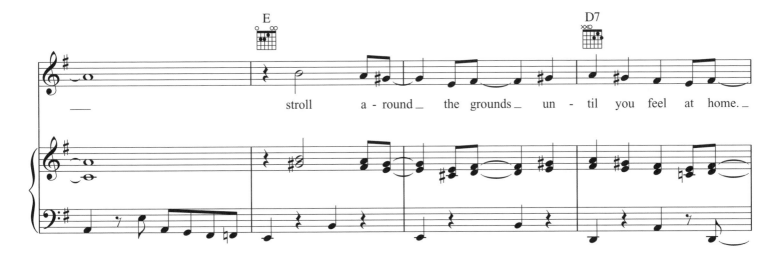

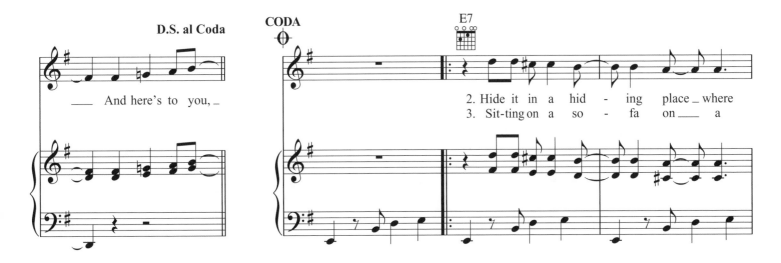

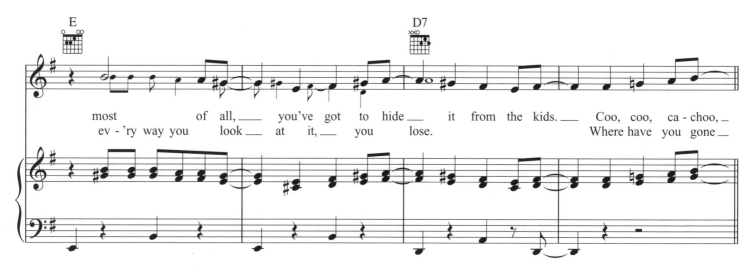

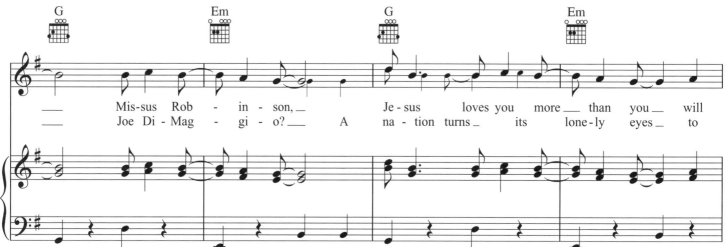

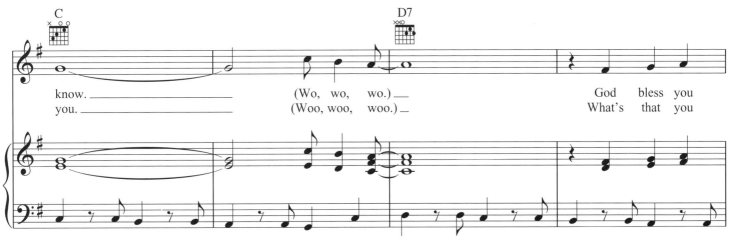

know. _____ (Wo, wo, wo.) _ God bless you
you. _____ (Woo, woo, woo.) _ What's that you

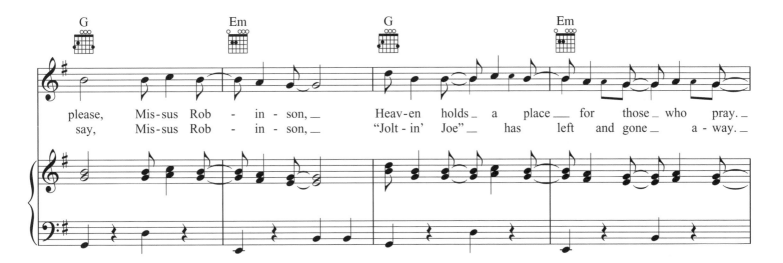

please, Mis-sus Rob - in - son, _ Heav-en holds _ a place _ for those _ who pray. _
say, Mis-sus Rob - in - son, _ "Jolt - in' Joe" _ has left and gone _ a - way. _

(Hey, hey, hey, _____ hey, hey, hey.) _
(Hey, hey, hey, _____ hey, hey, hey.) _

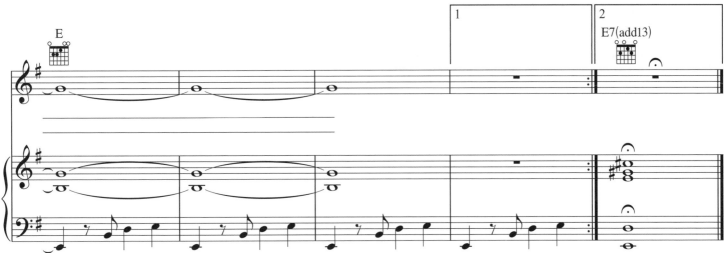

MR. BOJANGLES

Words and Music by
JERRY JEFF WALKER

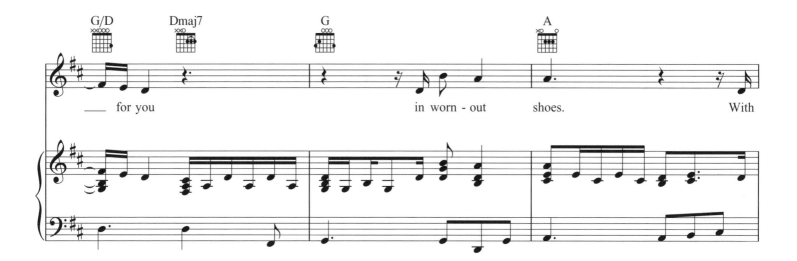

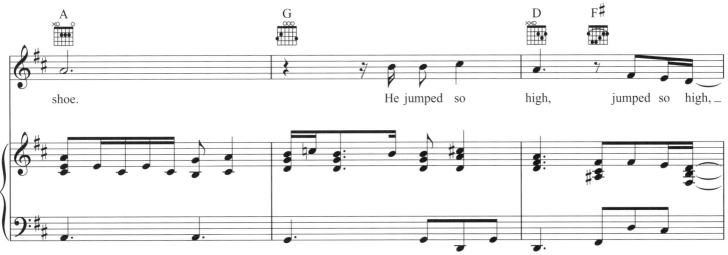

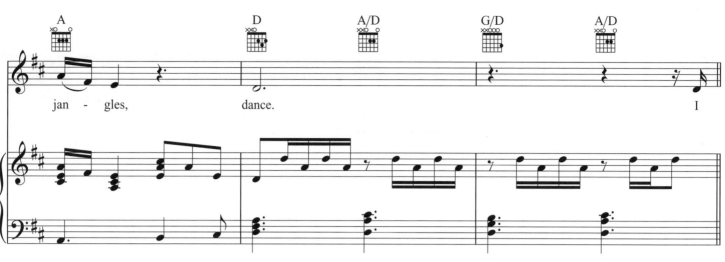

jan - gles, dance. I

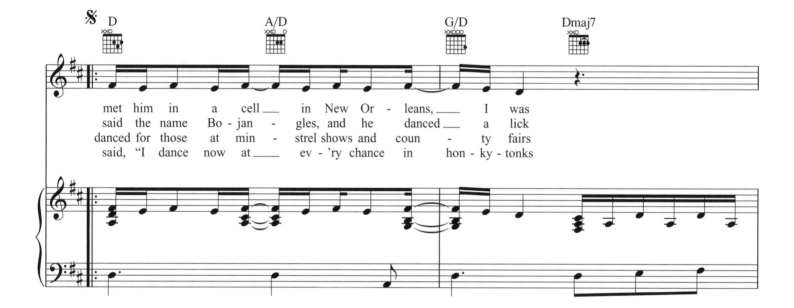

met him in a cell___ in New Or - leans,___ I was
said the name Bo - jan - gles, and he danced___ a lick
danced for those at min - strel shows and coun - ty fairs
said, "I dance now at___ ev - 'ry chance in hon - ky - tonks

down and out.___ He
a - cross the cell.___ He
through - out the South.___ He
for drinks and tips.___ But

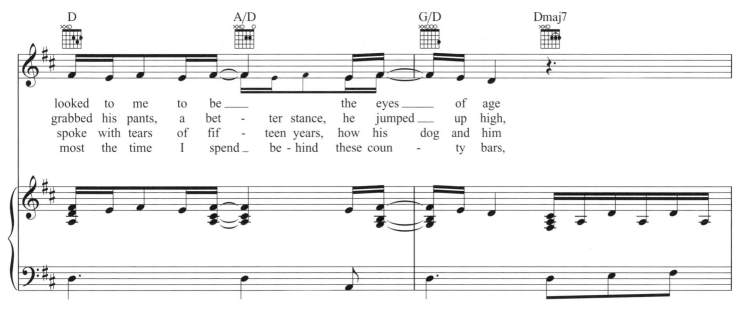

looked to me to be ____ the eyes ____ of age
grabbed his pants, a bet - ter stance, he jumped ____ up high,
spoke with tears of fif - teen years, how his dog and him
most the time I spend ____ be - hind these coun - ty bars,

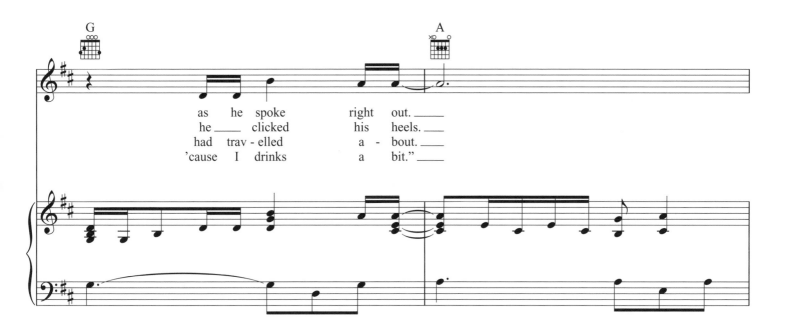

as he spoke right out. ____
he ____ clicked his heels. ____
had trav - elled a - bout. ____
'cause I drinks a bit." ____

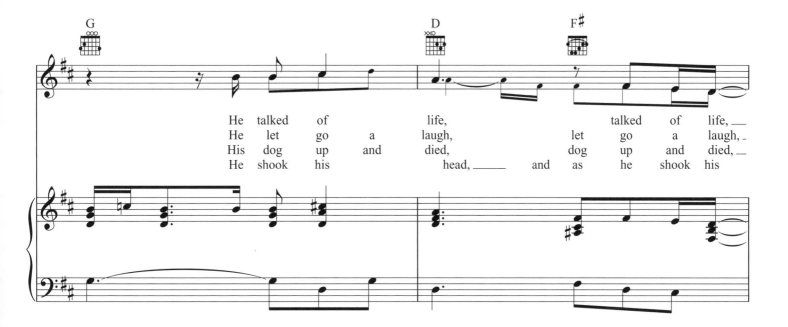

He talked of life, talked of life, ___
He let go a laugh, let go a laugh, _
His dog up and died, dog up and died, _
He shook his head, ____ and as he shook his

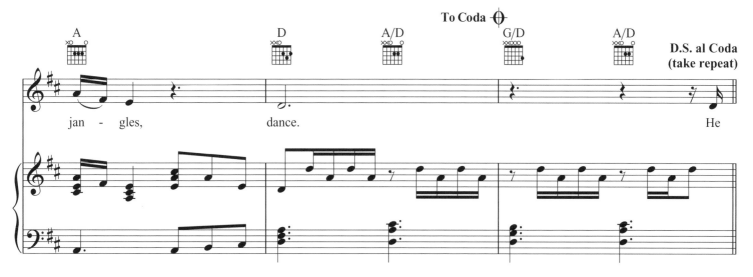

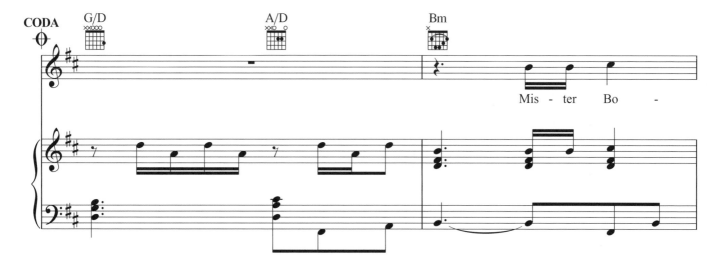

MR. TAMBOURINE MAN

Words and Music by
BOB DYLAN

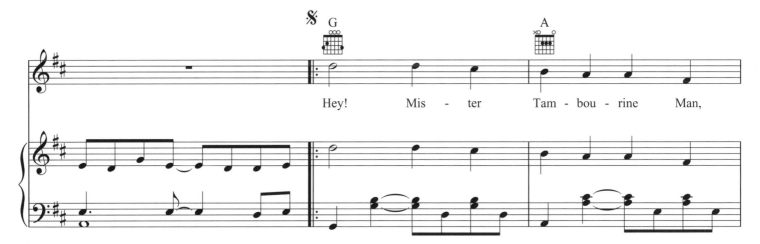

Hey! Mis- ter Tam- bou- rine Man,

play a song for me, I'm not sleep- y and there

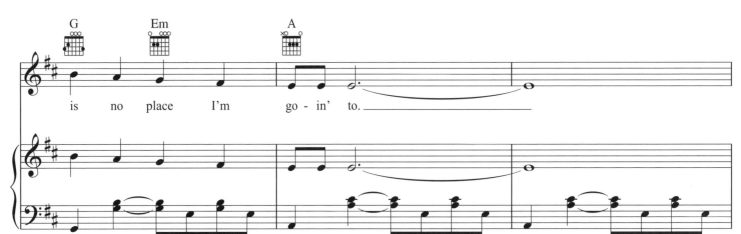

is no place I'm go- in' to. _____

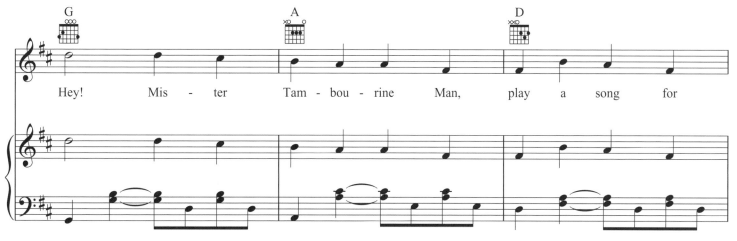

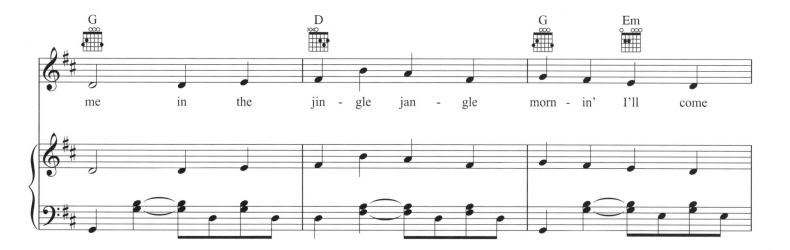

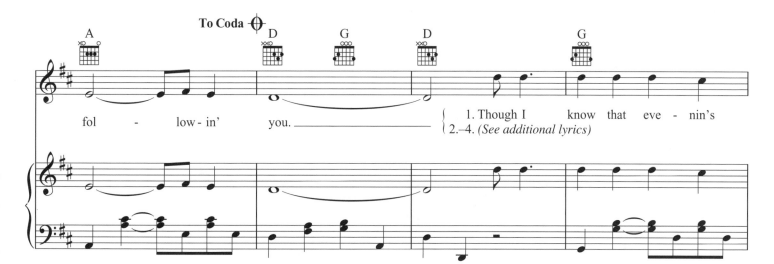

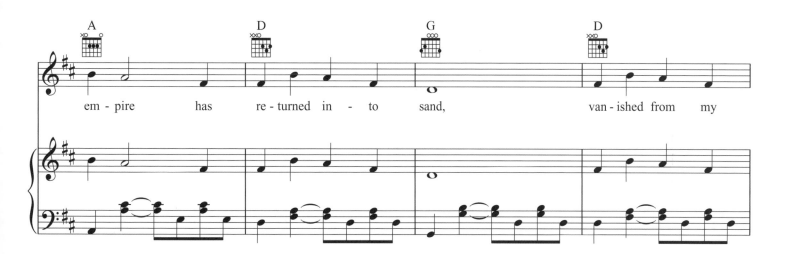

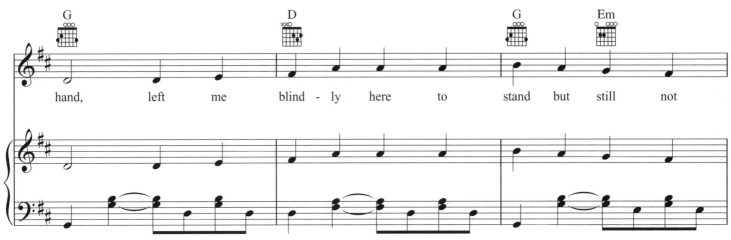

hand, left me blind - ly here to stand but still not

sleep - in'! _____ My wea - ri - ness a -

maz - es me, I'm brand - ed on my feet. I

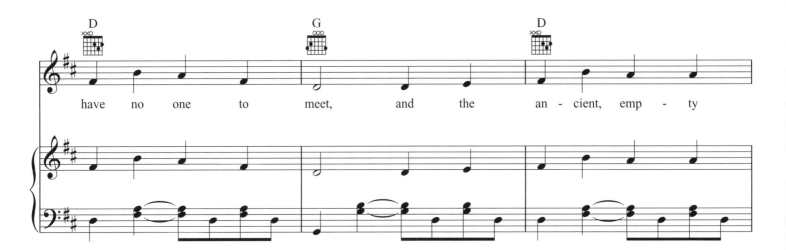

have no one to meet, and the an - cient, emp - ty

Additional Lyrics

2. Take me on a trip upon your magic swirlin' ship
My senses have been stripped, my hands can't feel to grip
My toes too numb to step, wait only for my boot heels
To be wanderin'
I'm ready to go anywhere, I'm ready for to fade
Into my own parade, cast your dancin' spell my way
I promise to go under it.

3. Though you might hear laughin' spinnin' swingin' madly across the sun
It's not aimed at anyone, it's just escapin' on the run
And but for the sky there are no fences facin'
And if you hear vague traces of skippin' reels of rhyme
To your tambourine in time, it's just a ragged clown behind
I wouldn't pay it any mind, it's just a shadow you're
Seein' that he's chasin'.

4. Then take me disappearin' through the smoke rings of my mind
Down the foggy ruins of time, far past the frozen leaves
The haunted, frightened trees out to the windy beach
Far from the twisted reach of crazy sorrow
Yes, to dance beneath the diamond sky with one hand wavin' free
Silhouetted by the sea, circled by the circus sands
With all memory and fate driven deep beneath the waves
Let me forget about today until tomorrow.

MONDAY, MONDAY

Words and Music by
JOHN PHILLIPS

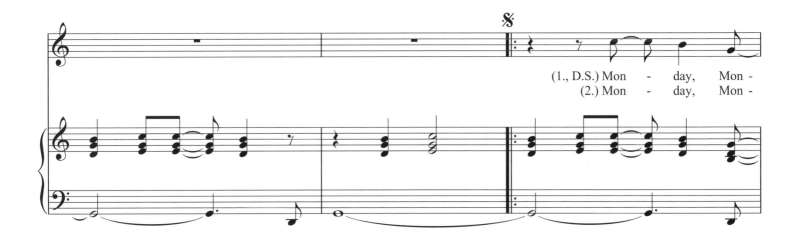

(1., D.S.) Mon - day, Mon -
(2.) Mon - day, Mon -

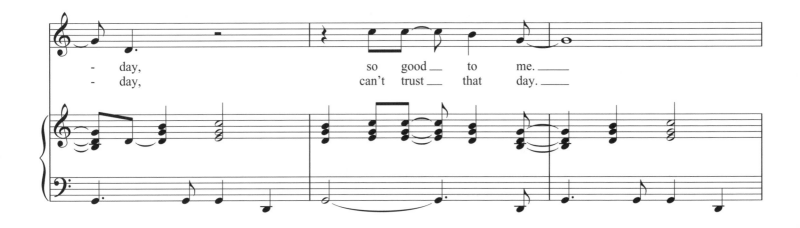

- day,   so good __ to   me. __
- day,   can't trust __ that day. __

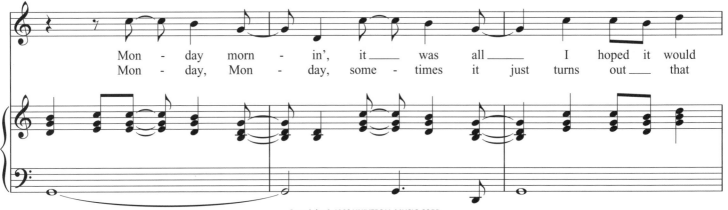

Mon - day morn - in', it __ was all __ I hoped it would
Mon - day, Mon - day, some - times it just turns out __ that

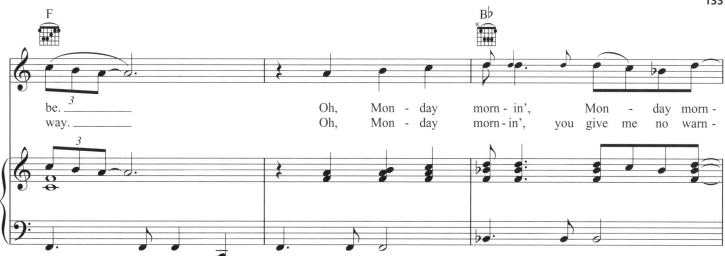

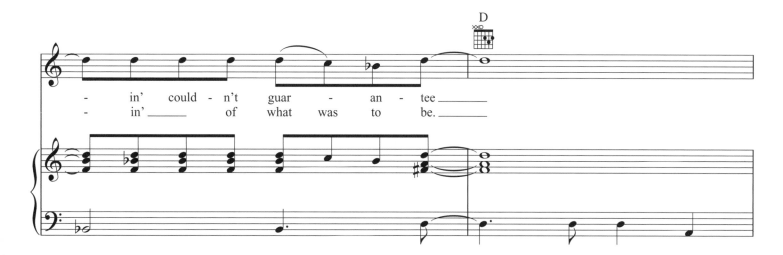

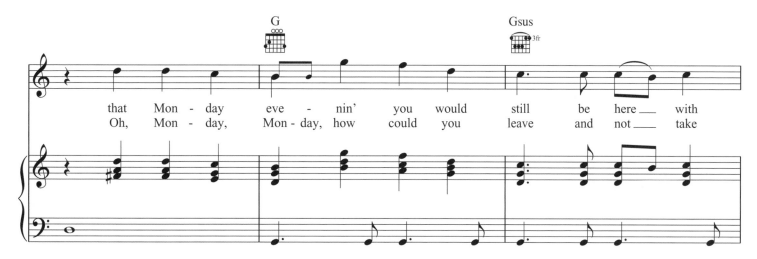

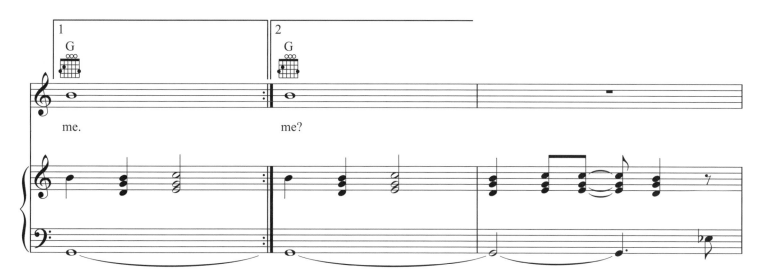

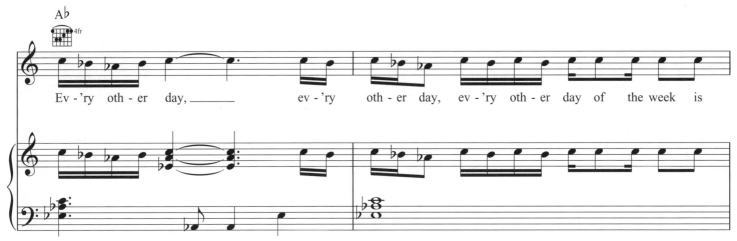

Ev-'ry oth-er day, _____ ev-'ry oth-er day, ev-'ry oth-er day of the week is

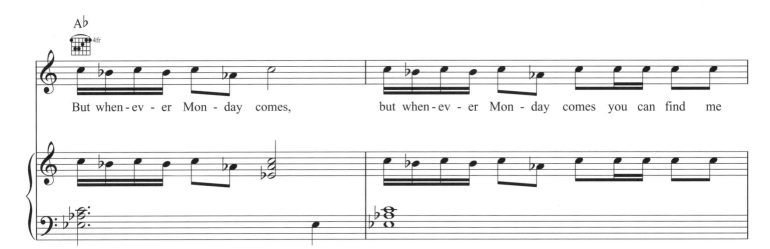

fine, yeah! _____

But when-ev-er Mon-day comes, but when-ev-er Mon-day comes you can find me

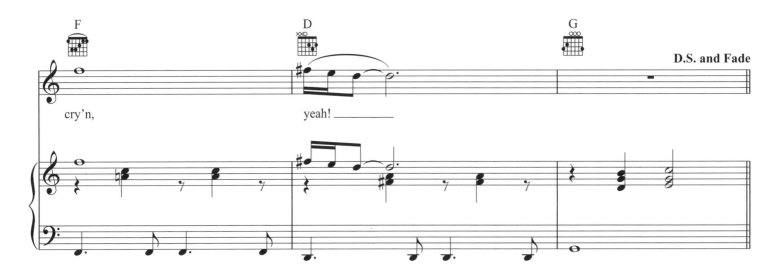

D.S. and Fade

cry'n, yeah! _____

MORNING HAS BROKEN

Words by ELEANOR FARJEON
Music by CAT STEVENS

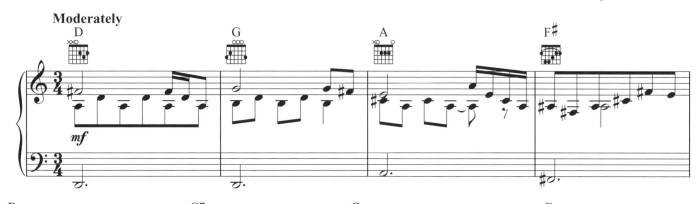

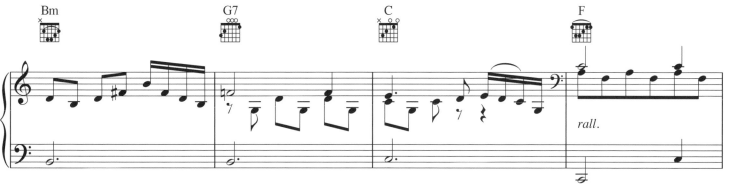

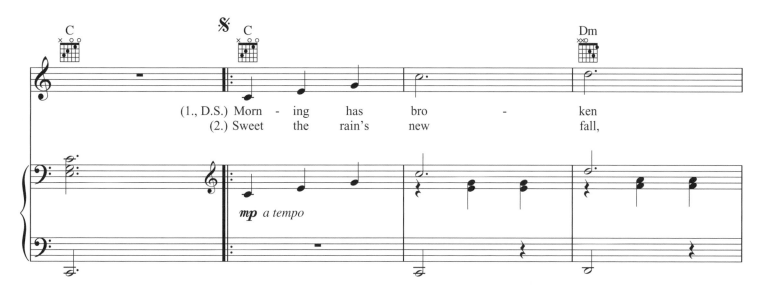

(1., D.S.) Morn - ing has bro - ken
(2.) Sweet the rain's new fall,

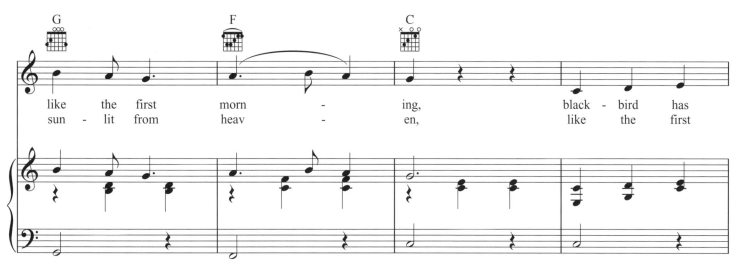

like the first morn - ing, black - bird has
sun - lit from heav - en, like the first

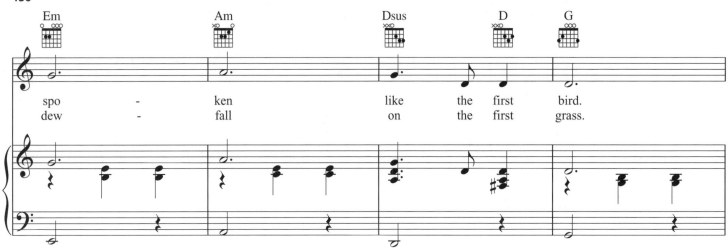

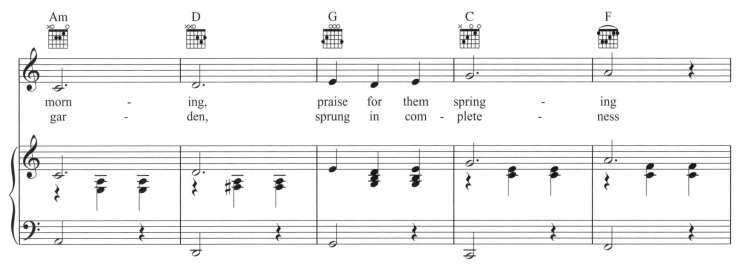

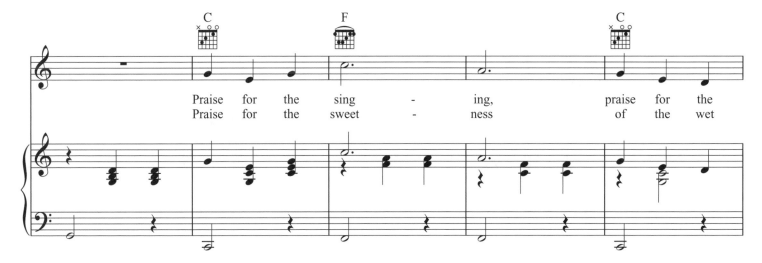

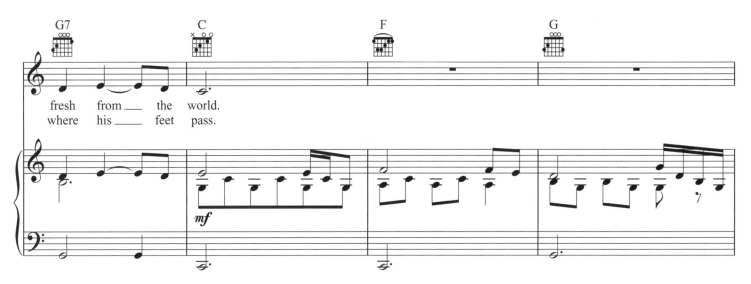

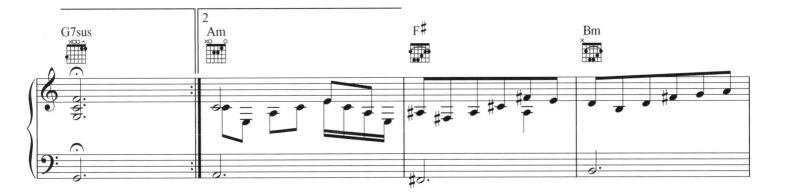

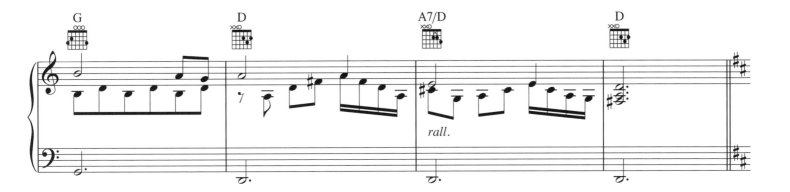

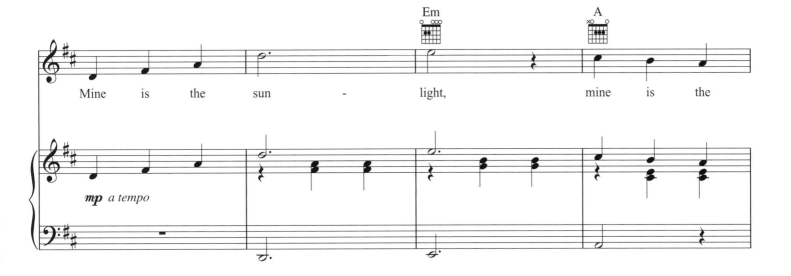

Mine is the sun - light, mine is the

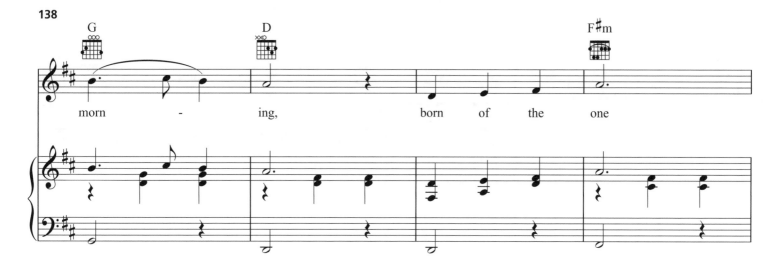

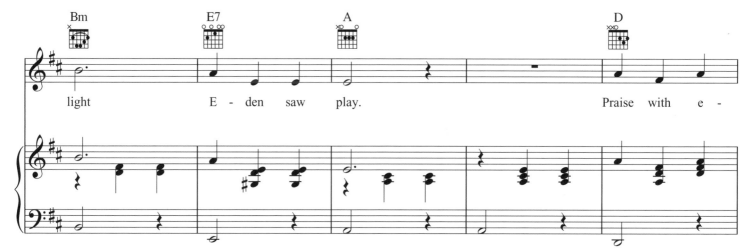

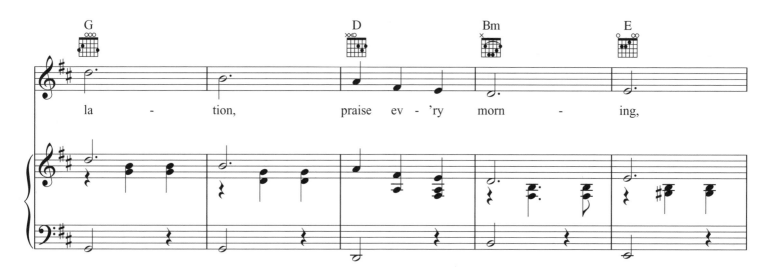

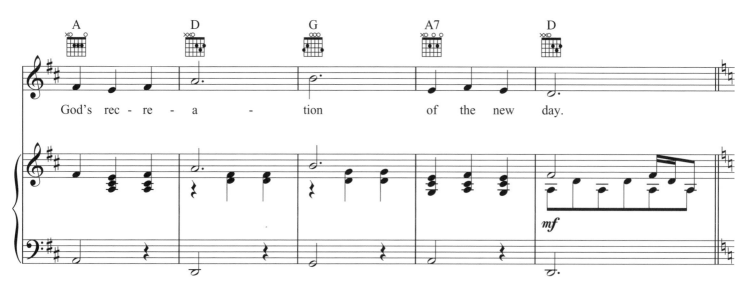

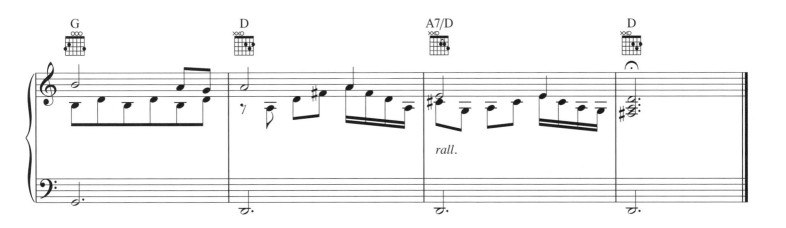

MOUNTAIN MUSIC

Words and Music by
RANDY OWEN

Brightly, in 2

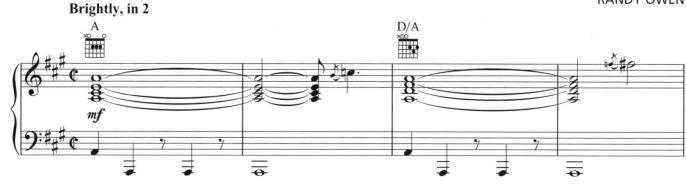

Oh, play me _____ some moun-tain mu - sic, ___ like

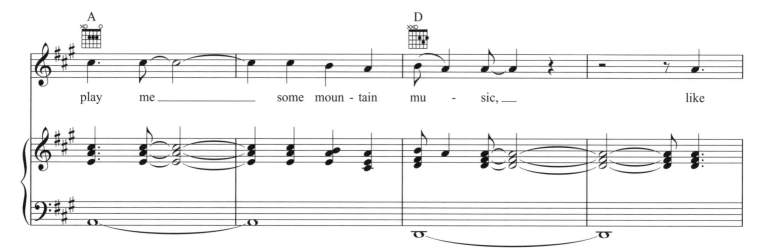

grand-ma and grand-pa used to play. ___ Then I'll

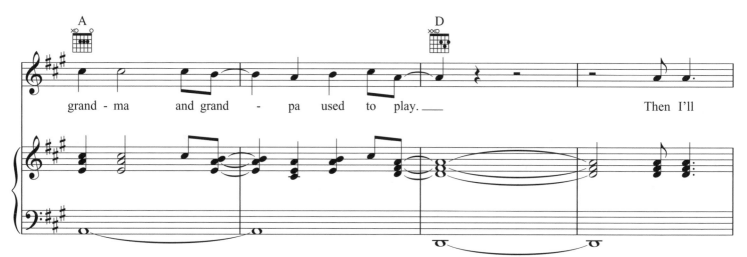

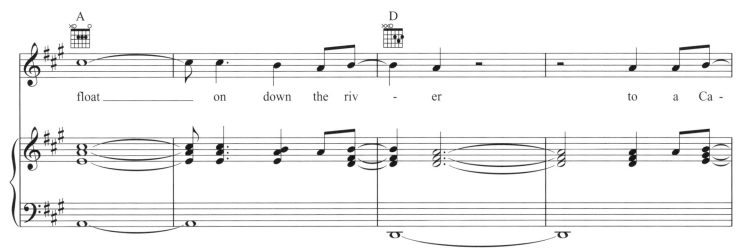

float _____ on down the riv - er _____ to a Ca -

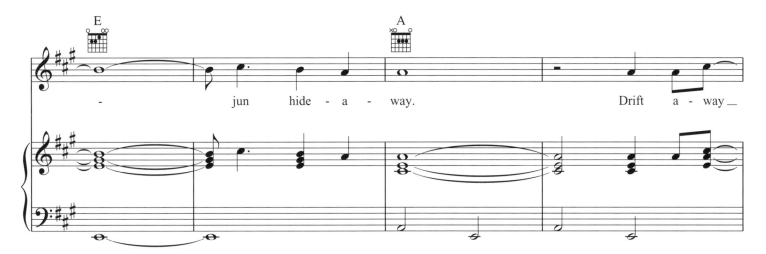

- jun hide - a - way. _____ Drift a - way _____

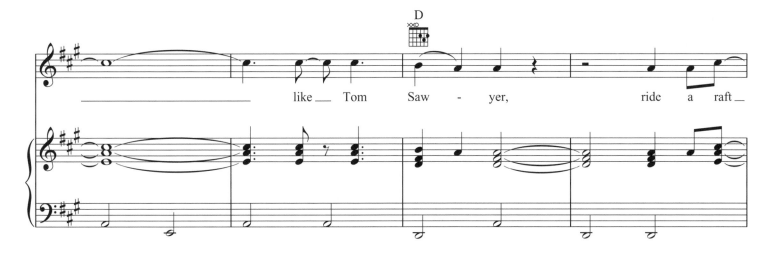

_____ like __ Tom Saw - yer, _____ ride a raft __

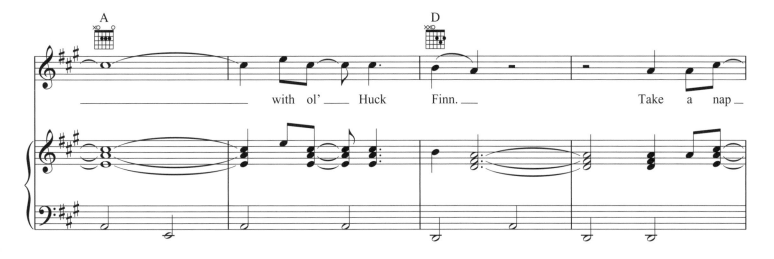

_____ with ol' ____ Huck Finn. ___ Take a nap _____

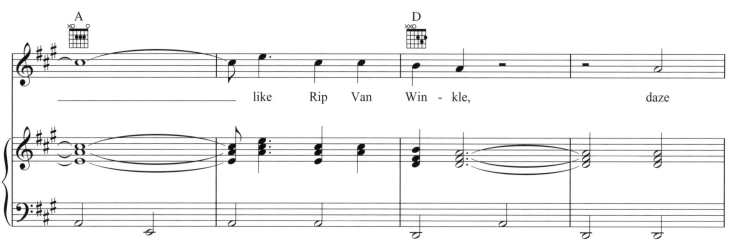

like Rip Van Win - kle, daze

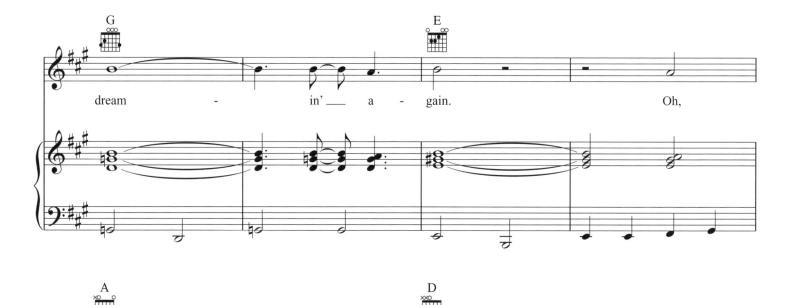

dream - in' __ a - gain. Oh,

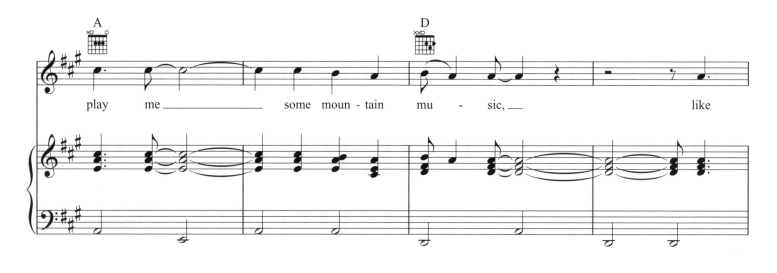

play me ___ some moun - tain mu - sic, __ like

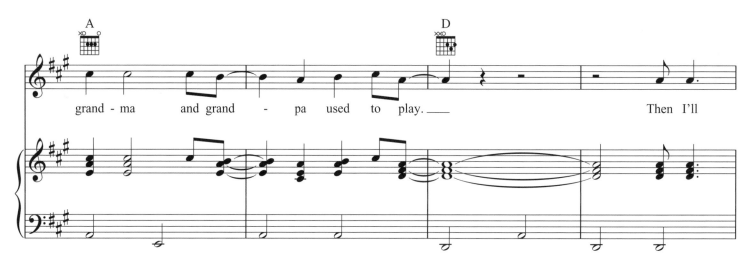

grand - ma and grand - pa used to play. __ Then I'll

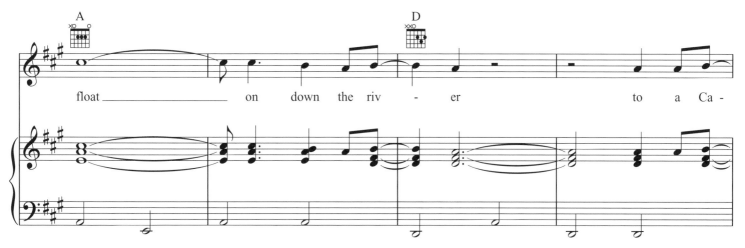

float _____ on down the riv - er to a Ca -

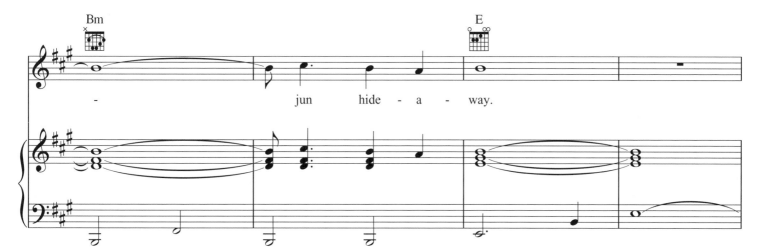

- jun hide - a - way.

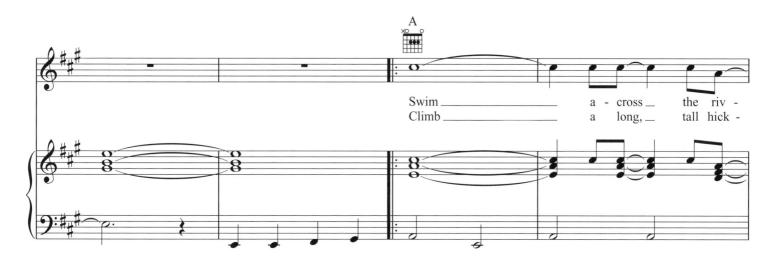

Swim _____ a - cross _ the riv -
Climb _____ a long, _ tall hick -

- er, just to prove _____ that I'm _ a man. _
- 'ry. Bend it o - ver "skin - nin' cats." _

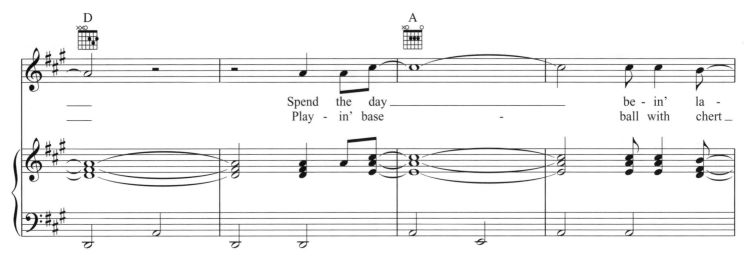

Spend the day _____ be - in' la -
Play - in' base - ball with chert __

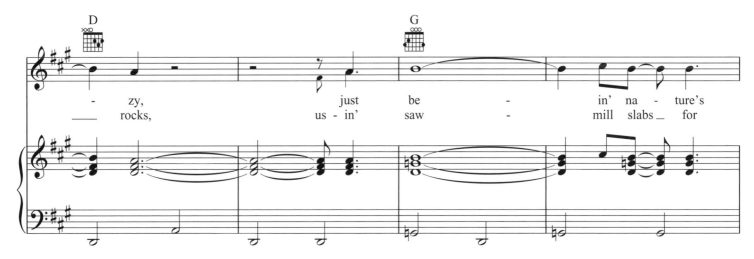

- zy, just be - in' na - ture's
____ rocks, us - in' saw - mill slabs __ for

1.
friend.

2.
bats.

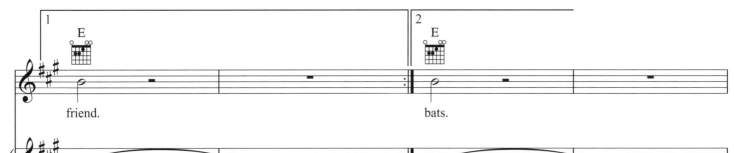

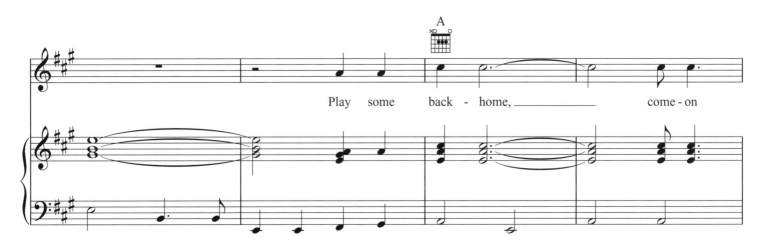

Play some back - home, _____ come - on

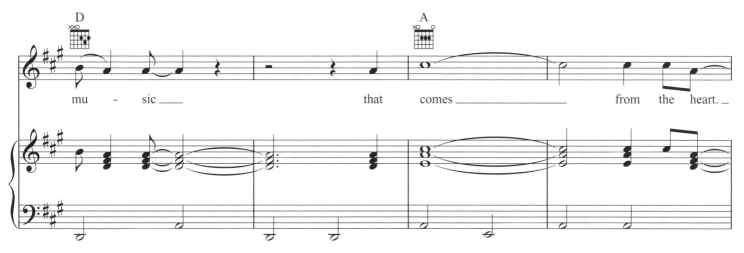

mu - sic ___ that comes ___ from the heart. ___

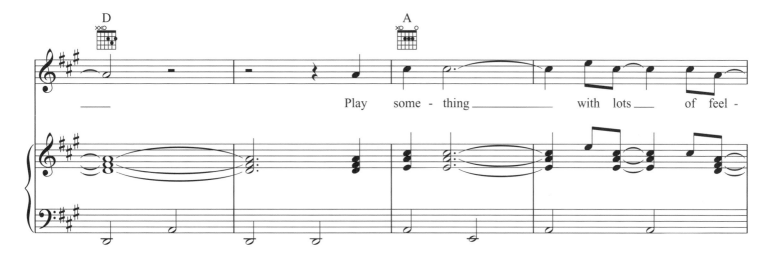

___ Play some - thing ___ with lots ___ of feel -

- in', 'cause that's where mu - sic has ___ to

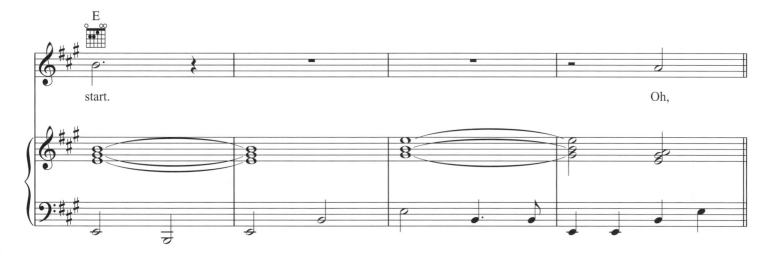

start. Oh,

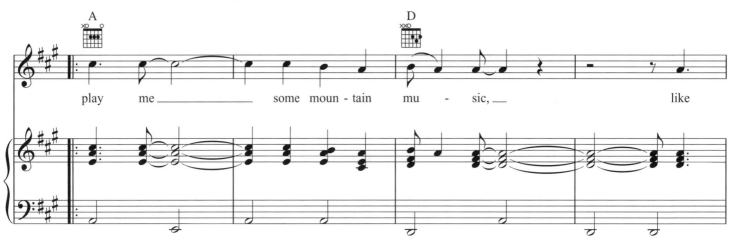

play me _____ some moun-tain mu-sic, ___ like

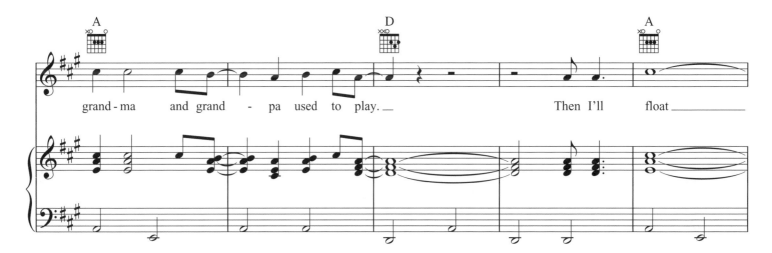

grand-ma and grand-pa used to play. ___ Then I'll float _____

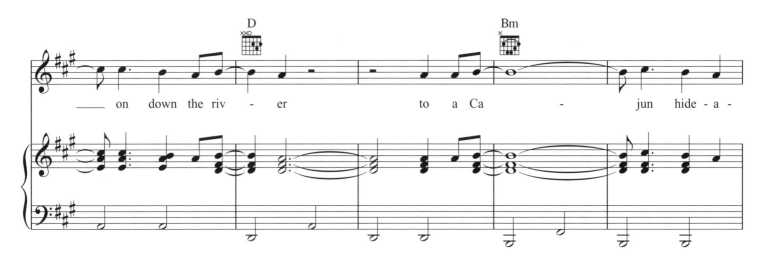

___ on down the riv - er to a Ca - jun hide-a-

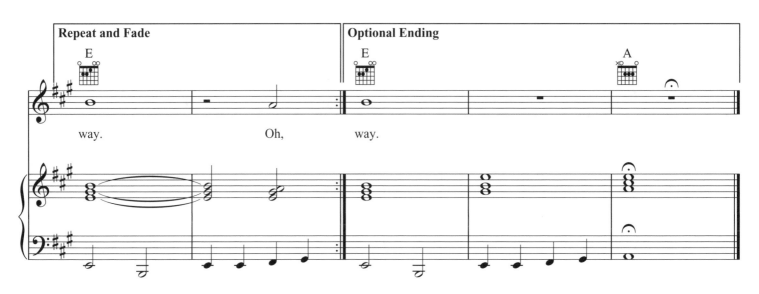

Repeat and Fade

Optional Ending

way. Oh, way.

PEACEFUL EASY FEELING

Words and Music by
JACK TEMPCHIN

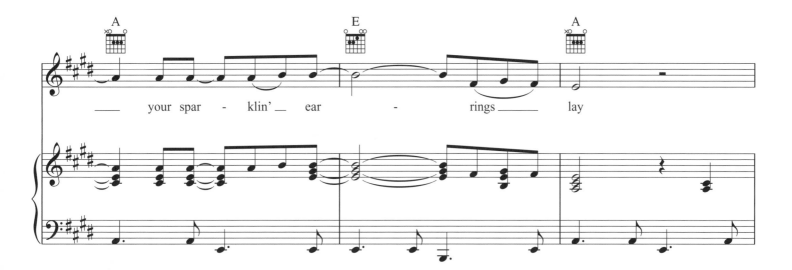

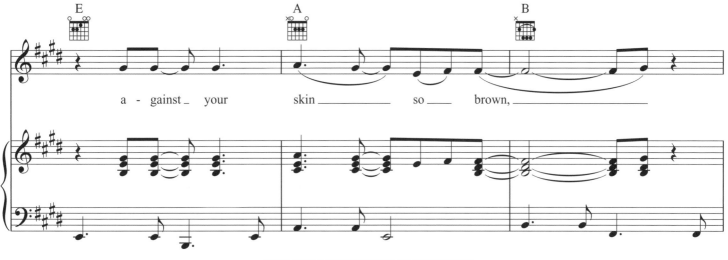

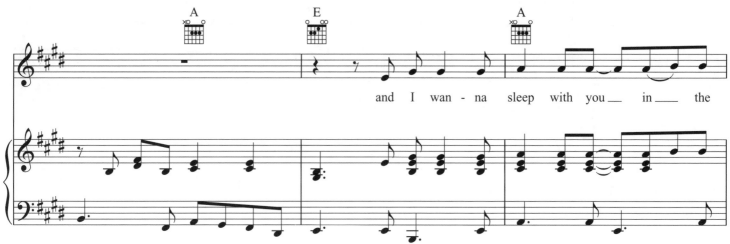

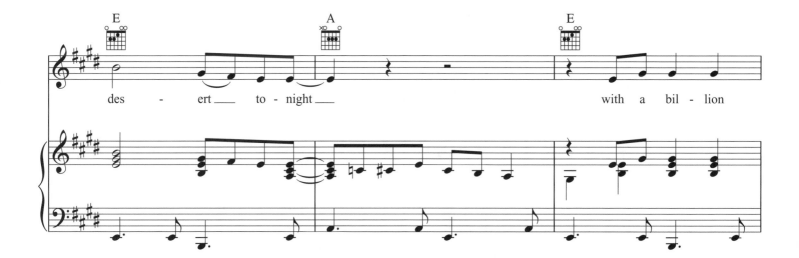

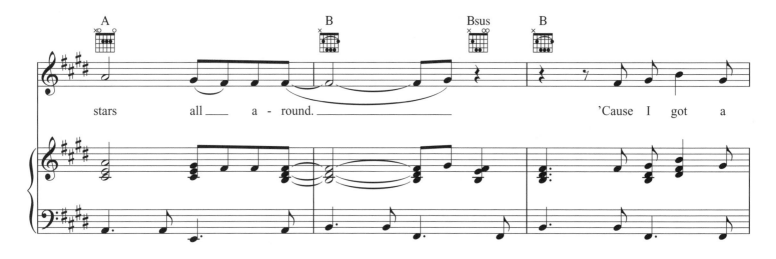

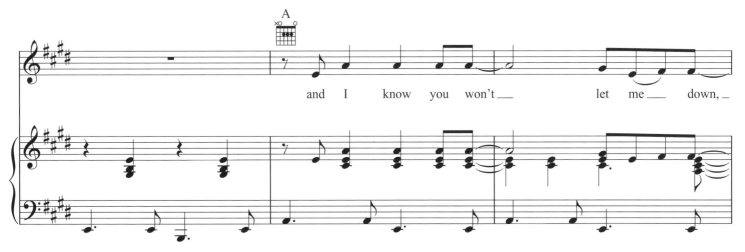

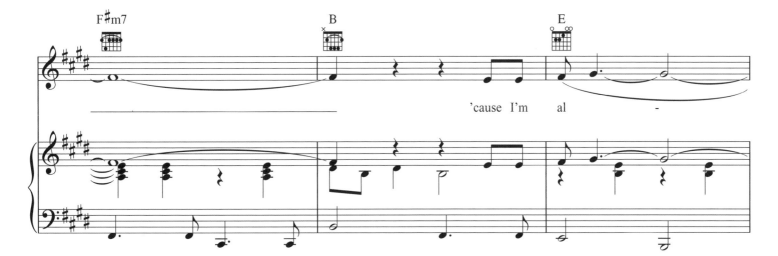

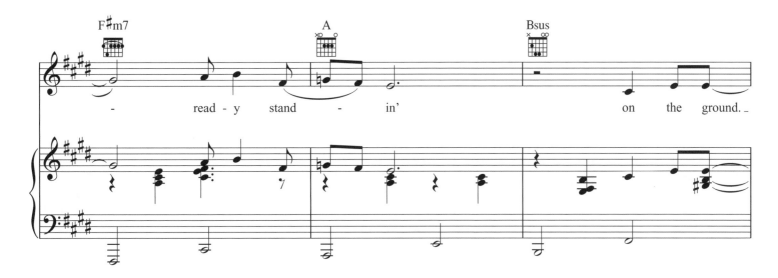

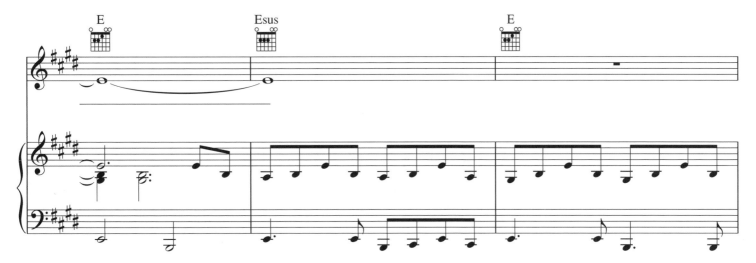

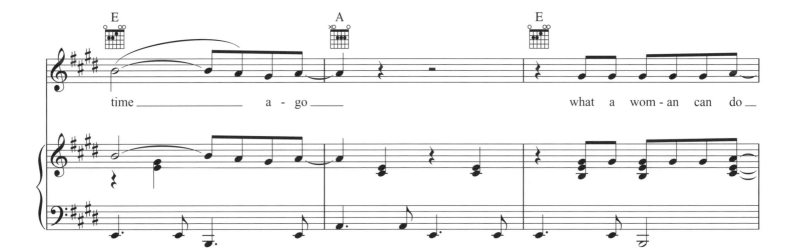

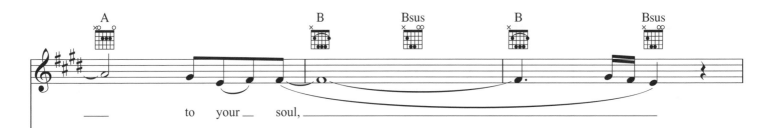

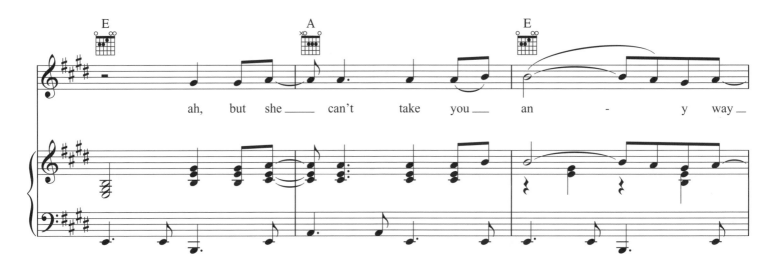

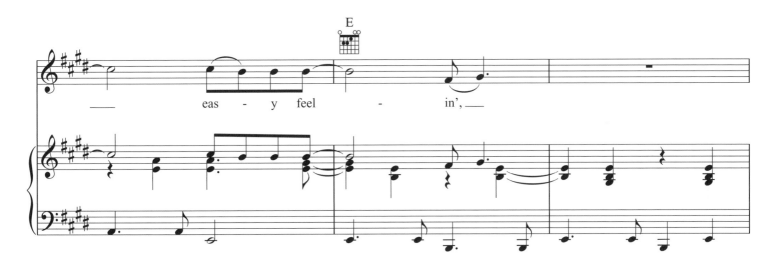

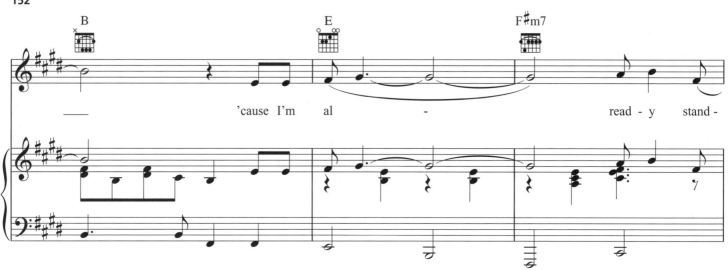

'cause I'm al - read - y stand -

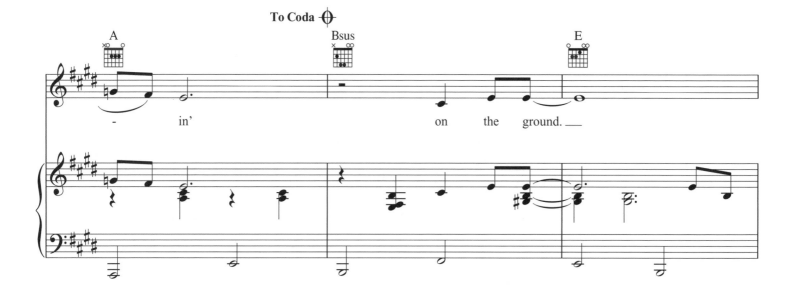

To Coda ⊕

- in' on the ground. ___

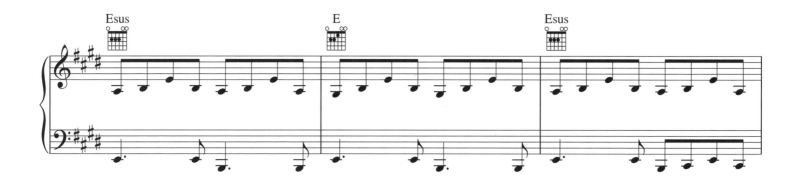

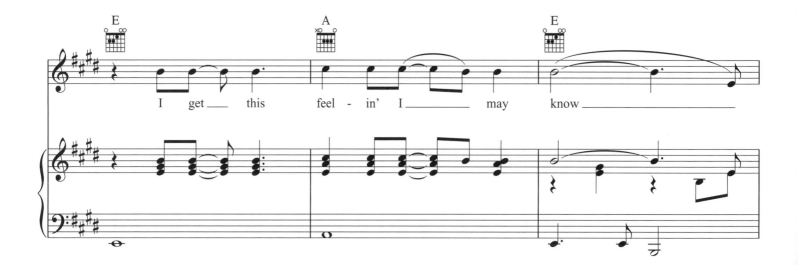

I get ___ this feel - in' I ___ may know ___

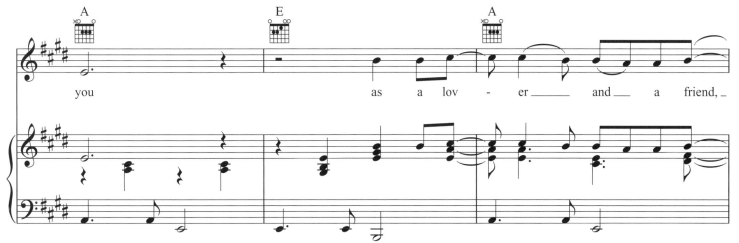

you as a lov - er _____ and _ a friend, _

but this voice keeps

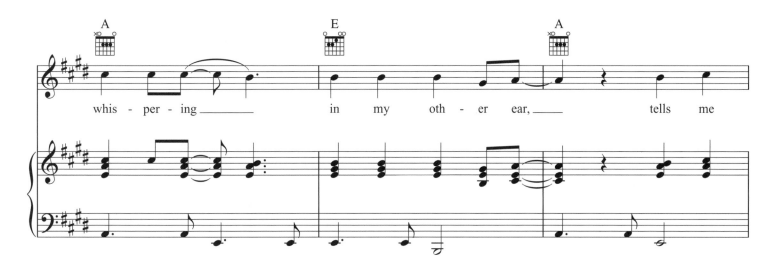

whis - per - ing _____ in my oth - er ear, _____ tells me

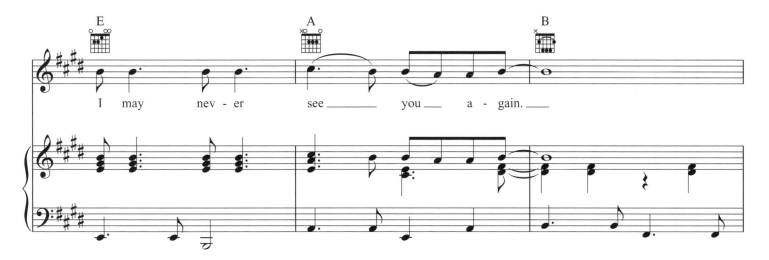

I may nev - er see _____ you _ a - gain. _____

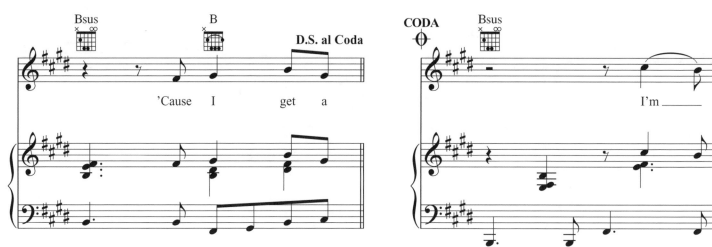

'Cause I get a

D.S. al Coda

CODA

I'm _____

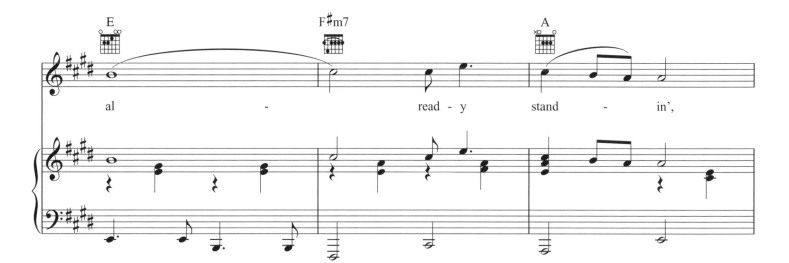

al - read-y stand-in',

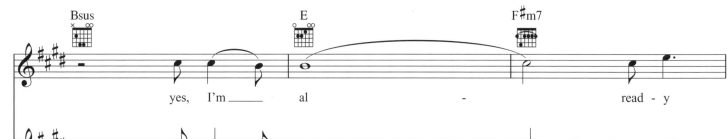

yes, I'm _____ al - read-y

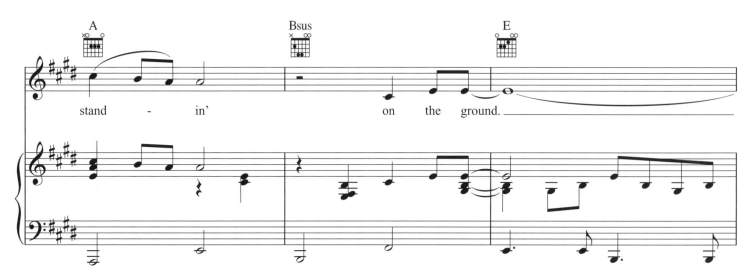

stand-in' on the ground. _____

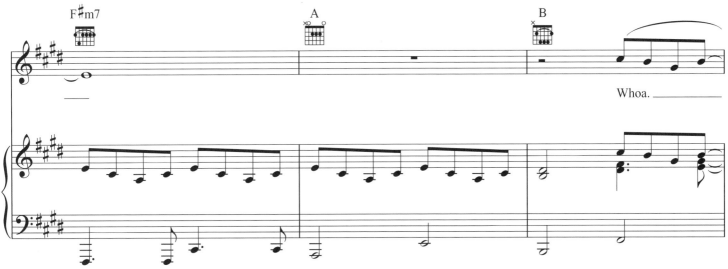

Whoa.

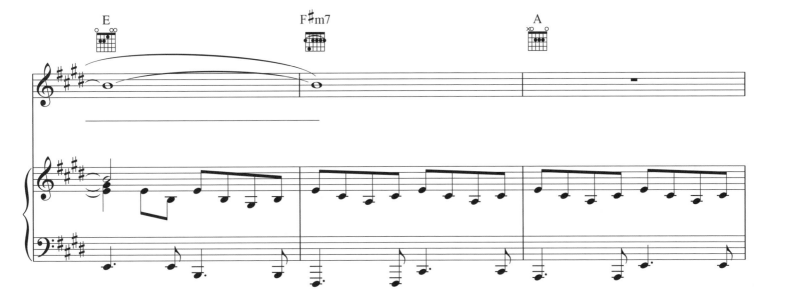

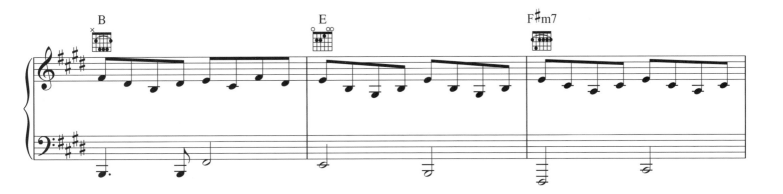

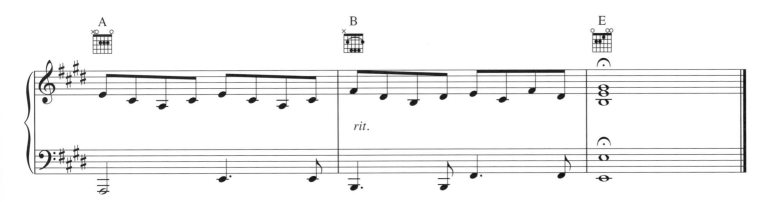

rit.

PEOPLE GOT TO BE FREE

Words and Music by FELIX CAVALIERE
and EDWARD BRIGATI, JR.

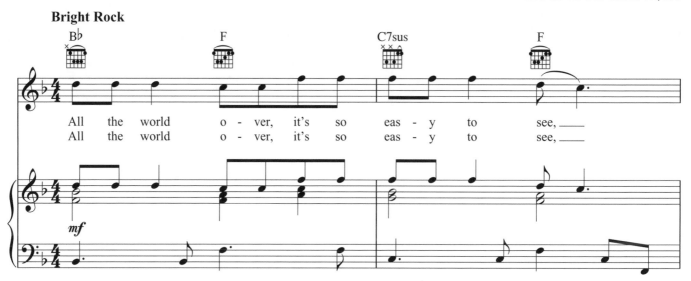

Bright Rock

All the world o-ver, it's so eas-y to see,
All the world o-ver, it's so eas-y to see,

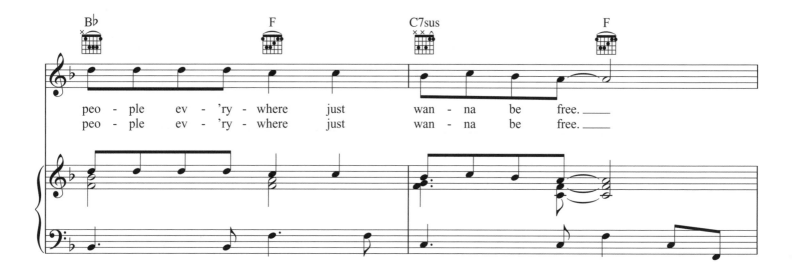

peo-ple ev-'ry-where just wan-na be free.
peo-ple ev-'ry-where just wan-na be free.

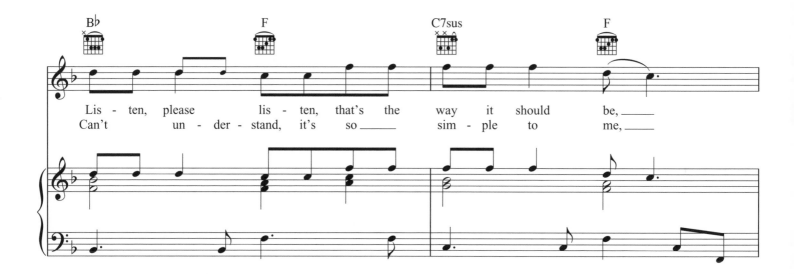

Lis-ten, please lis-ten, that's the way it should be,
Can't un-der-stand, it's so sim-ple to me,

peace in the val - ley, peo - ple got to be free. _____
peo - ple ev - 'ry - where _ just _ got to be free. _____

You should see _____ what a love - ly, love - ly world this would be ____
If there's a man _____ who is down and needs a help - ing hand, _

_____ if ev - er - y - one ____ learned to live to - geth -
_____ all it takes is you to un - der - stand ____ and to pull him through. _

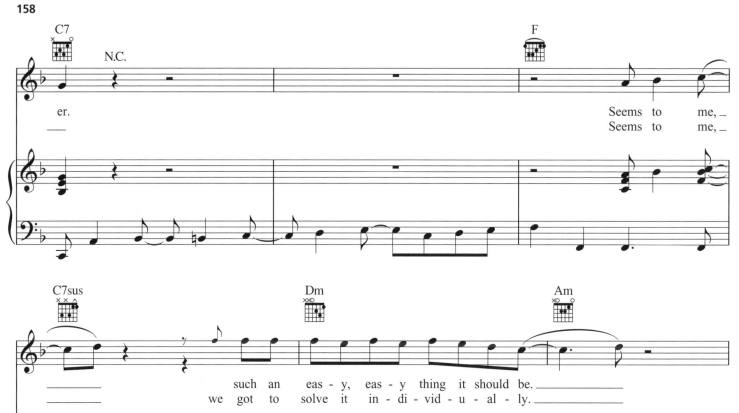

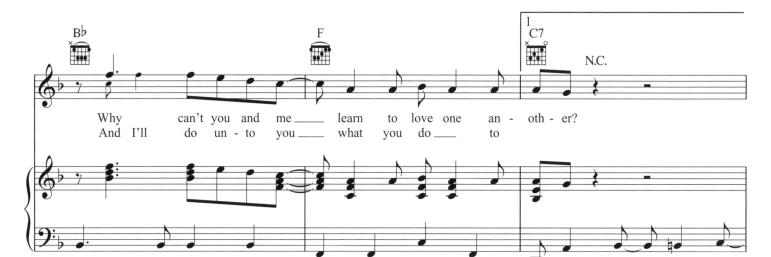

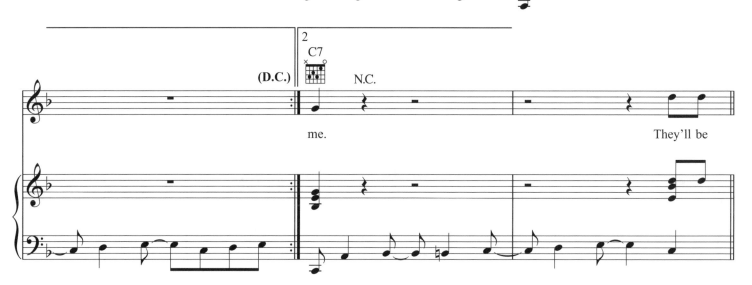

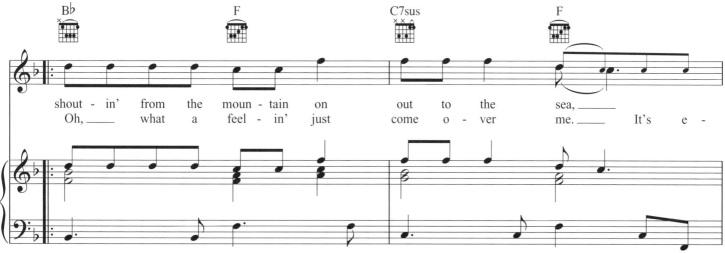

shout - in' from the moun - tain on out to the sea, _____
Oh, _____ what a feel - in' just come o - ver me. _____ It's e -

no two ways a - bout it, peo - ple have to be free. _____
nough to move a moun - tain, make a blind _____ man see. _____

Ask me my o - pin - ion, my o - pin - ion will be, _____ it's a
Ev - 'ry - bod - y's danc - in'; come on, let's _____ go see. _____ There's _

nat - 'ral sit - u - a - tion for a man to be free. _____
peace _ in the val - ley, now we all can be free. _____

THE RAINBOW CONNECTION

from THE MUPPET MOVIE

Words and Music by PAUL WILLIAMS
and KENNETH L. ASCHER

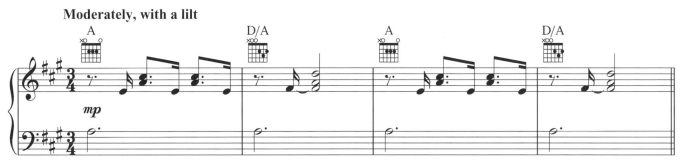

Why are there so man-y songs a-bout rain-bows, and
Who said that ev-'ry wish would be heard and an-swered when

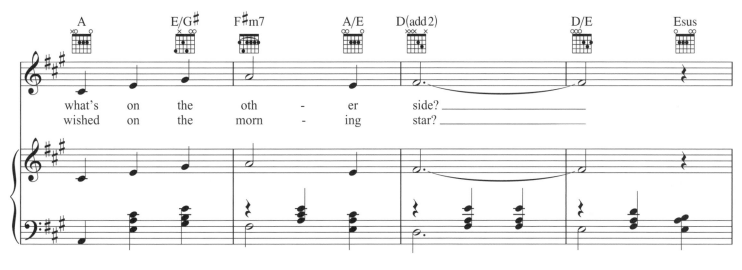

what's on the oth-er side? ____
wished on the morn-ing star? ____

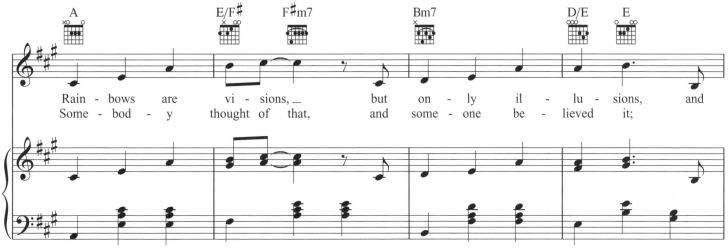

Rain-bows are vi-sions, ___ but on-ly il-lu-sions, and
Some-bod-y thought of that, and some-one be-lieved it;

rain - bows have noth - ing to hide. _____
look what it's done _____ so far. _____

Dmaj7

So we've been told, and some choose to be - lieve it.
What's so a - maz - ing that keeps us star - gaz - ing, and

G#m/C#

I know they're wrong; wait and see. _____
what do we think we might see? _____

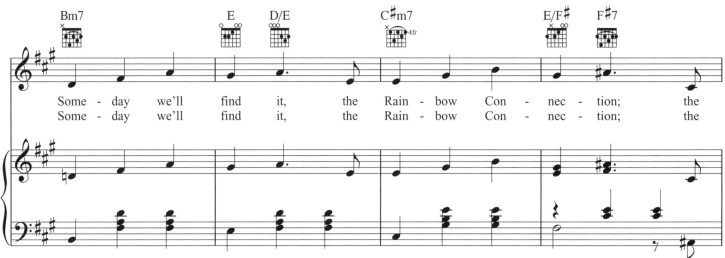

Bm7   E   D/E   C#m7   E/F#   F#7

Some - day we'll find it, the Rain - bow Con - nec - tion; the
Some - day we'll find it, the Rain - bow Con - nec - tion; the

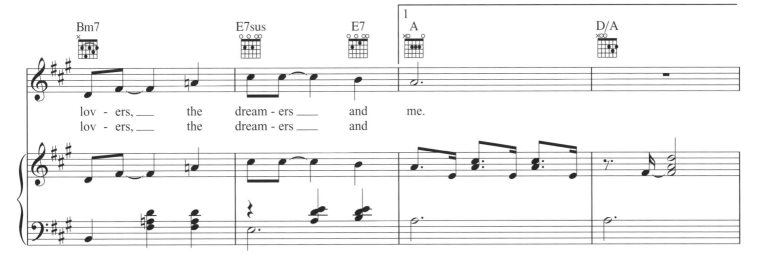

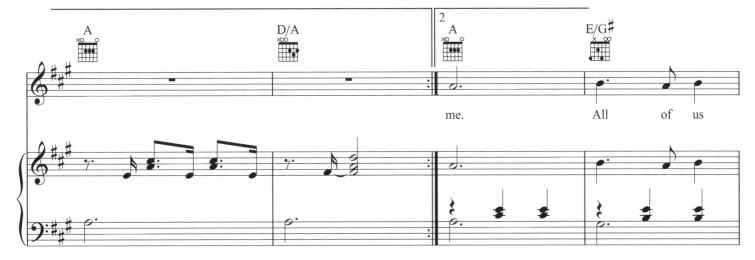

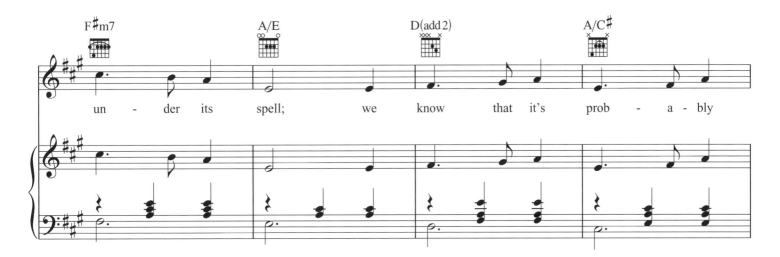

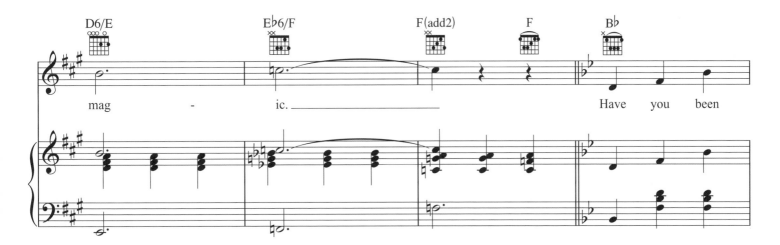

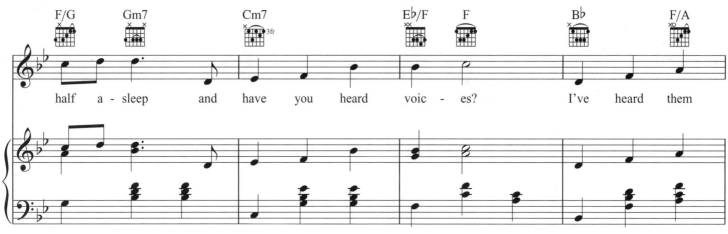

half a-sleep and have you heard voic-es? I've heard them

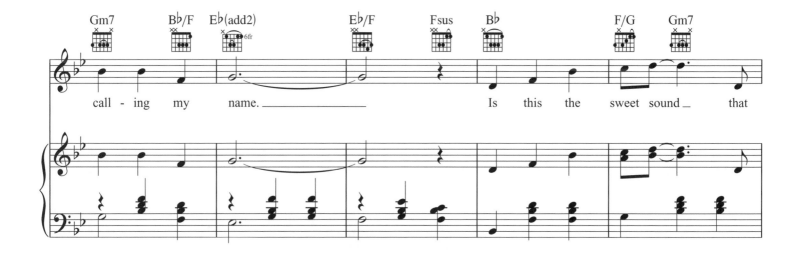

call - ing my name._____ Is this the sweet sound __ that

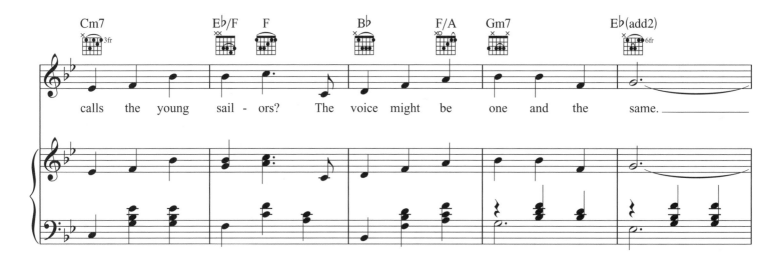

calls the young sail-ors? The voice might be one and the same._____

____ I've heard it too man-y times to ig -

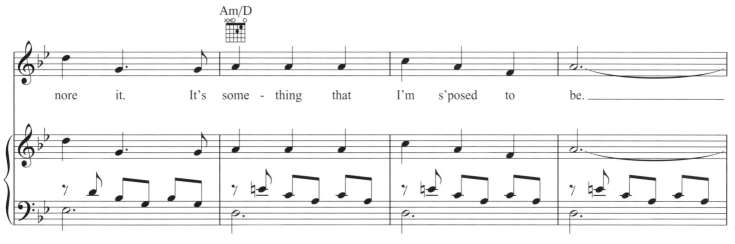

nore it. It's some - thing that I'm s'posed to be. _____

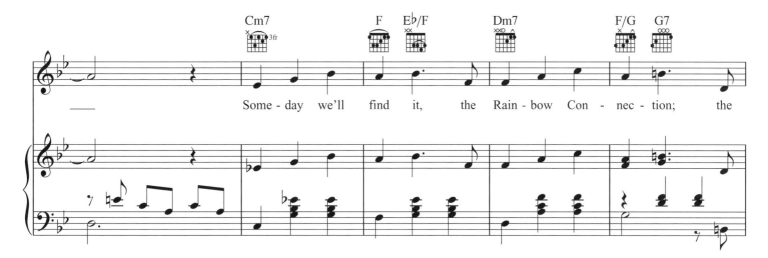

_____ Some - day we'll find it, the Rain - bow Con - nec - tion; the

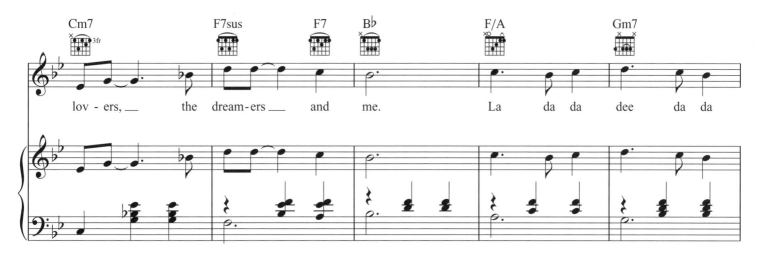

lov - ers, ___ the dream-ers ___ and me. La da da dee da da

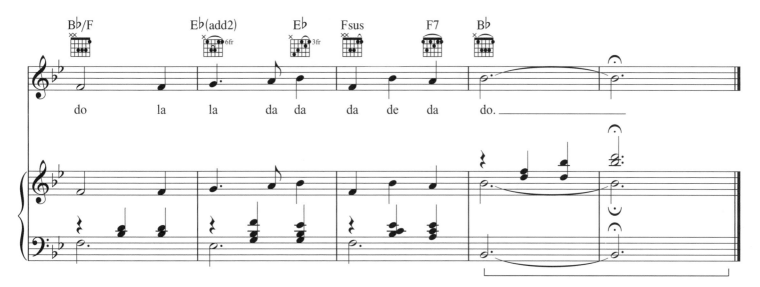

do la la da da da de da do. _____

PUFF THE MAGIC DRAGON

Words and Music by LENNY LIPTON
and PETER YARROW

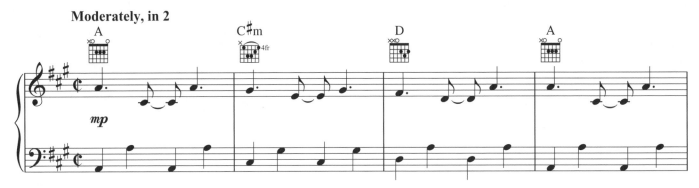

*3rd time, play verse twice
before proceeding to Chorus

1. Puff the Mag - ic Drag - on lived by ___ the
2.–5. (See additional lyrics)

sea and frol - icked in ___ the au - tumn mist ___ in a

land called Hon - a - lee. _____   Lit - tle   Jack - ie

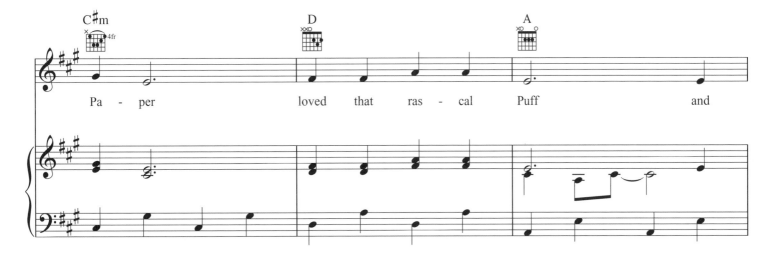

Pa - per   loved that ras - cal Puff   and

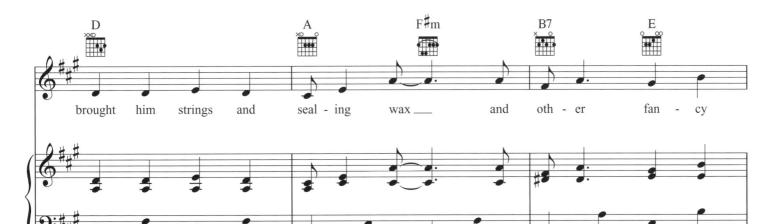

brought him strings and   seal - ing wax ___ and oth - er fan - cy

Chorus

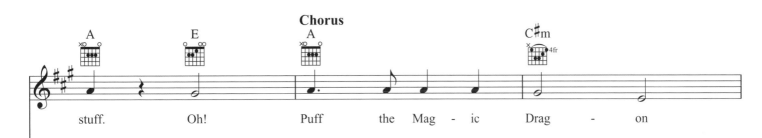

stuff.   Oh!   Puff   the Mag - ic Drag - on

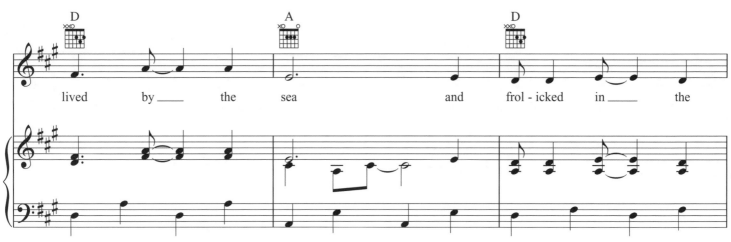

lived by ___ the sea and frol-icked in ___ the

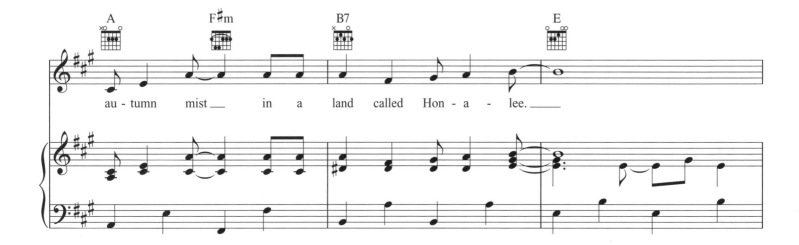

au-tumn mist ___ in a land called Hon-a-lee. ___

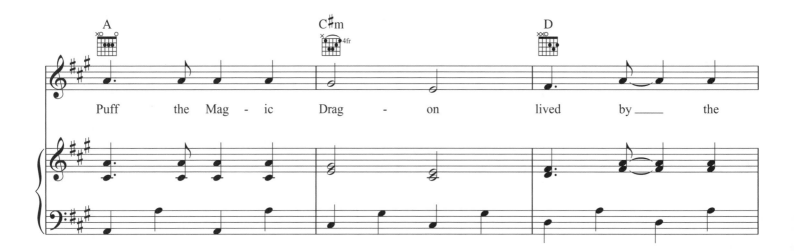

Puff the Mag - ic Drag - on lived by ___ the

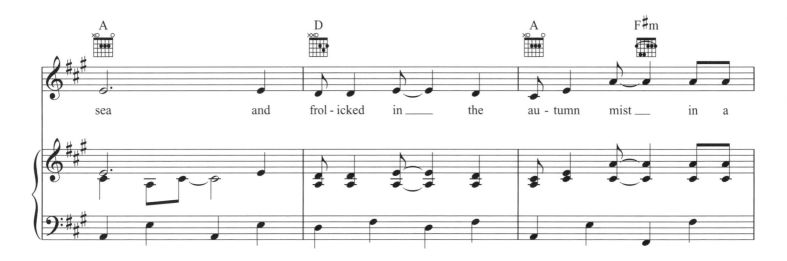

sea and frol-icked in ___ the au-tumn mist ___ in a

Additional Lyrics

2. Together they would travel on a boat with billowed sail.
   Jackie kept a lookout perched on Puff's gigantic tail.
   Noble kings and princes would bow whene'er they came.
   Pirate ships would low'r their flags when Puff roared out his name. Oh!
   Chorus

3. A dragon lives forever, but not so little boys.
   Painted wings and giant rings make way for other toys.
   One gray night it happened, Jackie Paper came no more,
   And Puff that mighty dragon, he ceased his fearless roar.

4. His head was bent in sorrow, green tears fell like rain.
   Puff no longer went to play along the Cherry Lane.
   Without his lifelong friend, Puff could not be brave,
   So Puff that mighty dragon sadly slipped into his cave. Oh!
   Chorus

THE RETURN OF PUFF

5. Puff the magic dragon danced down the Cherry Lane.
   He came upon a little girl, Julie Maple was her name.
   She'd heard that Puff had gone away, but that can never be,
   So together they went sailing to the land called Honalee.
   Chorus

PUT YOUR HAND IN THE HAND

Words and Music by
GENE MacLELLAN

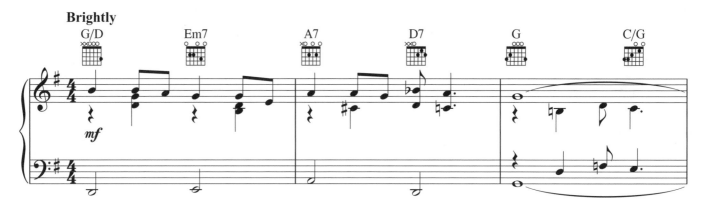

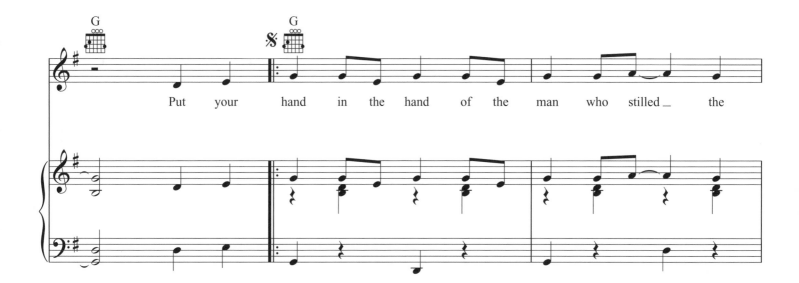

Put your hand in the hand of the man who stilled __ the

wa-ter. _____ Put your hand in the hand of the

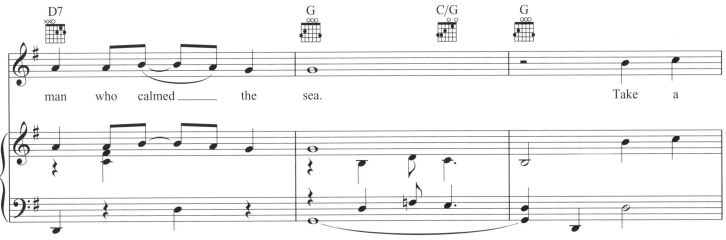

man who calmed _____ the sea.   Take a

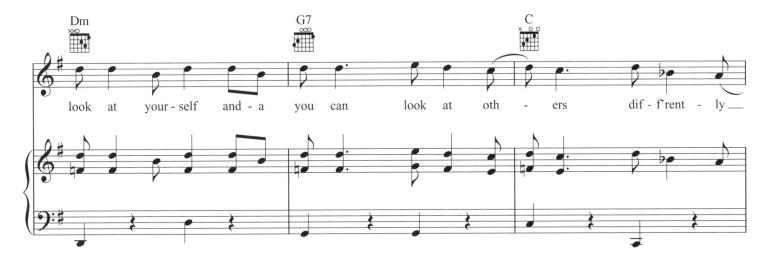

look at your-self and-a   you can   look at oth - ers   dif - f'rent - ly ___

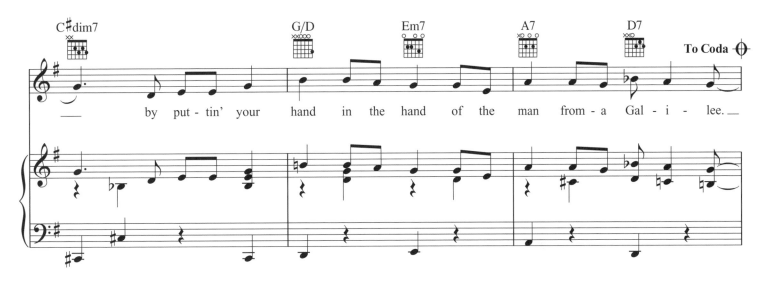

___   by put-tin' your   hand   in the hand   of the   man from-a Gal - i - lee. ___

To Coda

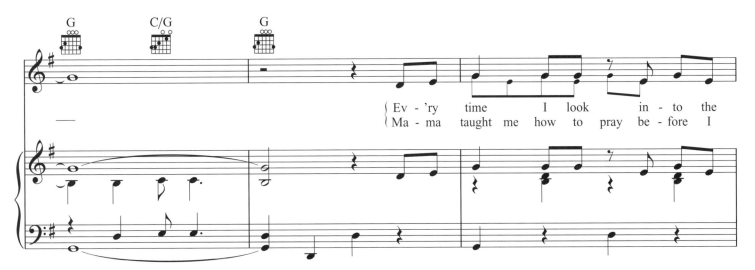

Ev - 'ry   time   I look   in - to the
Ma - ma   taught me how to   pray   be - fore I

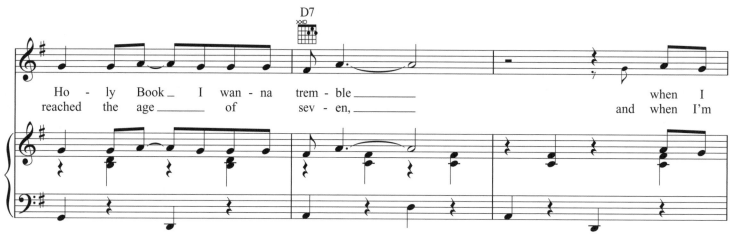

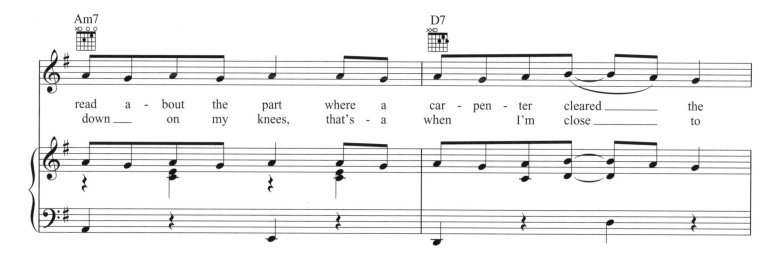

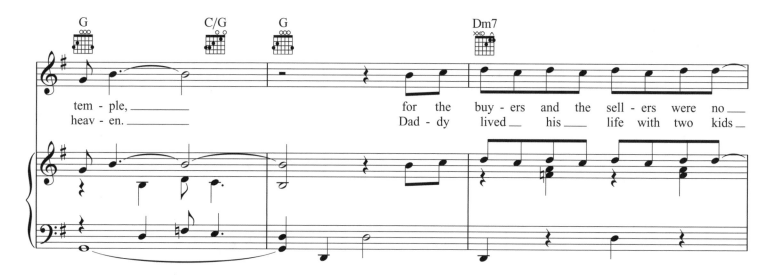

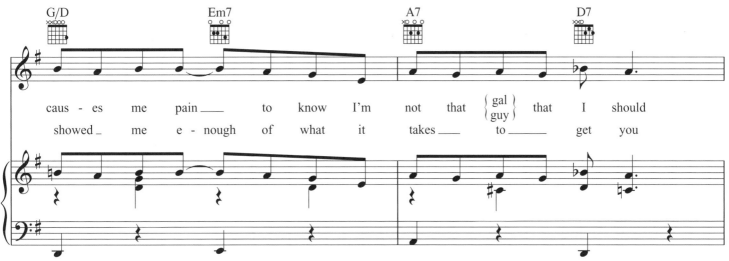

caus - es me pain ____ to know I'm not that { gal / guy } that I should
showed _ me e - nough of what it takes ____ to _____ get you

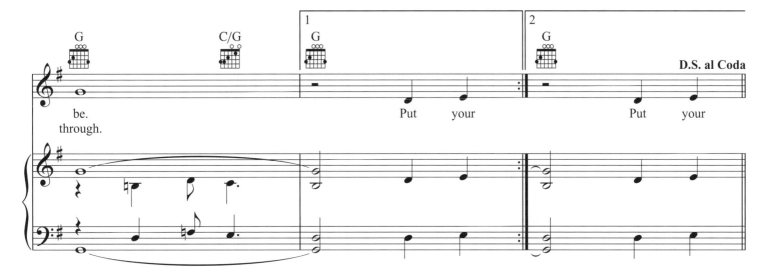

be.
through.

Put your   Put your

D.S. al Coda

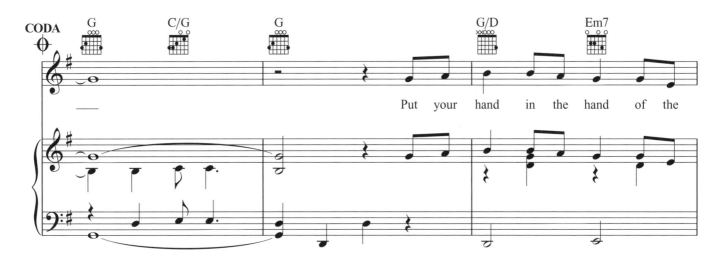

CODA

Put your hand in the hand of the

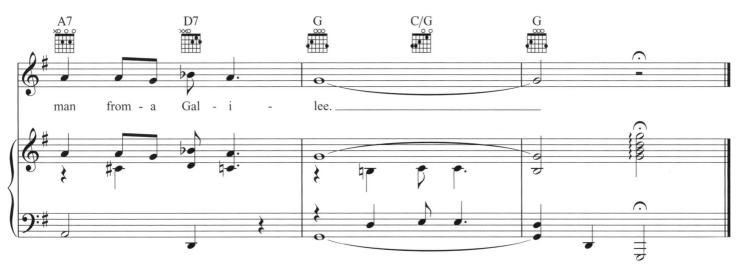

man from - a Gal - i - lee. _____

RAINDROPS KEEP FALLIN' ON MY HEAD

from BUTCH CASSIDY AND THE SUNDANCE KID

Lyric by HAL DAVID
Music by BURT BACHARACH

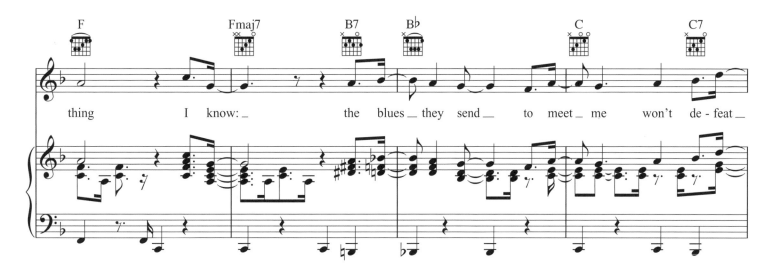

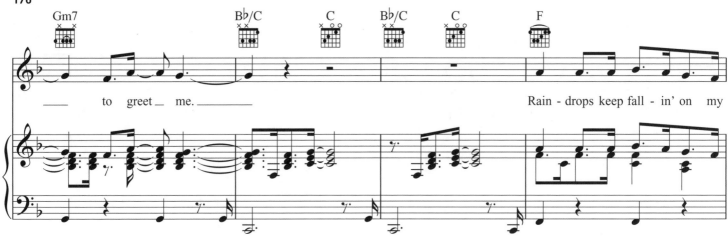

to greet me. Rain - drops keep fall - in' on my

head, but that does-n't mean my eyes will soon be turn - in' red. Cry-in's not for

me 'cause I'm nev - er gon - na stop the rain by com-plain - in'.

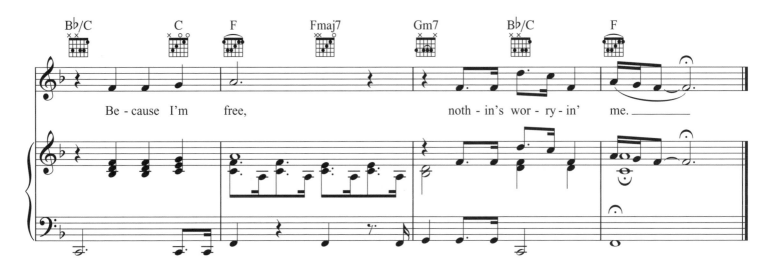

Be - cause I'm free, noth - in's wor - ry - in' me.

SAN FRANCISCO BAY BLUES

Words and Music by
JESSE FULLER

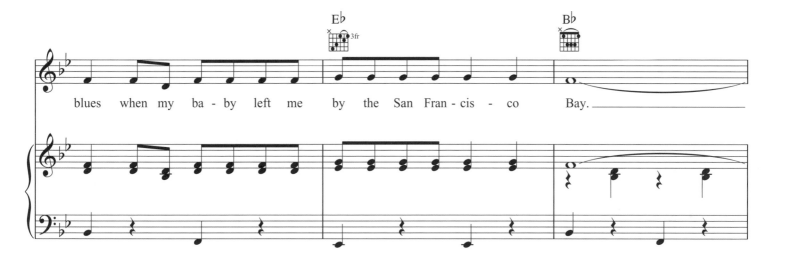

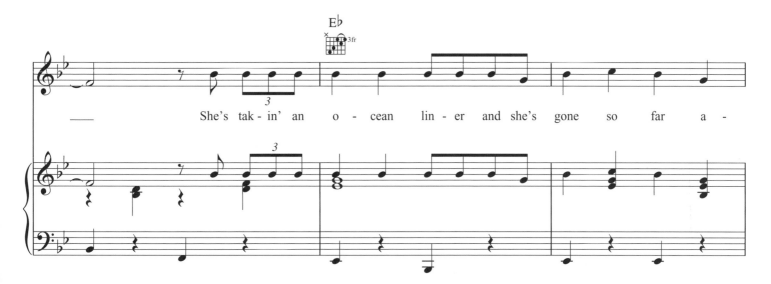

way. _____ I did-n't mean to treat her so bad. She's the

best gal I ev-er have had. She said good-bye, _ gon-na make me cry, _

I'm gon-na lay down and die. _____ I have-n't got a nick-el, ain't got a lous-y

dime. _____ If she don't come back, I think I'm gon-na lose my

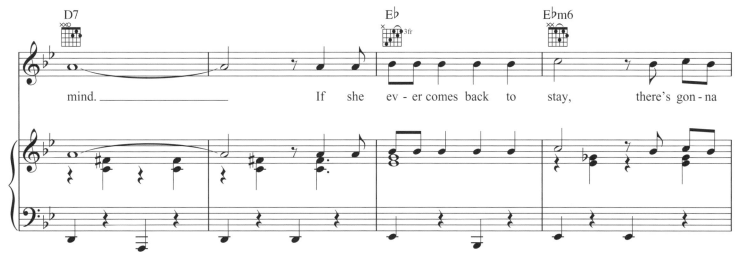

mind. _____ If she ev-er comes back to stay, there's gon-na

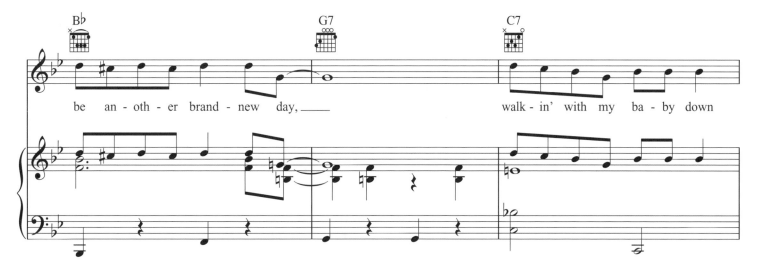

be an-oth-er brand-new day, _____ walk-in' with my ba-by down

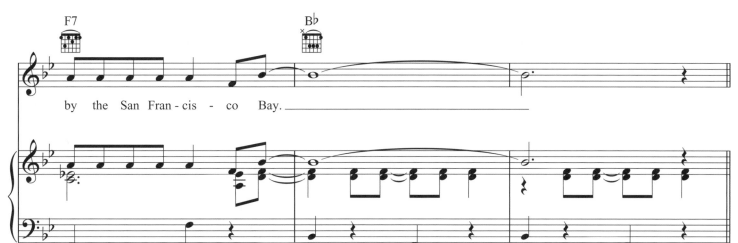

by the San Fran-cis-co Bay. _____

Sit-tin' down and look-in' through my back door, won-d'rin' which way to go. _

Wom - an I'm so cra - zy 'bout, she don't want me no

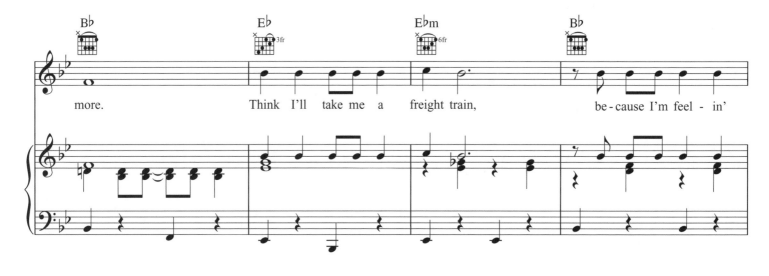

more. Think I'll take me a freight train, be - cause I'm feel - in'

blue. Ride all the way till the end of the line, think - in' on - ly of

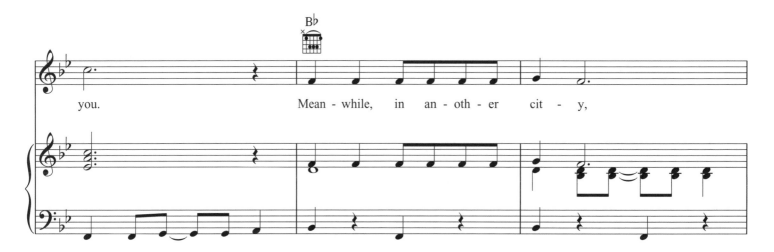

you. Mean - while, in an - oth - er cit - y,

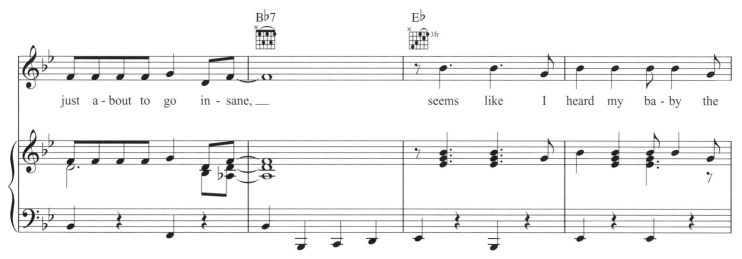

just a-bout to go in-sane, ___ seems like I heard my ba-by the

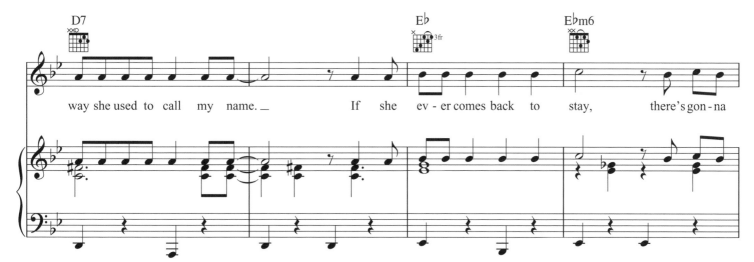

way she used to call my name. ___ If she ev-er comes back to stay, there's gon-na

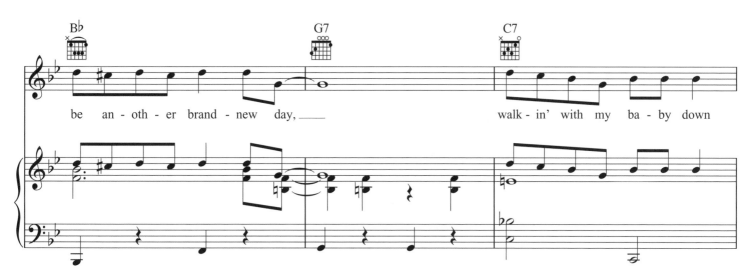

be an-oth-er brand-new day, ___ walk-in' with my ba-by down

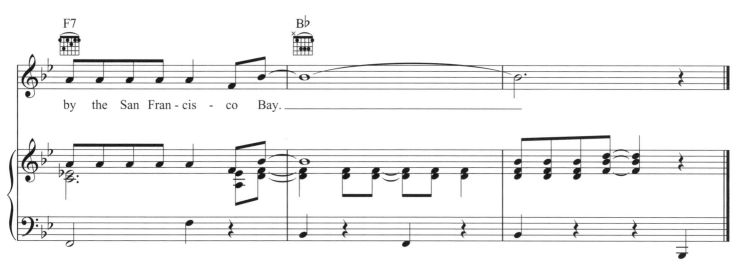

by the San Fran-cis-co Bay. ___

SAN FRANCISCAN NIGHTS

Words and Music by BARRY JENKINS,
DANNY McCULLOCH, JOHNNY WEIDER
and VIC BRAGGS

(Spoken:) This following program is dedicated to the city and people of San Francisco, who
and so is their city. This is a very personal song, so if the viewer cannot understand it,
European residents, save up all your bread and fly Trans Love Airways to San
maybe you'll understand the song. It will be worth it, if not for the sake of this song, but for

may not know it, but they are beautiful,
particularly those of you who are
Francisco, U.S.A. Then
the sake of your own peace of mind.

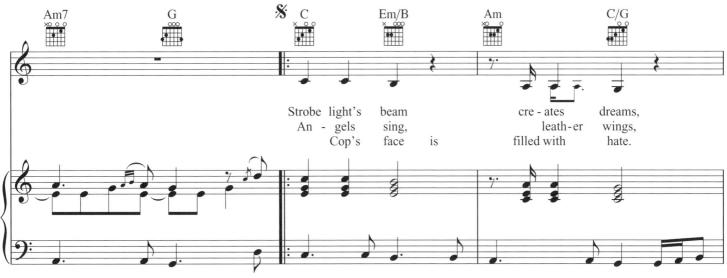

Strobe light's beam ... cre - ates dreams,
An - gels sing, ... leath-er wings,
Cop's face is ... filled with hate.

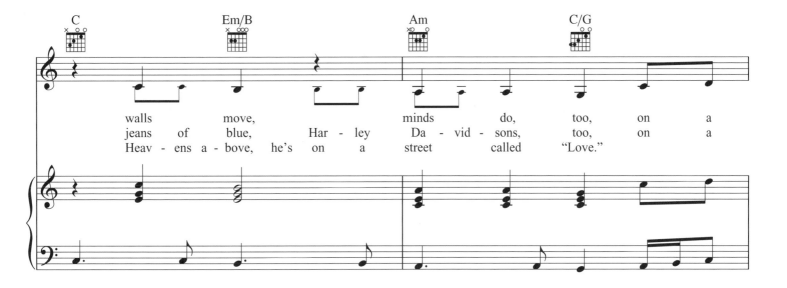

walls move, minds do, too, on a
jeans of blue, Har - ley Da - vid - sons, too, on a
Heav - ens a - bove, he's on a street called "Love."

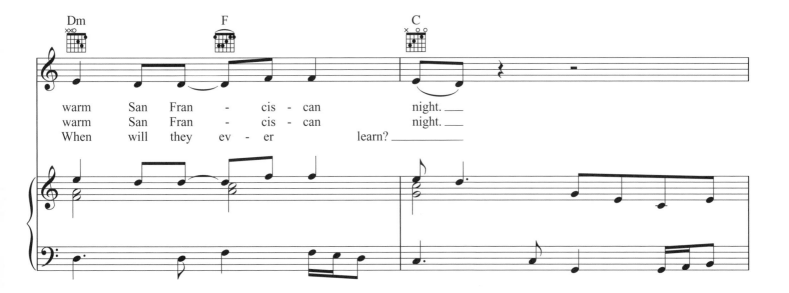

warm San Fran - cis - can night. ___
warm San Fran - cis - can night. ___
When will they ev - er learn? ___

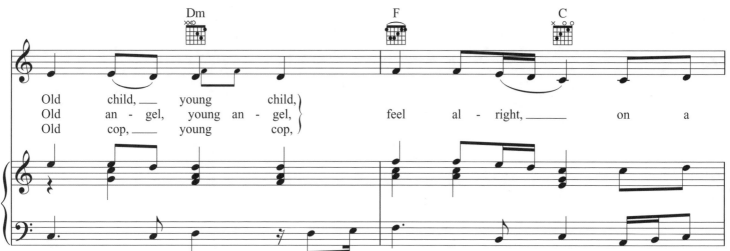

Old child, ___ young child,
Old an-gel, young an-gel, feel al-right, _____ on a
Old cop, ___ young cop,

warm _ San Fran - cis-can night. _ night. _

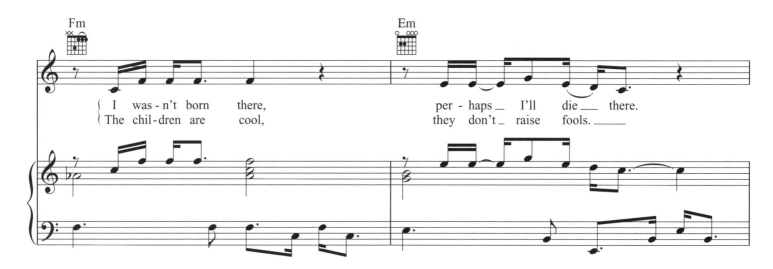

I was-n't born there, perhaps _ I'll die _ there.
The chil-dren are cool, they don't _ raise fools. _____

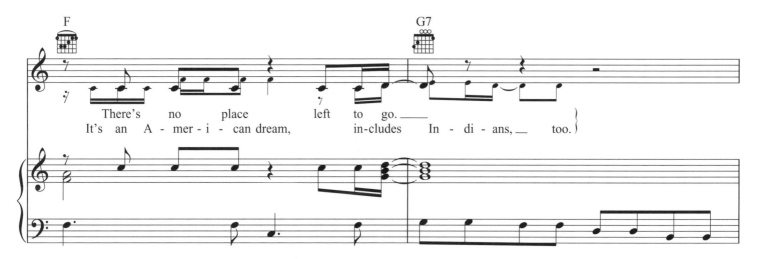

There's no place left to go. _____
It's an A - mer-i-can dream, in-cludes In - di - ans, _ too.

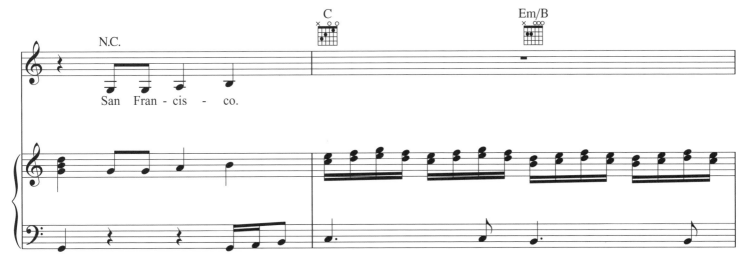

San Fran - cis - co.

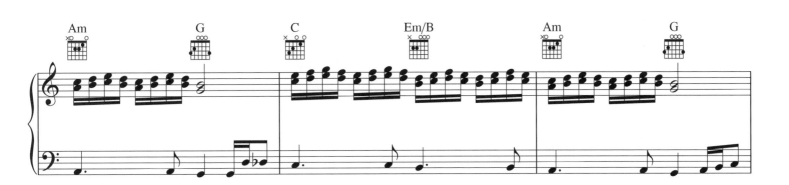

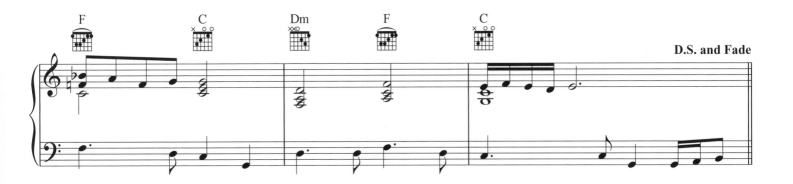

D.S. and Fade

SAN FRANCISCO
(Be Sure to Wear Some Flowers in Your Hair)

Words and Music by
JOHN PHILLIPS

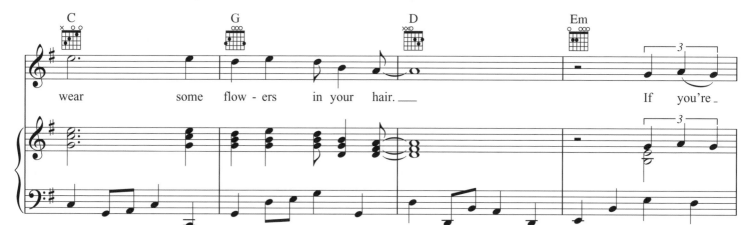

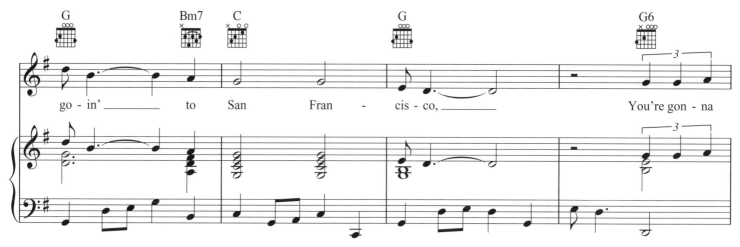

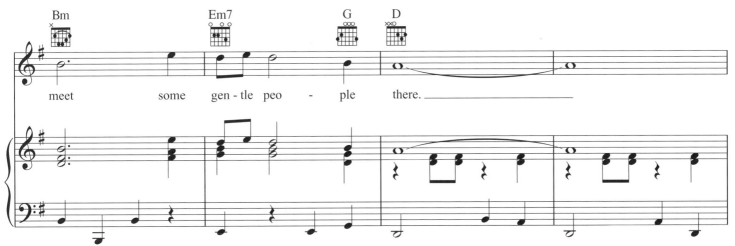

meet some gen - tle peo - ple there. _____

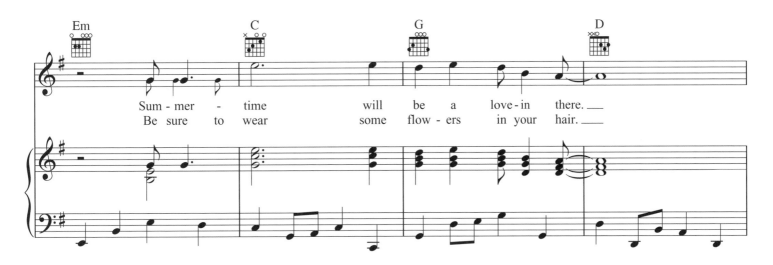

For those who come to San Fran - cis - co, _____
For those who come to San Fran - cis - co, _____

Sum - mer - time will be a love - in there. ___
Be sure to wear some flow - ers in your hair. ___

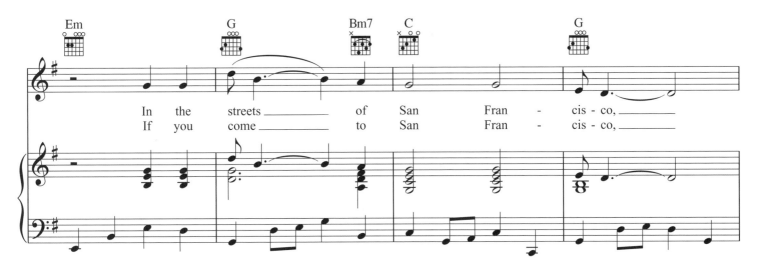

In the streets _____ of San Fran - cis - co, _____
If you come _____ to San Fran - cis - co, _____

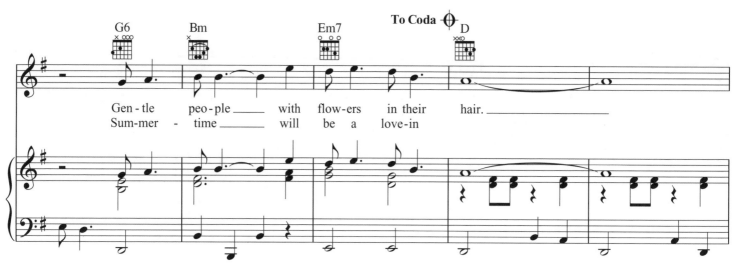

Gen-tle peo-ple _____ with flow-ers in their hair. _____
Sum-mer - time _____ will be a love-in

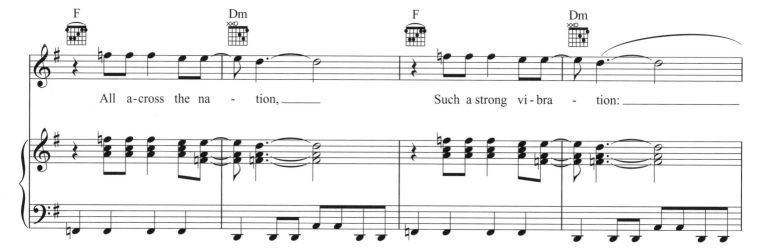

All a-cross the na - tion, _____ Such a strong vi-bra - tion: _____

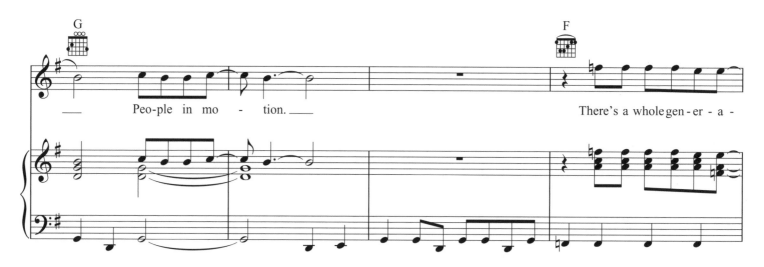

_____ Peo-ple in mo - tion. _____ There's a whole gen - er - a -

- tion _____ with a new ex-pla-na - tion, _____ Peo-ple in mo -

D.S. al Coda

-tion, ___ Peo-ple in mo - tion.

CODA

there. ___

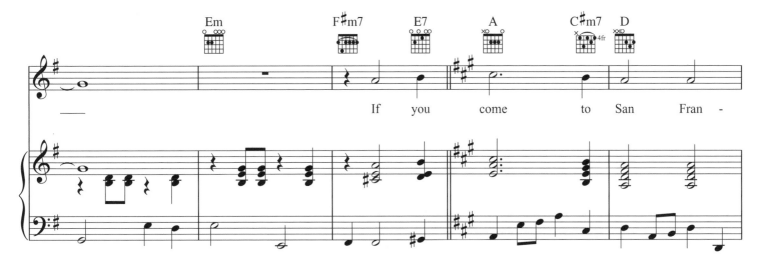

___ If you come to San Fran -

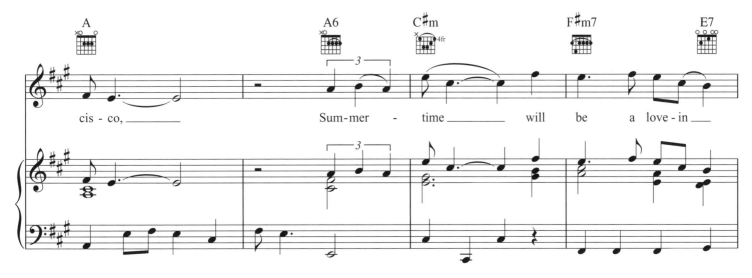

cis - co, ___ Sum-mer - time ___ will be a love - in ___

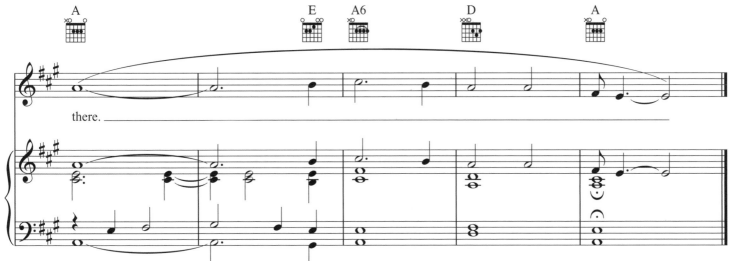

there. ___

SCARLET RIBBONS
(For Her Hair)

Words by JACK SEGAL
Music by EVELYN DANZIG

Moderately

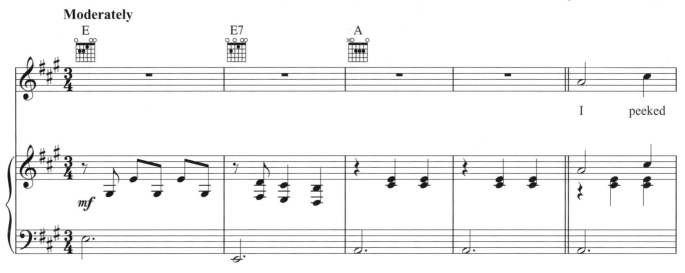

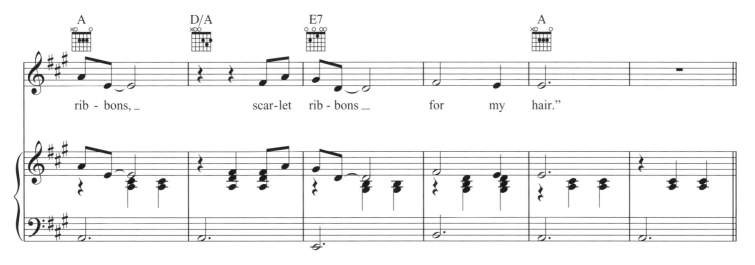

rib - bons, _ scar-let rib bons _ for my hair."

All our stores were closed and shut - tered. _ All the
I peeked in and on her bed, in gay pro -

streets were dark and bare. In our town, no
fu - sion ly - ing there, love - ly rib - bons,

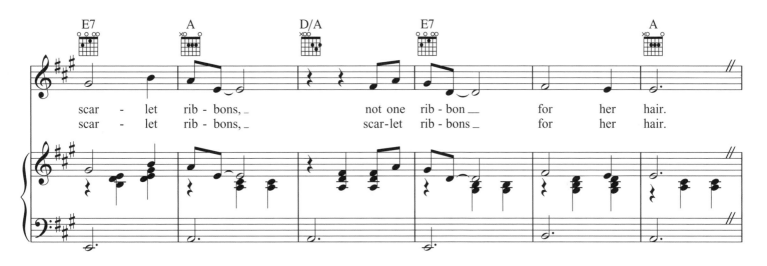

scar - let rib - bons, _ not one rib - bon _ for her hair.
scar - let rib - bons, _ scar-let rib - bons _ for her hair.

SLOOP JOHN B.

Words and Music by PHIL F. SLOAN,
STEVE BARRI, BARRY McGUIRE and BONES HOWE

With a Calypso beat

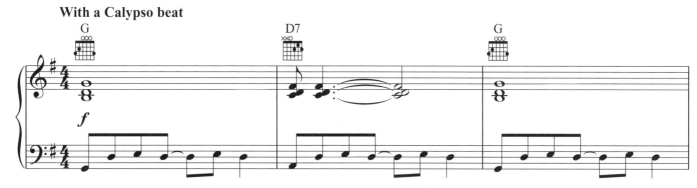

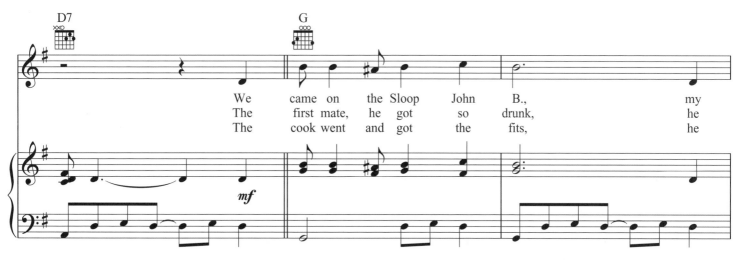

We came on the Sloop John B., my
The first mate, he got so drunk, he
The cook went and got the fits, he

grand - fa - ther and me. 'Round Nas - sau town _
broke o - pen my trunk. Poor sea - sick me _
poured beer on my grits. In - to my soup _

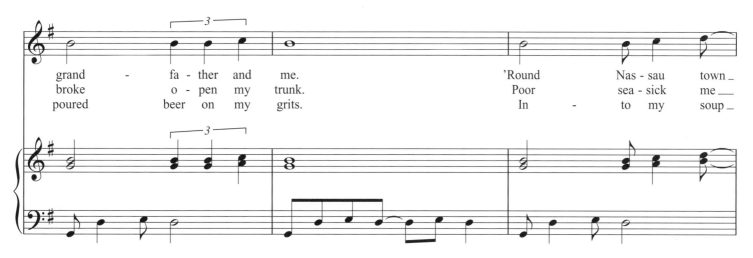

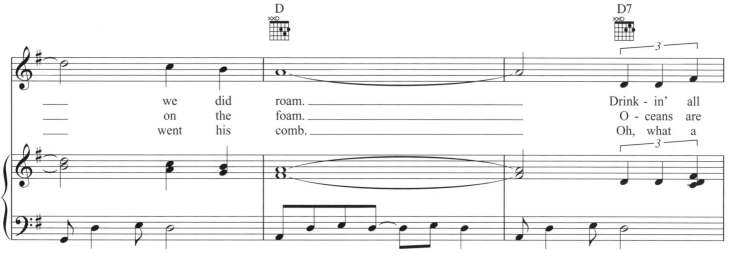

we did roam. Drink - in' all
on the foam. O - ceans are
went his comb. Oh, what a

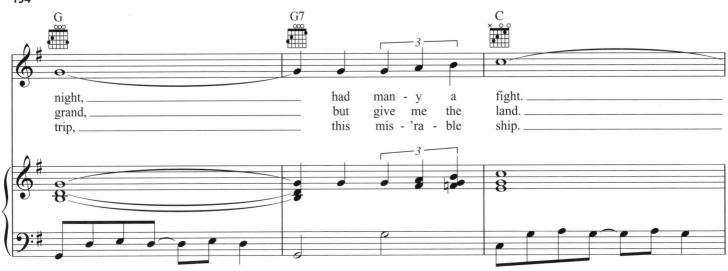

night, _____ had man-y a fight. _____
grand, _____ but give me the land. _____
trip, _____ this mis-'ra-ble ship. _____

I feel so broke up, I wan-na go

home. _____ So hoist up the John B.

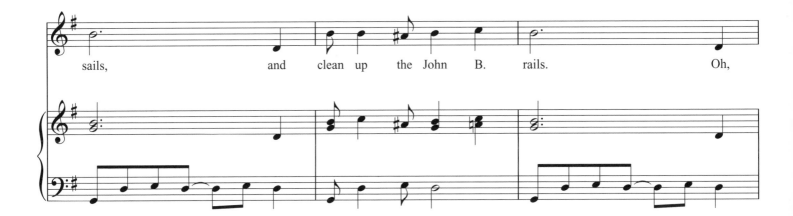

sails, and clean up the John B. rails. Oh,

cap - tain, please come a - board and sail me back home. _____

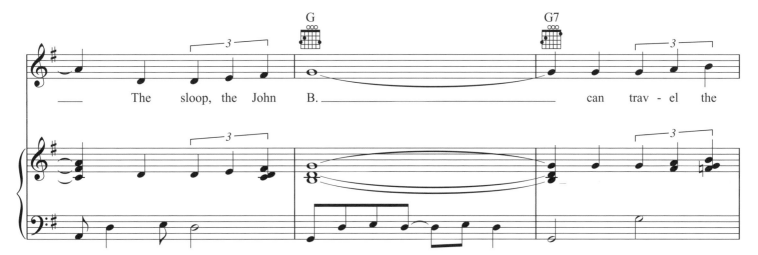

_____ The sloop, the John B. _____ can trav - el the

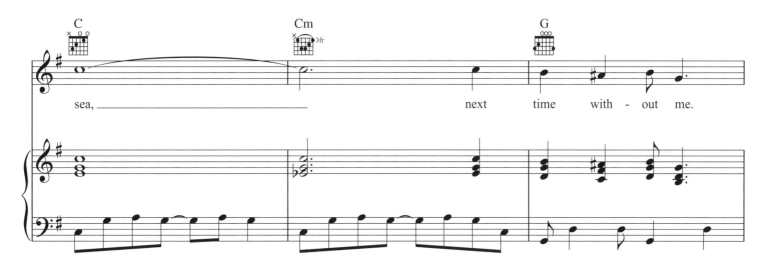

sea, _____ next time with - out me.

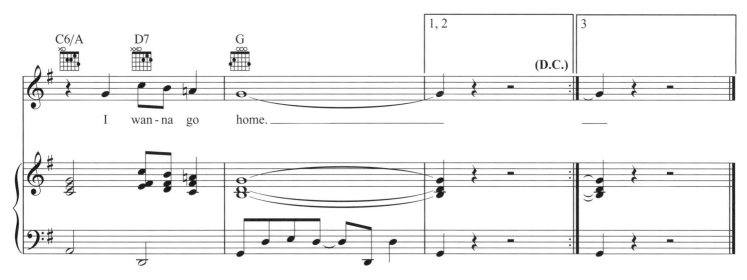

I wan - na go home. _____

SING
from SESAME STREET

Words and Music by
JOE RAPOSO

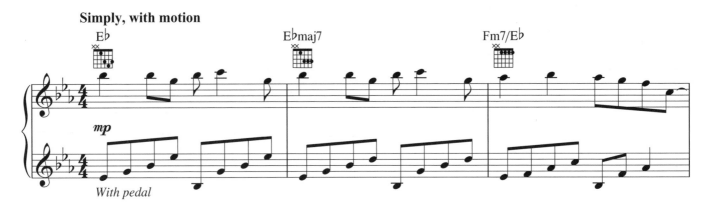

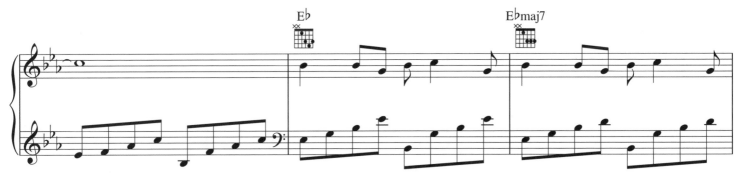

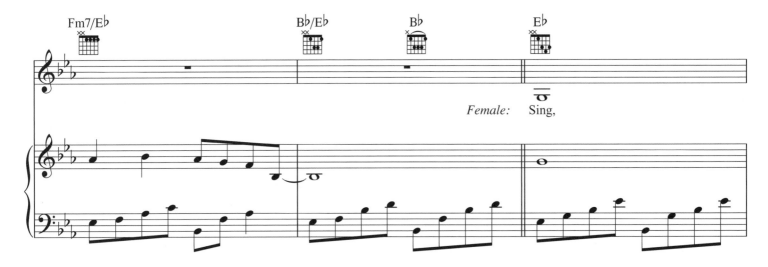

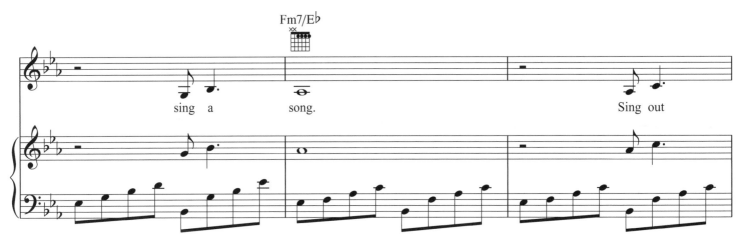

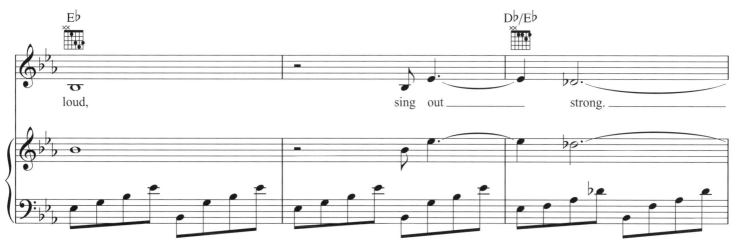

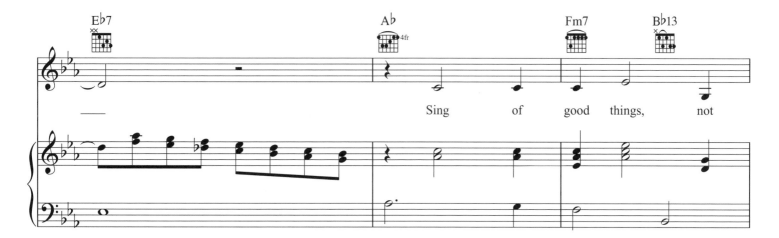

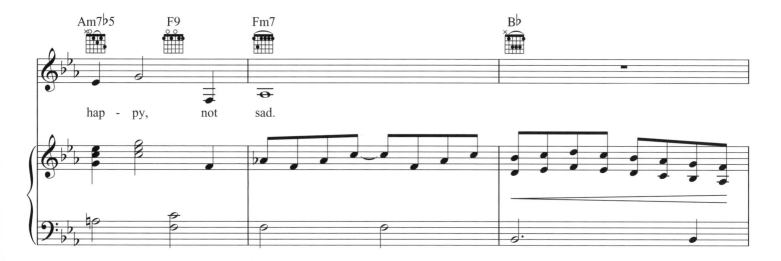

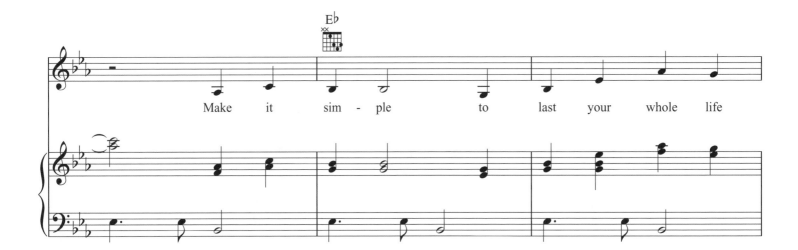

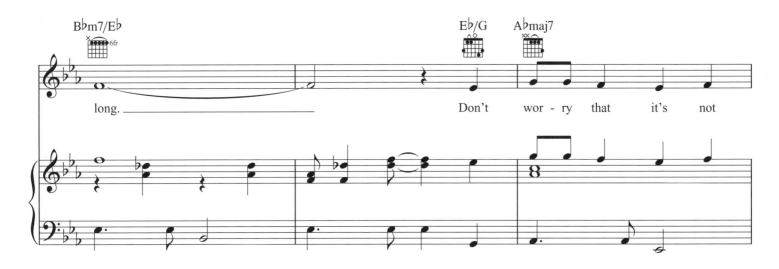

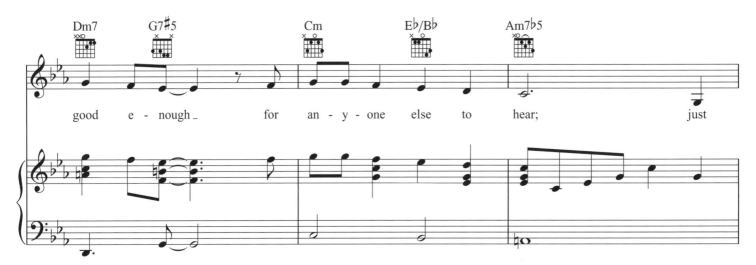

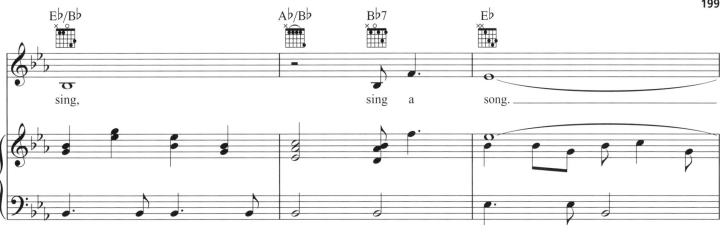

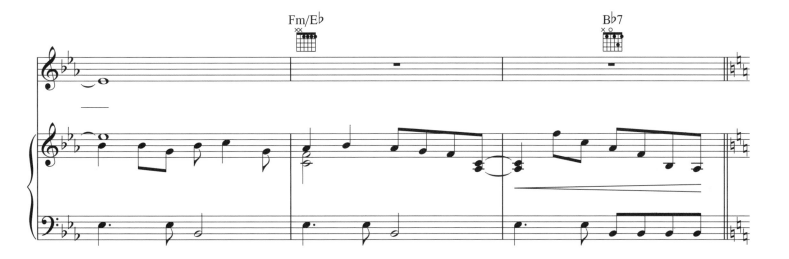

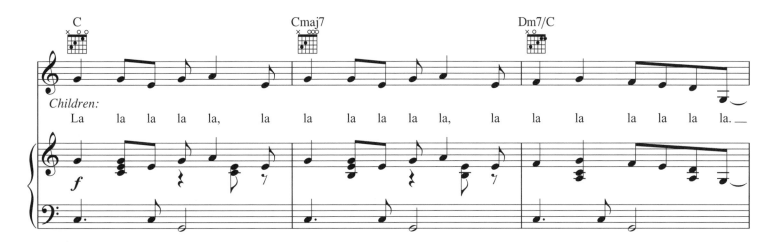

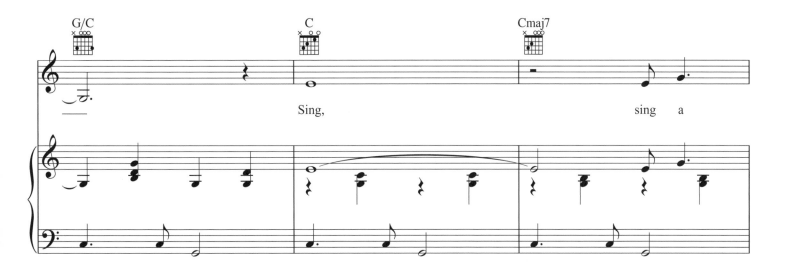

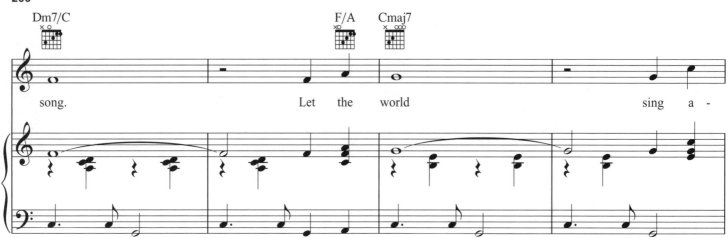

song.   Let the world   sing a-

long. _____   Sing   of

love there could be.   Sing   for

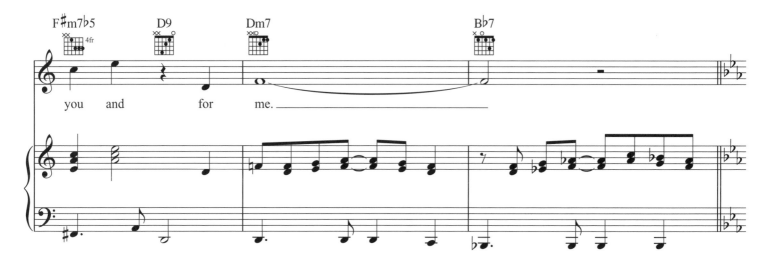

you   and   for   me. _____

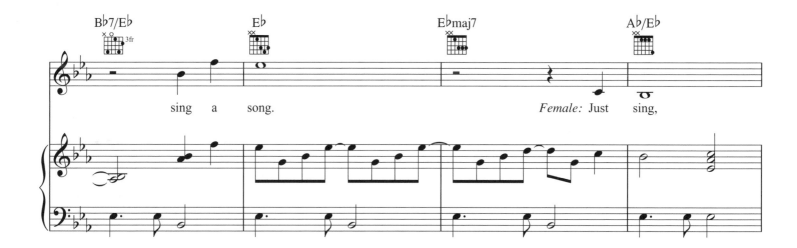

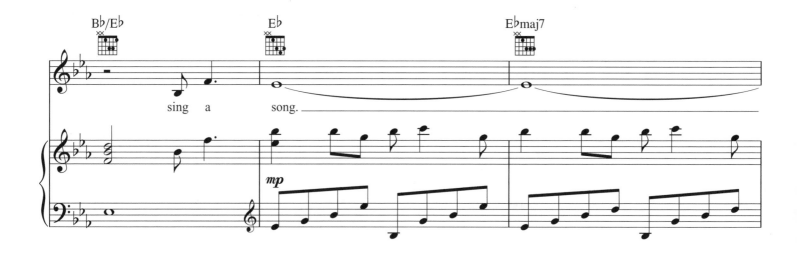

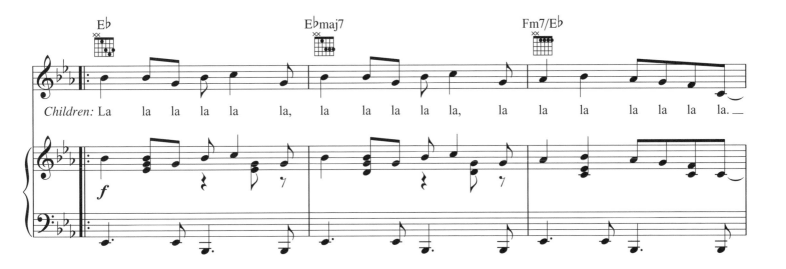

Children: La la la la la la, la la la la la, la la la la la la la.

La la la la la, la la la la la la, la

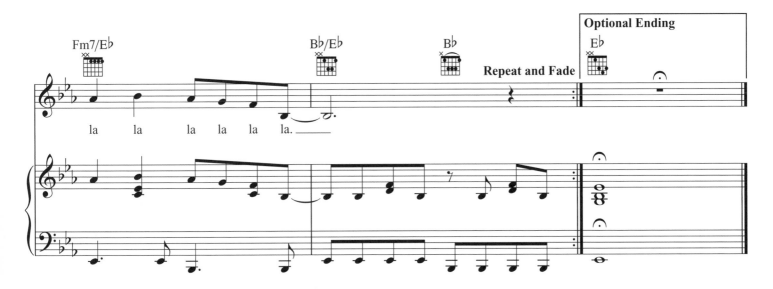

la la la la la la. _

Optional Ending

Repeat and Fade

SOUTHERN CROSS

Words and Music by STEPHEN STILLS,
RICHARD CURTIS and MICHAEL CURTIS

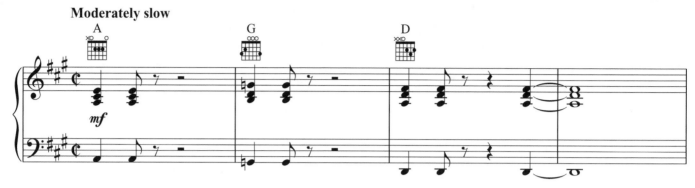

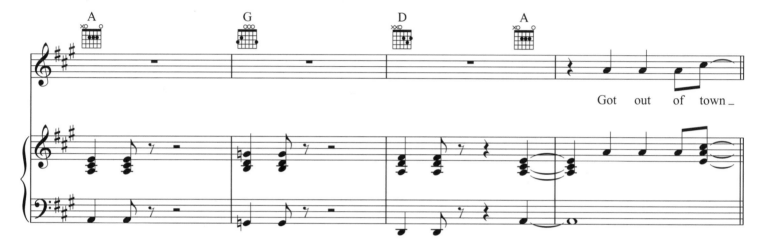

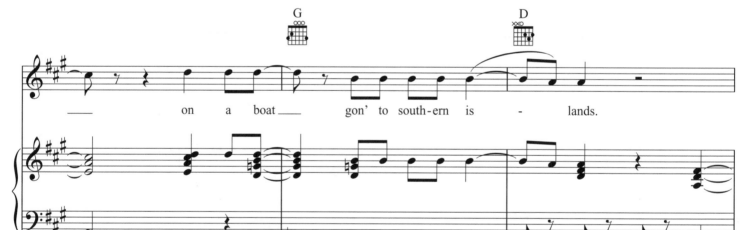

sea. She was mak - ing for the trades __

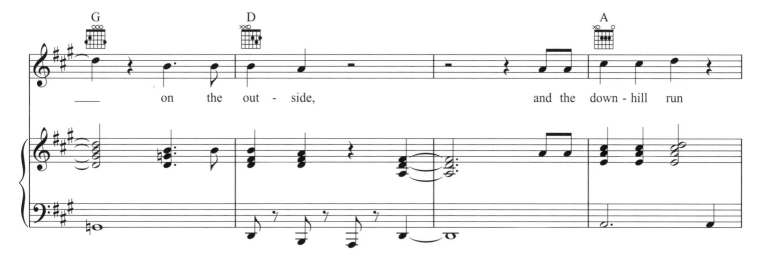

__ on the out - side, and the down - hill run

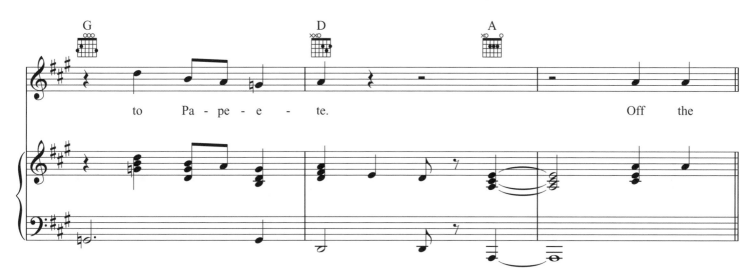

to Pa - pe - e - te. Off the

wind on this head - ing, lie ____ the Mar - que - sas.
sail - ing for to - mor - row. My dreams are a - dy - ing.

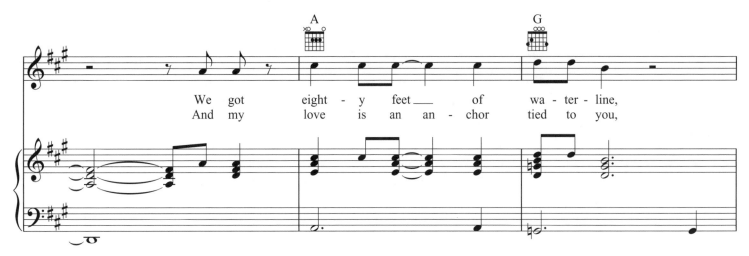

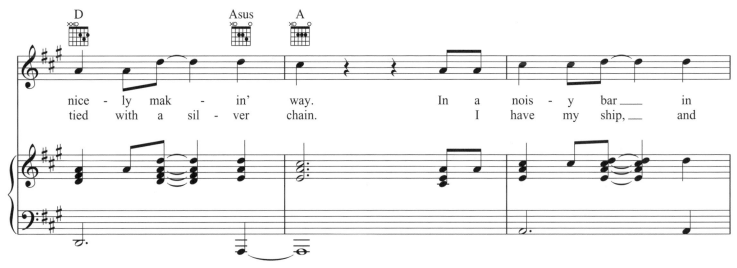

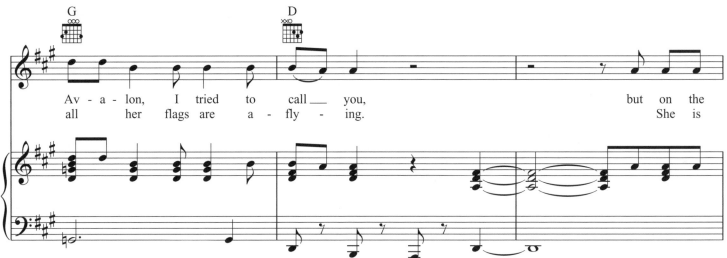

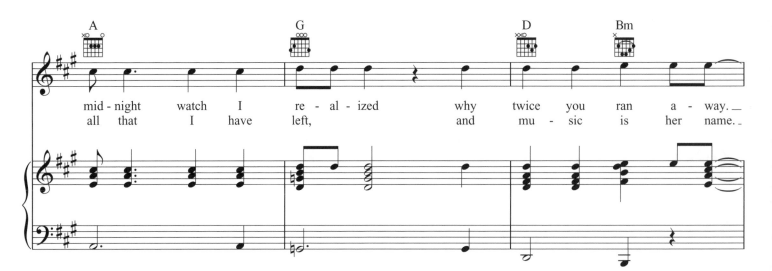

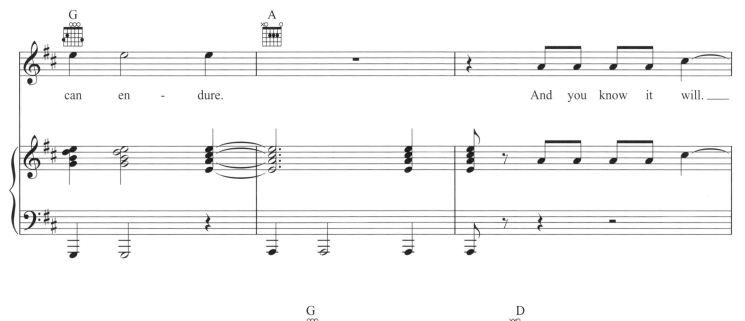

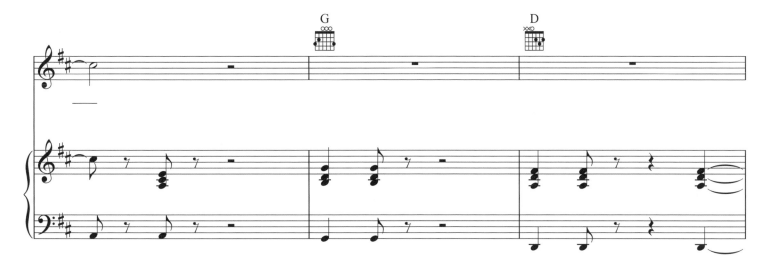

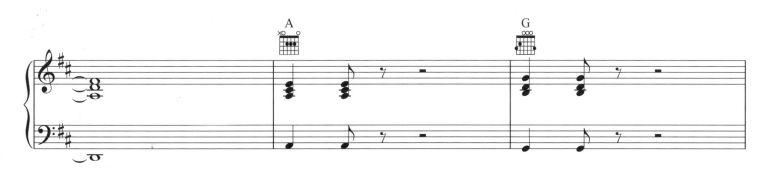

can en - dure.　And you know it will.___

When you see _____ the South - ern

So we cheat - ed and we

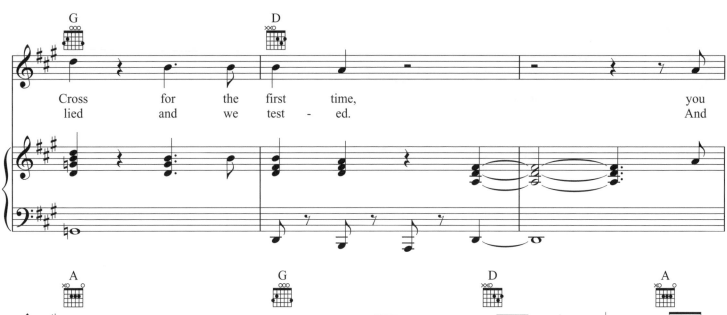

Cross for the first time, you
lied and we first test - ed.

un - der - stand ___ now why you came ___ this way.
we nev - er failed to fail; it was ___ the eas - i - est thing to do.

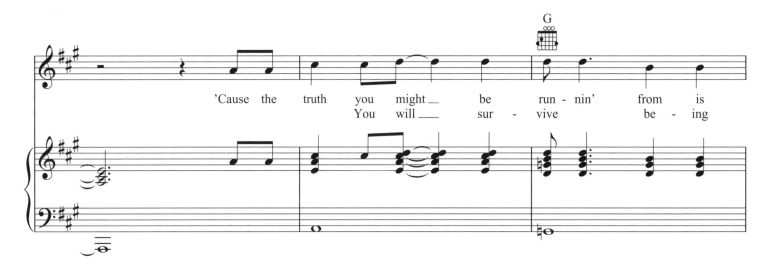

'Cause the truth you might ___ be run - nin' from is
You will ___ sur - vive be - ing

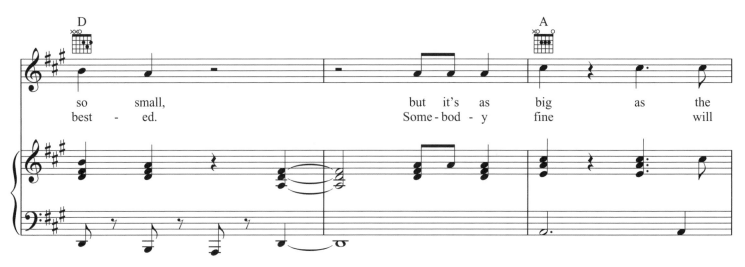

so small, but it's as big as the
best - ed. Some - bod - y fine will

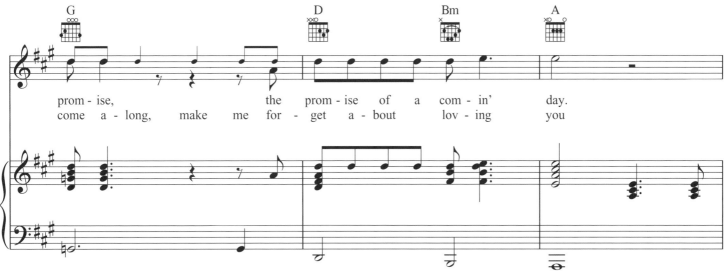

prom - ise,   the prom - ise of a com - in' day.
come a - long, make me for - get a - bout lov - ing you

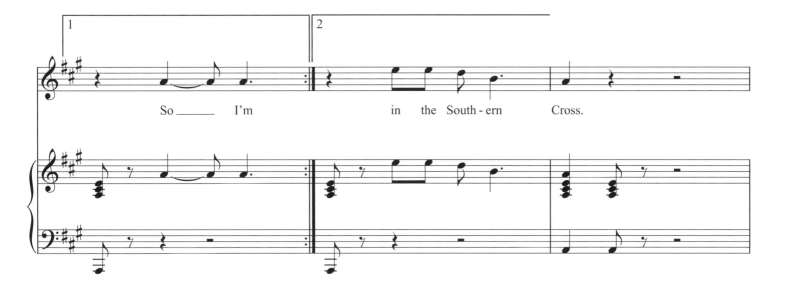

So _____ I'm   in the South - ern Cross.

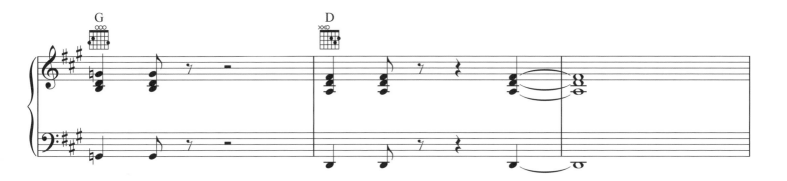

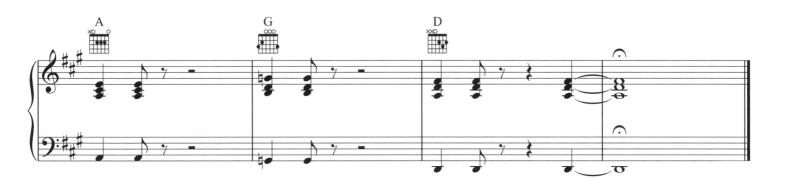

SUMMER IN THE CITY

Words and Music by JOHN SEBASTIAN,
STEVE BOONE and MARK SEBASTIAN

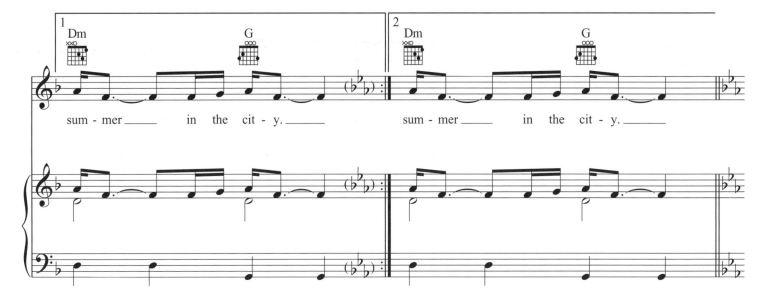

1 Dm · G · summer ___ in the cit - y. ___

2 Dm · G · summer ___ in the cit - y. ___

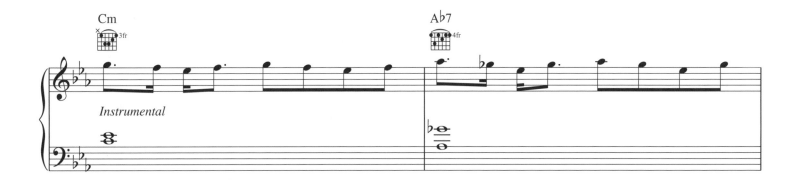

Cm · Ab7

Instrumental

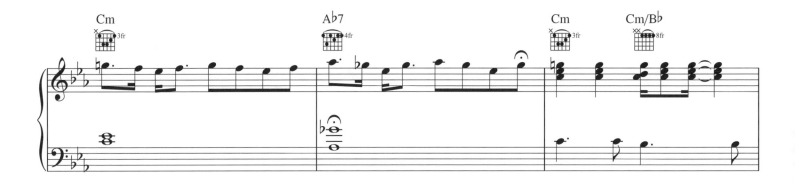

Cm · Ab7 · Cm · Cm/Bb

D.S. and Fade
(Instrumental)

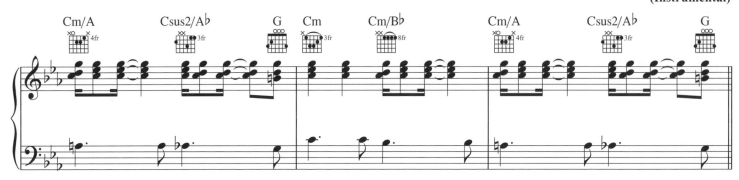

Cm/A · Csus2/Ab · G · Cm · Cm/Bb · Cm/A · Csus2/Ab · G

SUNSHINE
(Go Away Today)

Written by
JONATHAN EDWARDS

Moderately

Sun-shine go __ a - way to - day, __ I don't feel much __ like __
Sun-shine go __ a - way to - day, __ I don't feel much __ like __

danc - in'. __ Some man's gone __ and tried to run my __ life. __ He
danc - in'. __ Some man's gone __ and tried to run my __ life. __ He

don't know what __ he's __ ask - in'. When
don't know what __ he's __ ask - in'.

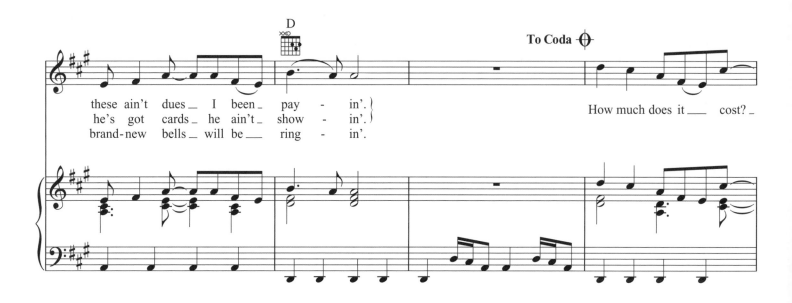

I'll buy __ it. The time is all __ we've __ lost. __ I'll try __ it, 'n'

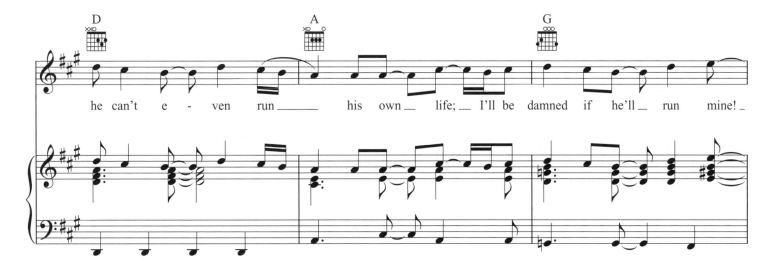

he can't e - ven run _____ his own __ life; __ I'll be damned if he'll __ run mine! __

D.S. al Coda

Sun - shine, __ Sun - shine, __

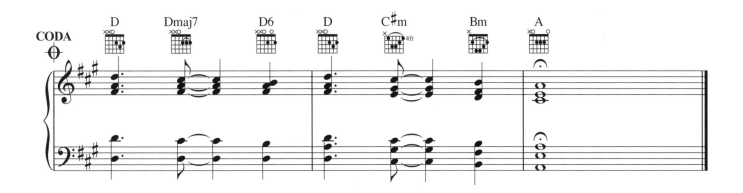

CODA

SUNSHINE ON MY SHOULDERS

Words by JOHN DENVER
Music by JOHN DENVER,
MIKE TAYLOR and DICK KNISS

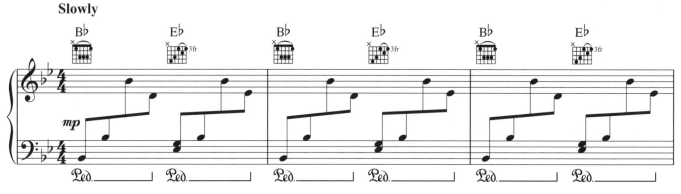

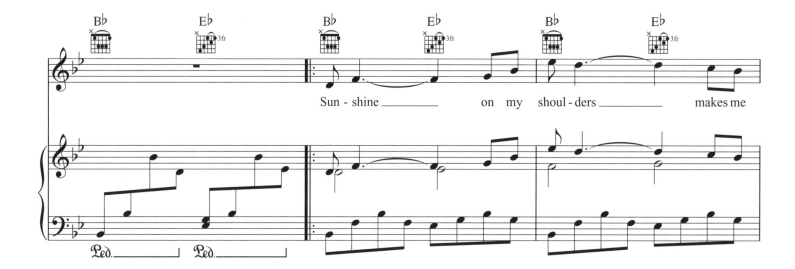

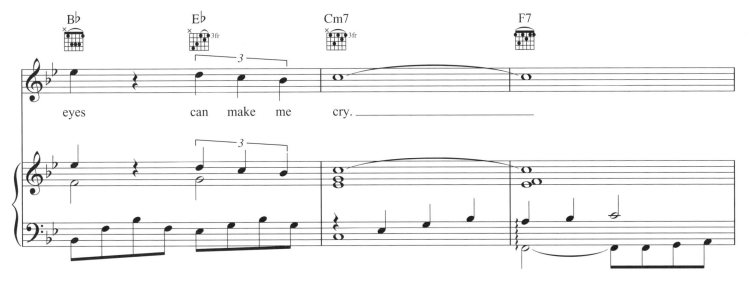

eyes can make me cry. _____

Sun - shine _____ on the wa - ter _____ looks so love - ly. _____

Sun - shine _____ al - most al - ways _____ makes me

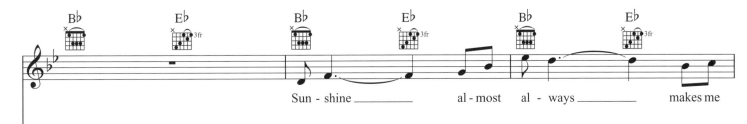

high. _____

If I had a
If I had a

day that I could give you, _____ I'd
tale that I could tell you, _____ I'd

give to you _____ a day just like to - day. _____
tell a tale _____ sure to make you smile. _____

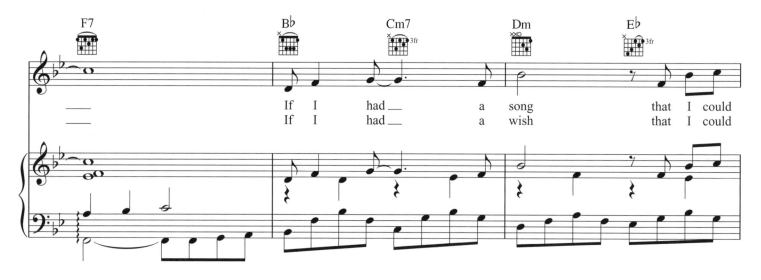

_____ If I had _____ a song that I could
_____ If I had _____ a wish that I could

sing for you, _ I'd sing a song _____ to
wish for you, _ I'd make a wish _____ for

make you feel this way. _____

sun - shine all the while. _____

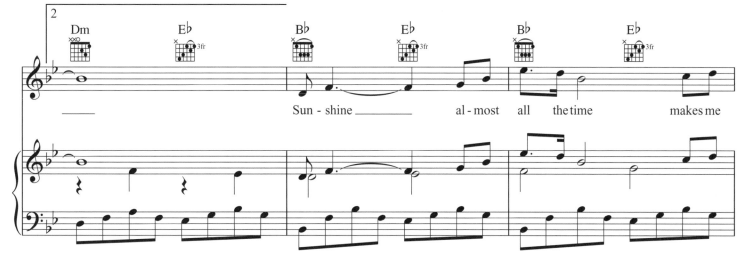

___ Sun - shine _____ al - most all the time makes me

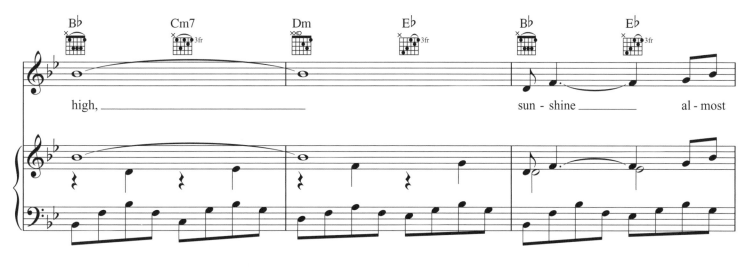

high, _____ sun - shine _____ al - most

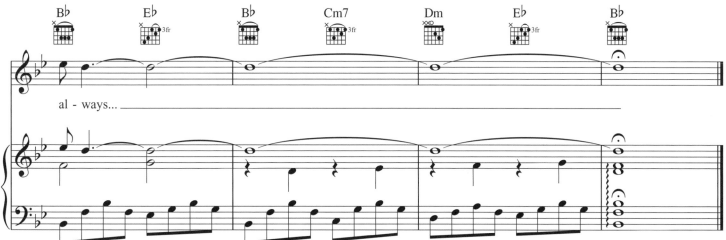

al - ways... _____

SUZANNE

Words and Music by
LEONARD COHEN

Madrigal mode

1. Su - zanne takes you
Je - sus was a
zanne takes you

down _____ to her place by the riv - er. You can
sail - or when He walked up - on the wa - ter. And He
down _____ to her place by the riv - er. You can

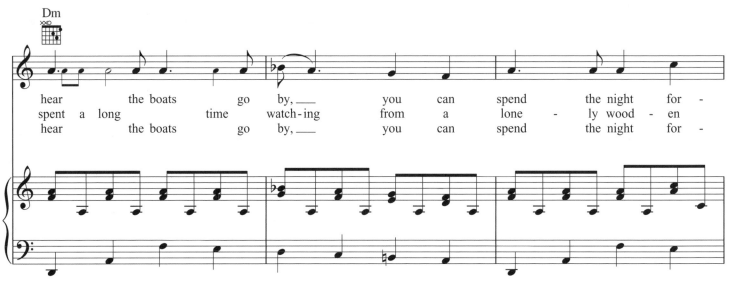

hear the boats go by, ___ you can spend the night for -
spent a long time watch - ing from a lone - ly wood - en
hear the boats go by, ___ you can spend the night for -

THIS LAND IS YOUR LAND

Words and Music by
WOODY GUTHRIE

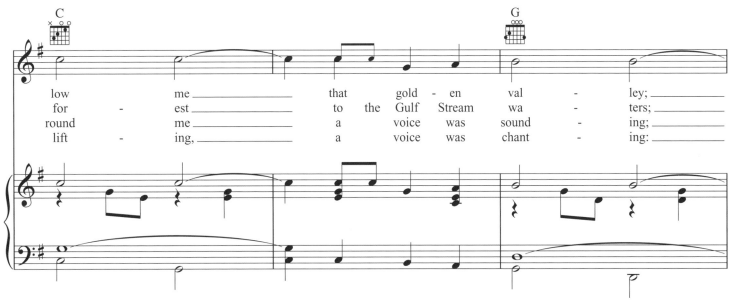

low me _____ that gold - en val - ley; _____
for - est _____ to the Gulf Stream wa - ters; _____
round me _____ a voice was sound - ing; _____
lift - ing, _____ a voice was chant - ing: _____

this land was made for you and

me. _____

{ 2.,4.,6. This land is
3. I've roamed and
5. Well, the sun came

me. _____

rit.

THOSE WERE THE DAYS

Words and Music by
GENE RASKIN

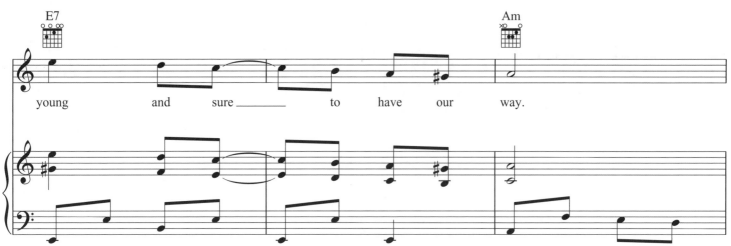

young and sure _____ to have our way.

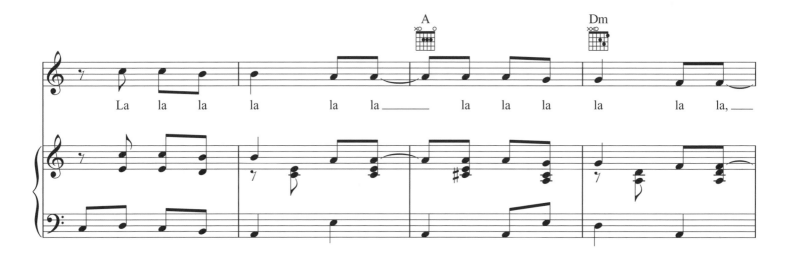

La la la la la la _____ la la la la la la, _____

_____ those were the days, oh yes, those were the

days.

days. _____

THE TIMES THEY ARE A-CHANGIN'

Words and Music by
BOB DYLAN

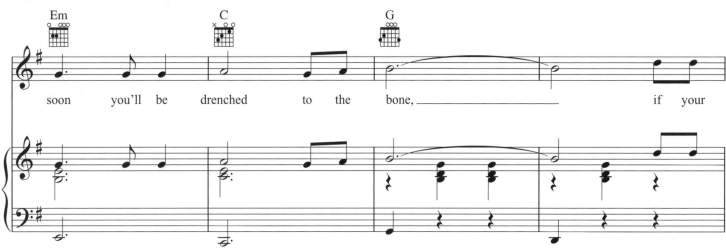

soon you'll be drenched to the bone, _____ if your

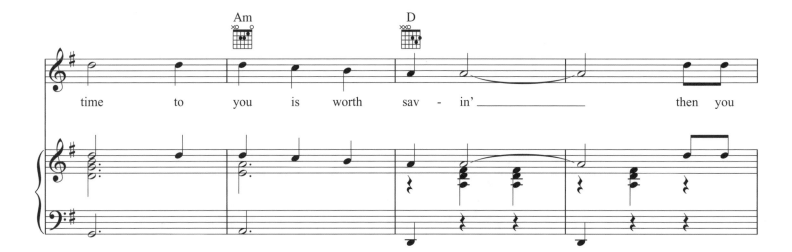

time to you is worth sav - in' _____ then you

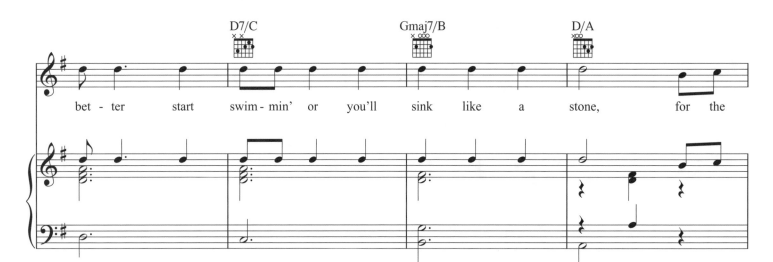

bet - ter start swim - min' or you'll sink like a stone, for the

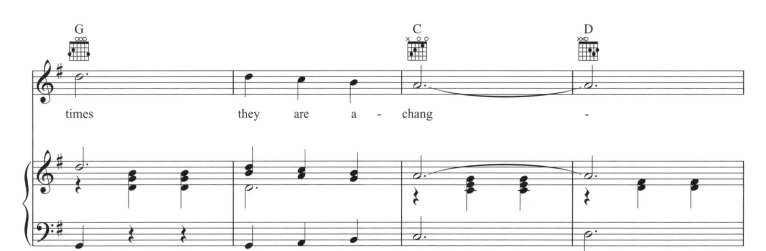

times they are a - chang -

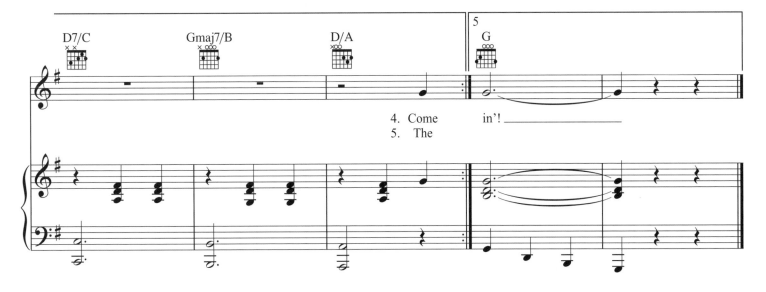

Additional Lyrics

2. Come writers and critics
   Who prophesy with your pen
   And keep your eyes wide
   The chance won't come again.
   And don't speak too soon
   For the wheel's still in spin,
   And there's no tellin' who
   That it's namin'.
   For the loser now
   Will be later to win
   For the times they are a-changin'!

3. Come senators, congressmen
   Please heed the call
   Don't stand in the doorway
   Don't block up the hall.
   For he that gets hurt
   Will be he who has stalled,
   There's a battle
   Outside and it's ragin'.
   It'll soon shake your windows
   And rattle your walls
   For the times they are a-changin'!

4. Come mothers and fathers
   Throughout the land
   And don't criticize
   What you can't understand.
   Your sons and your daughters
   Are beyond your command,
   Your old road is
   Rapidly agin'.
   Please get out of the new one
   If you can't lend your hand
   For the times they are a-changin'!

5. The line it is drawn
   The curse it is cast
   The slow one now will
   Later be fast.
   As the present now
   Will later be past,
   The order is rapidly fadin'.
   And the first one now
   Will later be last
   For the times they are a-changin'!

TIE A YELLOW RIBBON
ROUND THE OLE OAK TREE

Words and Music by L. RUSSELL BROWN
and IRWIN LEVINE

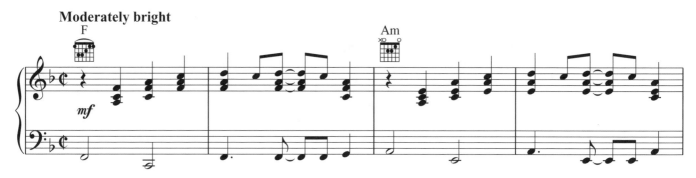

I'm com-in' home, ___ I've done my time, ___ now I've
Bus driv-er, please ___ look for me, ___ 'cause I

got to know ___ what is ___ and is-n't mine. ___ If
could-n't bear ___ to see ___ what I might see. ___ I'm

you re-ceived my let-ter tell-in' you ___ I'd soon be free, ___
real-ly still in pris-on and my love ___ she holds the key, ___ a

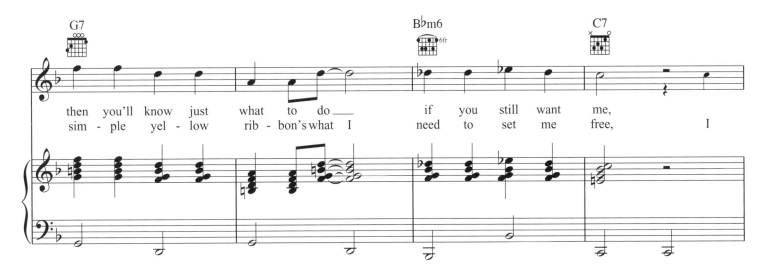

then you'll know just what to do ___ if you still want me,
sim-ple yel-low rib-bon's what I need to set me free, I

if you still want me.
wrote you and told her please: }

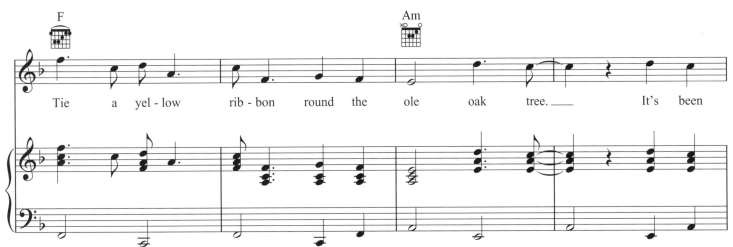

Tie a yel-low rib-bon round the ole oak tree. ___ It's been

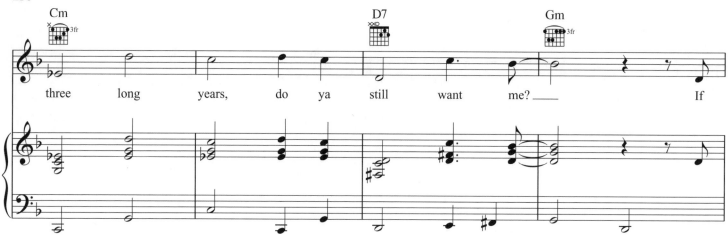

three long years, do ya still want me? ___ If

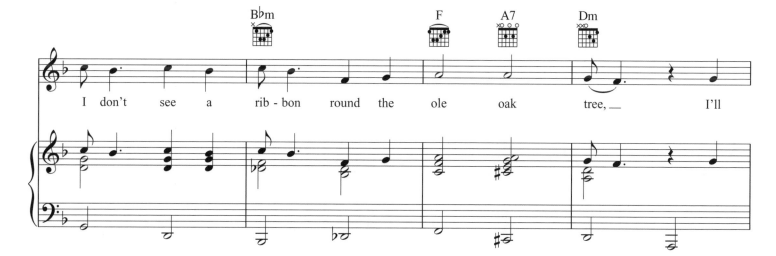

I don't see a rib-bon round the ole oak tree, ___ I'll

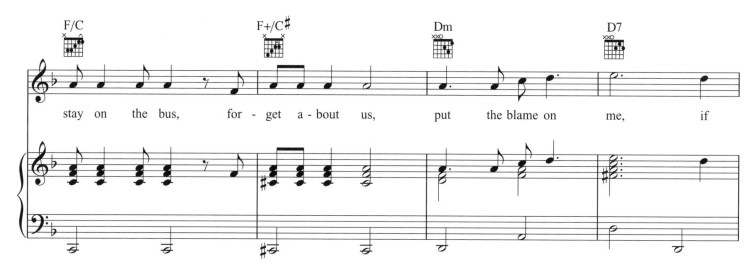

stay on the bus, for-get a-bout us, put the blame on me, if

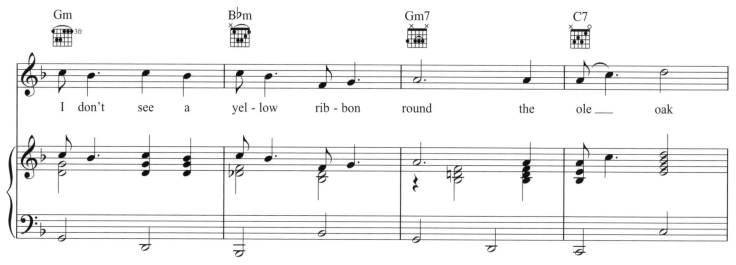

I don't see a yel-low rib-bon round the ole ___ oak

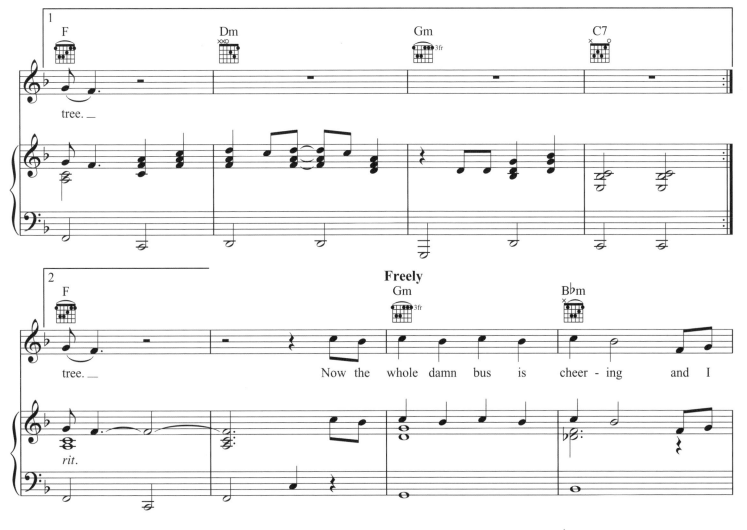

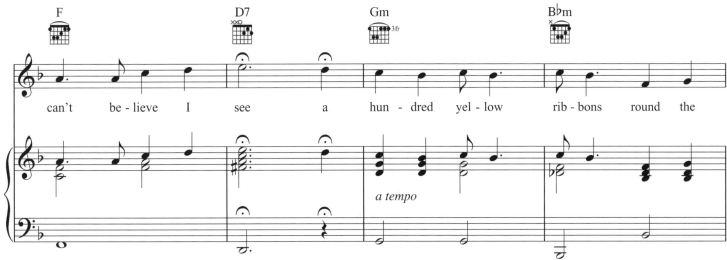

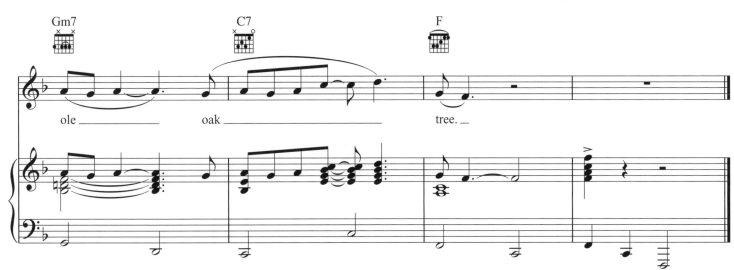

TOM DOOLEY

Words and Music Collected, Adapted and Arranged by
FRANK WARNER, JOHN A. LOMAX and ALAN LOMAX
From the singing of FRANK PROFFITT

Hang down your head, Tom Doo-ley, hang down your head and cry.

Hang down your head, Tom Doo-ley. Poor boy, you're bound __ to die. I

met her on the moun-tain, and there I took her life. I
This time to-mor-row, reck-on where I'll be? If it
This time to-mor-row, reck-on where I'll be?

met her on the moun-tain, and stabbed her with __ my knife.)
had-n'-a been for Gray-son, I'd-a been in Ten-nes-see.
In some lone-some val-ley, a-hang-in' on a white __ oak tree.)

Hang down your head, Tom Doo-ley, hang down your head and

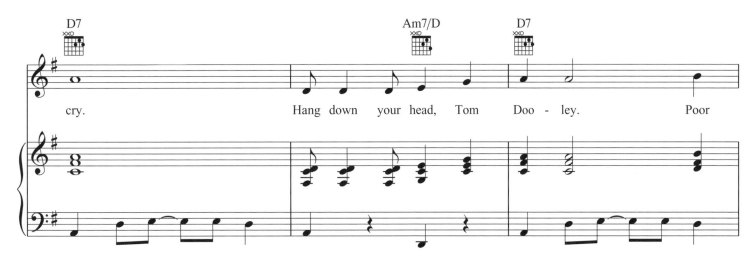

cry. Hang down your head, Tom Doo-ley. Poor

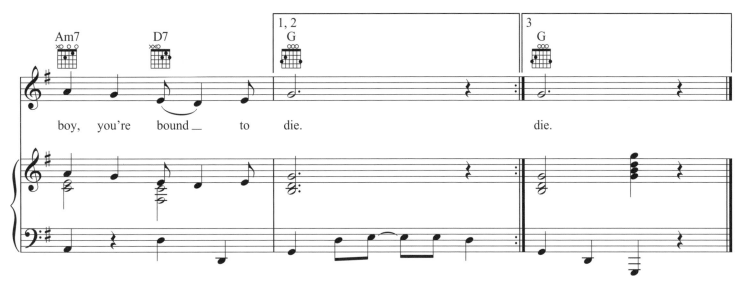

boy, you're bound __ to die. die.

TURN! TURN! TURN!
(To Everything There Is a Season)

Adaptation and Music by PETE SEEGER
Words from the Book of Ecclesiastes

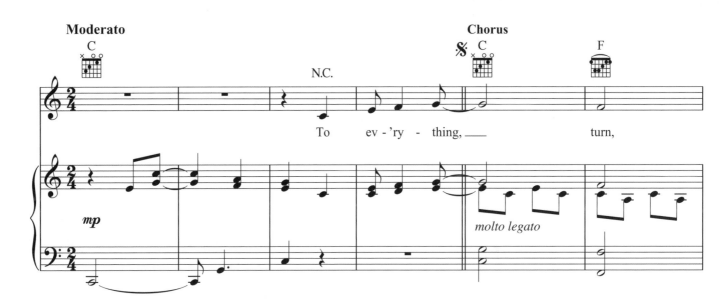

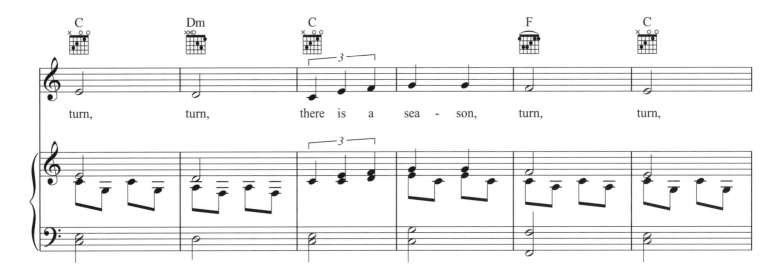

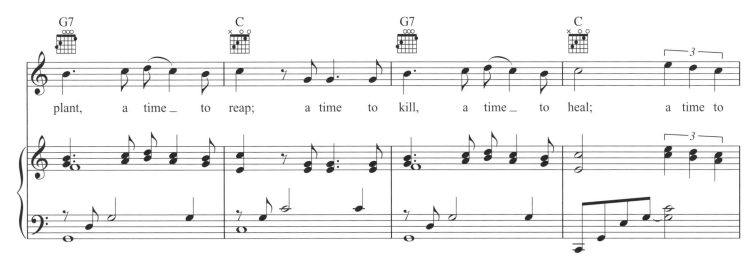

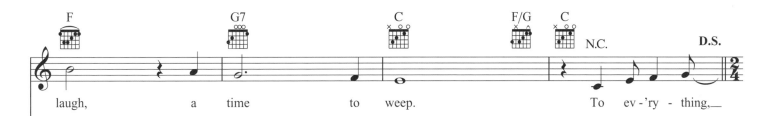

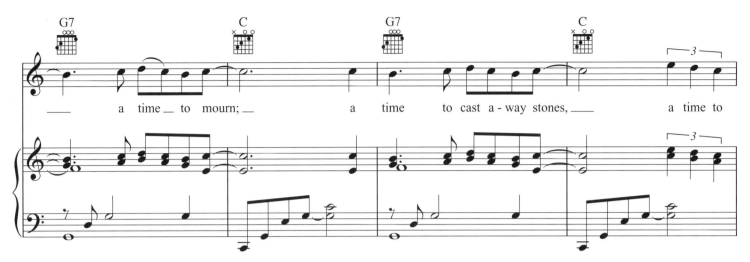

Verse 3

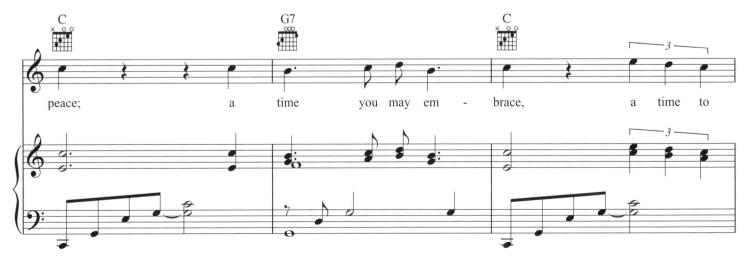

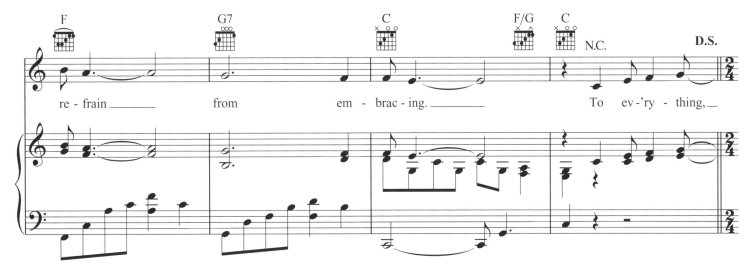

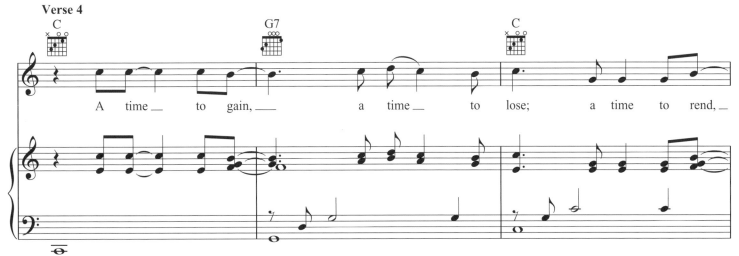

26 MILES
(Santa Catalina)

Words and Music by GLEN LARSON
and BRUCE BELLAND

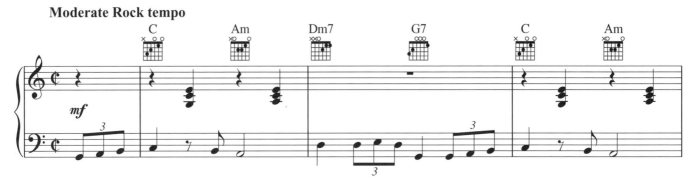

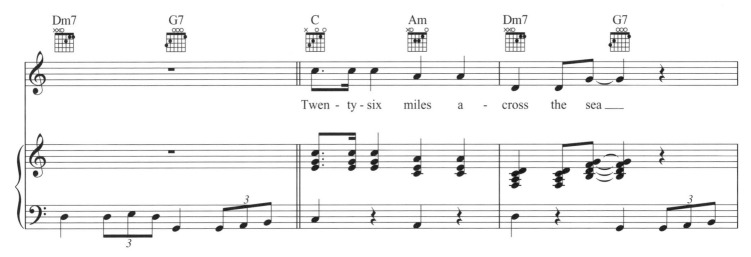

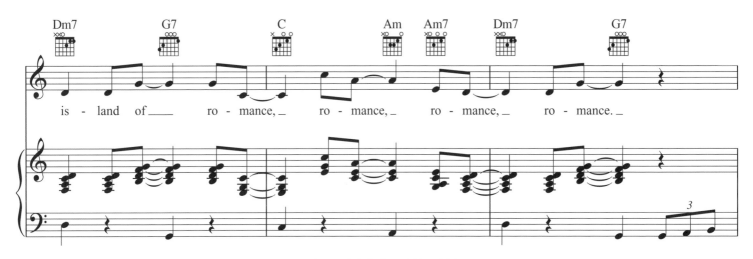

Wa - ter all a - round it ev - 'ry - where, ___ trop - i - cal trees and the

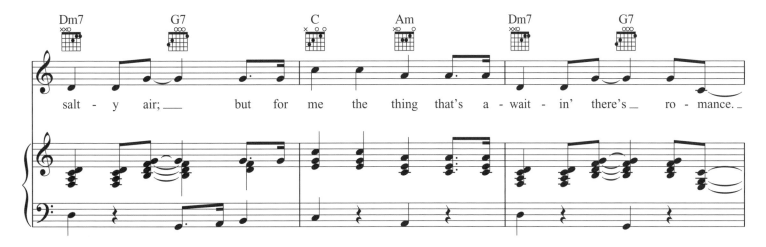

salt - y air; ___ but for me the thing that's a - wait - in' there's ___ ro - mance. ___

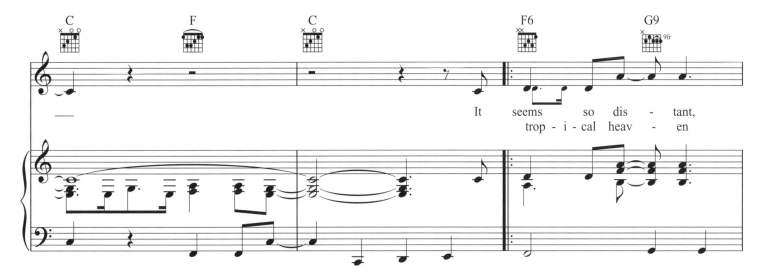

___ It seems so dis - tant, trop - i - cal heav - en

twen - ty - six miles ___ a - way, rest - in' in the wa - ter se - rene. ___ I'd
out in the o - cean cov - ered with ___ trees and girls. ___ If I

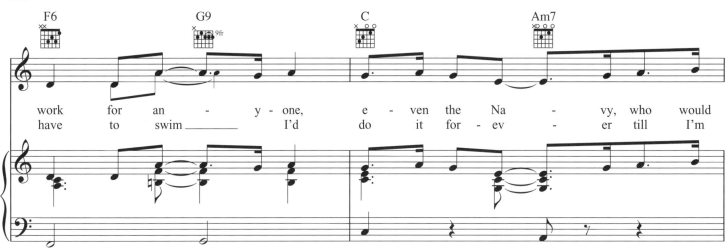

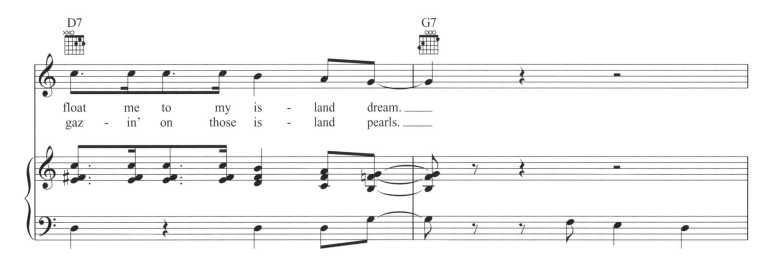

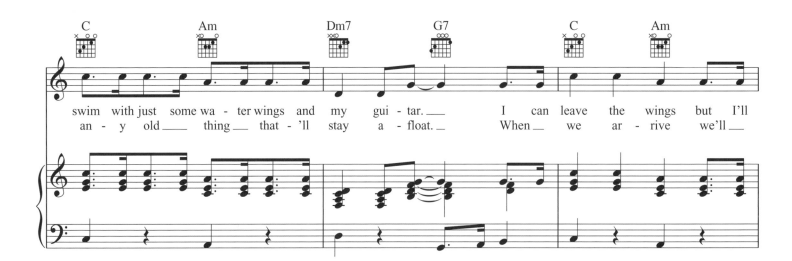

need the gui - tar ___ for ro - mance, ___ ro - mance, ___ ro - mance, ___ ro - mance. ___
all ___ pro - mote _____ ro - mance, ___ ro - mance, ___ ro - mance, _

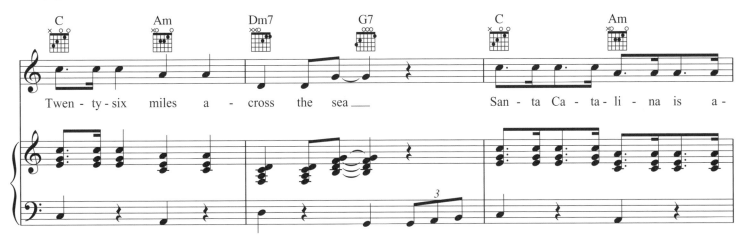

Twen - ty - six miles a - cross the sea ___ San - ta Ca - ta - li - na is a -

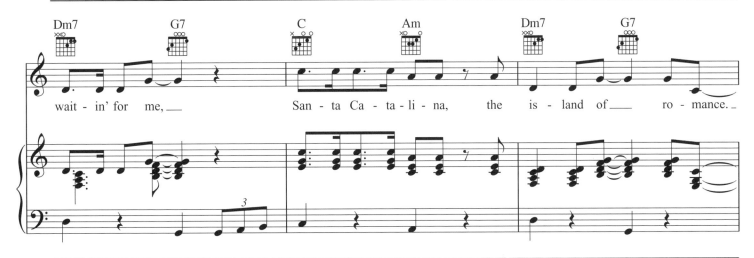

wait - in' for me, ___ San - ta Ca - ta - li - na, the is - land of ___ ro - mance. ___

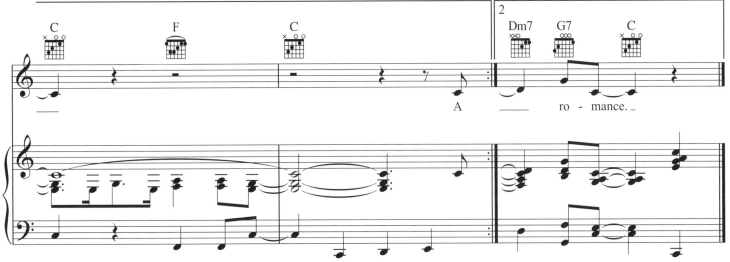

A ___ ro - mance. _

THE UNICORN

Words and Music by
SHEL SILVERSTEIN

Moderately slow

1. A long time a-go when the earth was green,＿ there was more kinds of an-i-mals than
2.–6. *(See additional lyrics)*
you've ev-er seen. And they'd run a-round free while the world was be-ing born, and the

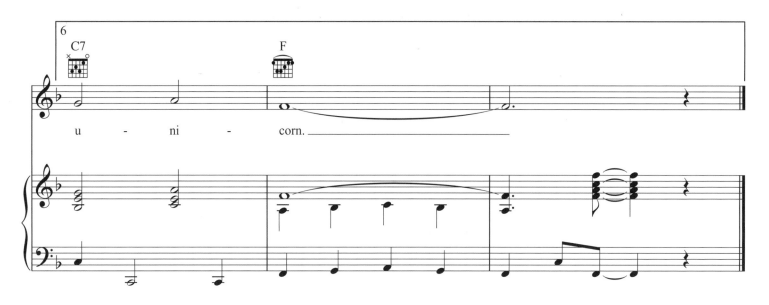

u - ni - corn. _____

Additional Lyrics

2. But the Lord seen some sinnin' and it caused him pain.
   He says, "Stand back, I'm gonna make it rain.
   So hey, Brother Noah, I'll tell you what to do.
   Go and build me a floating zoo."
Chorus
   "And you take two alligators and a couple of geese,
   Two humpback camels and two chimpanzees,
   Two cats, two rats, two elephants. But, sure as you're born,
   Noah, don't you forget my unicorns."

3. Now Noah wsa there and he answered the callin'
   And he finished up the ark as the rain started fallin'.
   Then he marched in the animals two by two,
   And he sung out as they went through:
Chorus
   "Hey Lord, I got you two alligators and a couple of geese,
   Two humpback camels and two chimpanzees,
   Two cats, two rats, two elephants. But, sure as you're born,
   Lord, I just don't see your unicorns."

4. Well, Noah looked out through the drivin' rain,
   But the unicorns was hidin' – playin' silly games.
   They were kickin' and a-splashin' while the rain was pourin'.
   Oh, them foolish unicorns.
Chorus
   "And you take two alligators and a couple of geese,
   Two humpback camels and two chimpanzees,
   Two cats, two rats, two elephants. But, sure as you're born,
   Noah, don't you forget my unicorns."

5. Then the ducks started duckin' and the snakes started snakin',
   And the elephants started elephantin' and the boat started shakin'.
   The mice started squeakin' and the lions started roarin',
   And everyone's aboard but them unicorns.
Chorus
   I mean the two alligators and a couple of geese,
   The humpback camels and the chimpanzees.
   Noah cried, "Close the door 'cause the rain is pourin',
   And we just can't wait for them unicorns."

6. And then the ark started movin' and it drifted with the tide,
   And the unicorns looked up from the rock and cried.
   And the water came up and sort of floated them away,
   That's why you've never seen a unicorn to this day.
Chorus
   You'll see a lot of alligators and a whole mess of geese,
   You'll see humpback camels and chimpanzees,
   You'll see cats and rats and elephants. But, sure as you're born,
   You're never gonna see no unicorn.

WALKING IN THE SUNSHINE

Words and Music by
ROGER MILLER

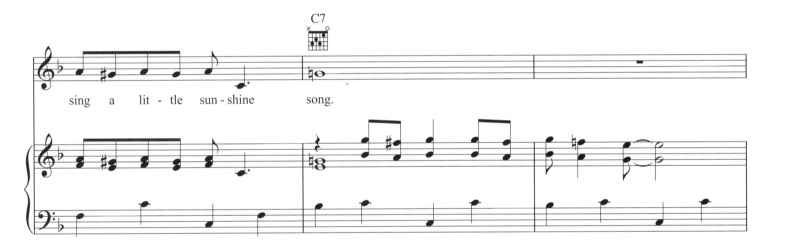

Think a-bout a good time had a long time a-go;

Bb

think a-bout for-get-ting a-bout your wor-ries and your woes.

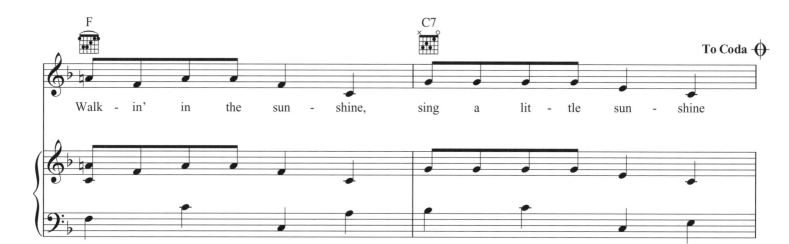

F   C7   To Coda ⊕

Walk-in' in the sun - shine, sing a lit - tle sun - shine

F   Bb

song.   La la la la

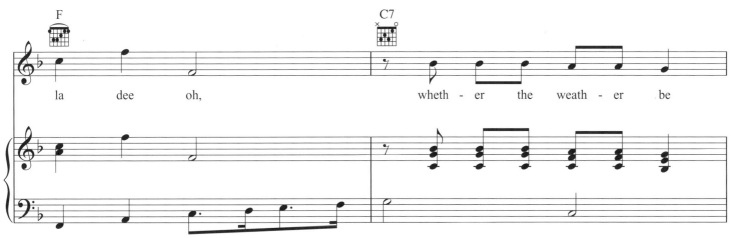

la dee oh, wheth - er the weath - er be

rain or snow, ____ pre - tend - ing can

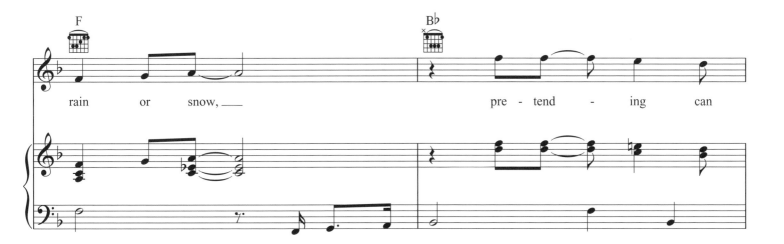

make it real; a snow - y pas - ture, a green and grass - y field.

D.S. al Coda

CODA

song. ____

WALK RIGHT IN

Words and Music by GUS CANNON
and H. WOODS

on.
Ev - 'ry - bod - y's talk - in' 'bout a new way o' walk - in'.

down.
Ev - 'ry - bod - y's talk - in' 'bout a new way o' walk - in'.

Do you want - a lose ___ your mind? _____ Walk right in, ___

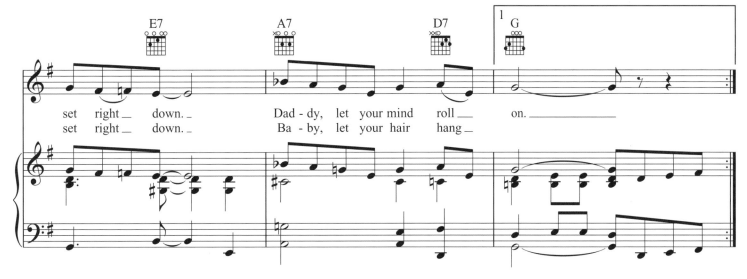

set right ___ down. ___ Dad - dy, let your mind roll ___ on. _____

set right ___ down. ___ Ba - by, let your hair hang ___

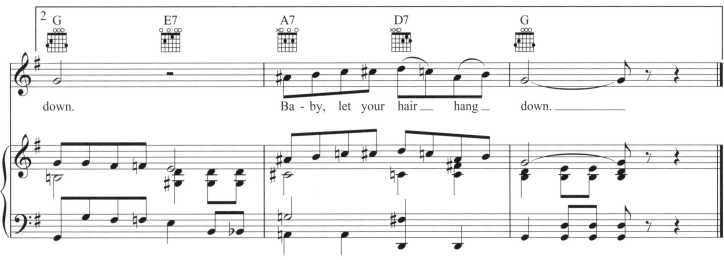

down.
Ba - by, let your hair ___ hang ___ down. _____

WE'LL SING IN THE SUNSHINE

Words and Music by
GALE GARNETT

We'll sing in the sun - shine, _____ we'll laugh ev - 'ry day; _____

we'll sing in the sun - shine _____ and I'll be on my way.

I will nev - er love _____ you; _____ the cost of love's too dear. _____
sing to you each morn - ing, _____ I'll kiss you ev - 'ry night. _____
dad - dy, he once told _____ me, don't love you an - y {man.
{wom -
when our year has end - ed _____ and I have gone a - way, _____

WHAT HAVE THEY DONE TO MY SONG, MA?

Words and Music by
MELANIE SAFKA

In slow 2

1. Look what they've done to my song, Ma.
2. Look what they've done to my brain, Ma.
3. I wish I could find a good book to live in.

4–8. *(See additional lyrics)*

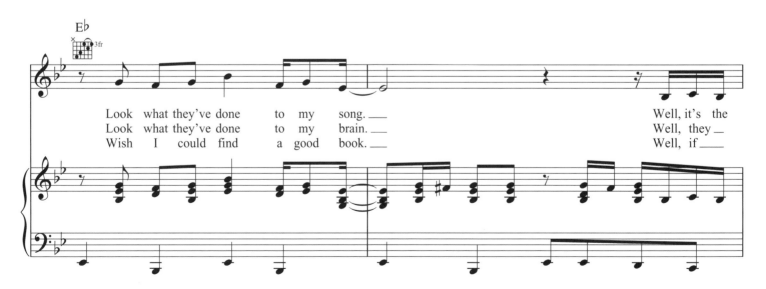

Look what they've done to my song. Well, it's the
Look what they've done to my brain. Well, they
Wish I could find a good book. Well, if

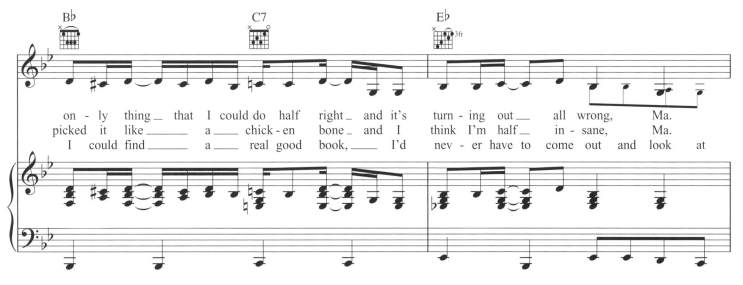

on-ly thing _ that I could do half right _ and it's turn-ing out _ all wrong, Ma.
picked it like _____ a _ chick-en bone _ and I think I'm half _ in-sane, Ma.
I could find _____ a _ real good book, _____ I'd nev-er have to come out and look at

Play 8 times

Look what they've done _ to my song.
Look what they've done _ to my song.
what they've done _ to my song.

9. Look what they've done _ to my song, Ma, Ma. _

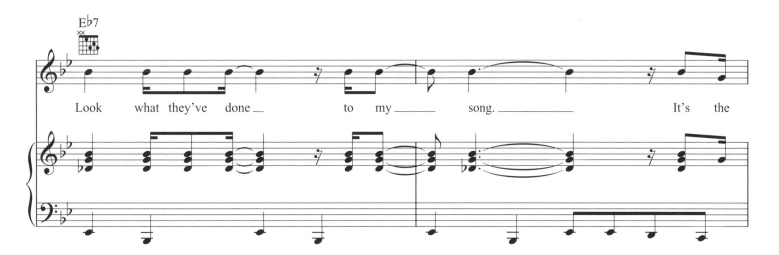

Look what they've done _ to my _____ song. _____ It's the

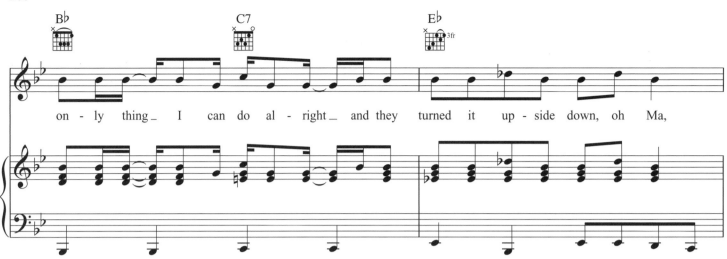

on-ly thing _ I can do al - right _ and they turned it up - side down, oh Ma,

look _ what they've done _ to my song. _ song.

Additional Lyrics

4. La da da da...
   Look what they've done to my song.

5. Maybe it'll all be alright, Ma
   Maybe it'll all be okay
   Well, if the people are buying tears
   I'll be rich some day, Ma.
   Look what they've done to my song.

6. Ils ont change ma chanson ma
   Ils ont change ma chanson
   C'est la seule chose que je peuz faire
   Et ce n'est pas bon ma
   Ils ont change ma chanson.

7. Look what they've done to my song, Ma
   Look what they've done to my song, Ma
   Well they tied it in a plastic bag
   And they turned it upside down, Ma.
   Look what they've done to my song.

8. Ils ont change ma chanson ma
   Ils ont change ma chanson
   C'est la seule chose que je peuz faire
   Et ce n'est pas bon ma
   Ils ont change ma chanson.

WHERE HAVE ALL THE FLOWERS GONE?

Words and Music by
PETE SEEGER

Moderately slow, with simplicity

1. Where have all the flow-ers gone? Long time pass - ing.
3., 5. *(See additional lyrics)*

Where have all the flow-ers gone? Long time a - go.

Where have all the flow-ers gone? The girls have picked them, ev - 'ry one.

Additional Lyrics

3. Where have all the young men gone? Long time passing.
   Where have all the young men gone? Long time ago.
   Where have all the young men gone?
   They're all in uniform.
   Oh, when will they ever learn?
   Oh, when will they ever learn?

4. Where have all the soldiers gone? Long time passing.
   Where have all the soldiers gone? Long time ago.
   Where have all the soldiers gone?
   They've gone to graveyards, every one.
   Oh, when will they ever learn?
   Oh, when will they ever learn?

5. Where have all the graveyards gone? Long time passing.
   Where have all the graveyards gone? Long time ago.
   Where have all the graveyards gone?
   They're covered with flowers, every one.
   Oh, when will they ever learn?
   Oh, when will they ever learn?

6. Where have all the flowers gone? Long time passing.
   Where have all the flowers gone? Long time ago.
   Where have all the flowerss gone?
   Young girls picked them, every one.
   Oh, when will they ever learn?
   Oh, when will they ever learn?

A WHITER SHADE OF PALE

Words and Music by KEITH REID,
GARY BROOKER and MATTHEW FISHER

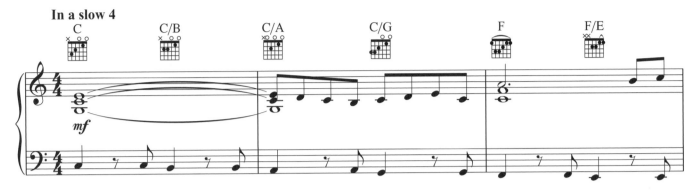

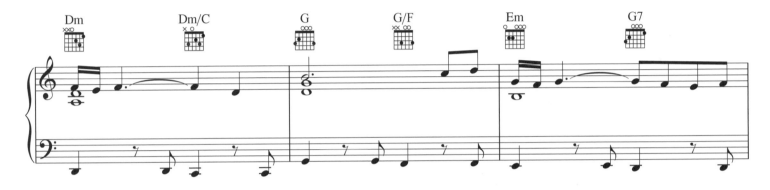

We skipped the light ___ fan - dan - go, ___
She said, "I'm home ___ on shore leave," ___
She said, "There is ___ no rea - son, ___

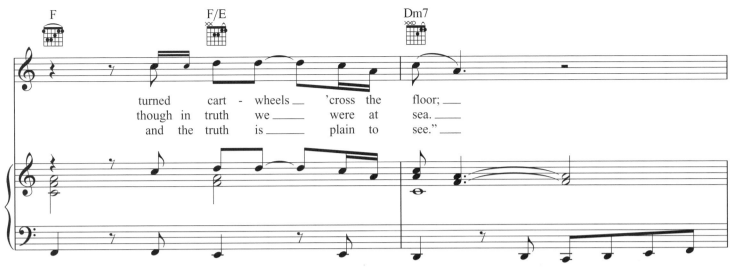

turned cart - wheels __ 'cross the floor; __
though in truth we ____ were at sea. __
and the truth is ____ plain to see."__

I was feel - ing kind of sea - sick,
So I took her by the look - ing glass
But I wan - dered through my play - ing cards

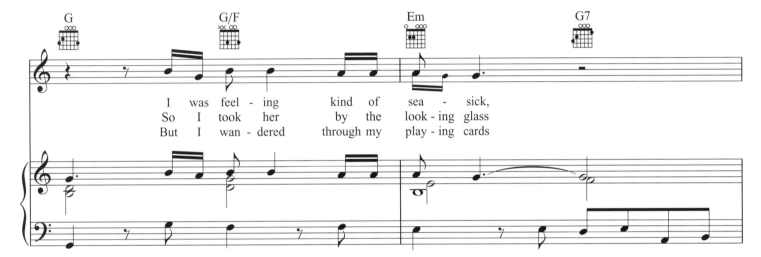

the crowd called _ out _____ for more.
and forced her __ to _____ a - gree,
and would not __ let _____ her be

The room was hum - ming hard - er
say - ing, "You must be the mer - maid
one of six - teen ves - tal vir - gins

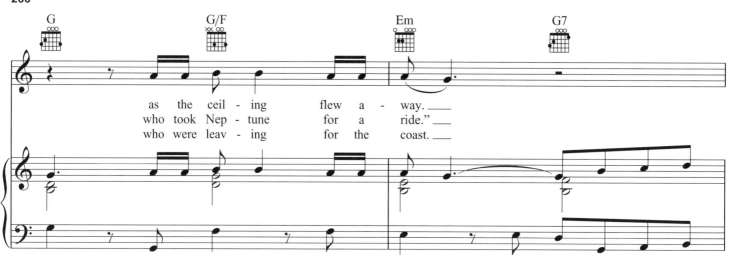

as the ceil - ing flew a - way. ___
who took Nep - tune for a ride." ___
who were leav - ing for the coast. ___

When we called out for an - oth - er drink ___
But she smiled at me so sad - ly ___
And al - though my eyes were o - pen, ___

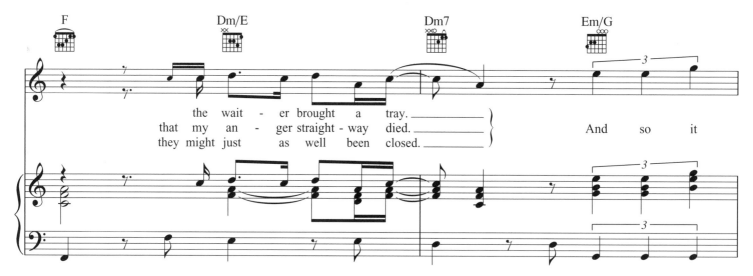

the wait - er brought a tray. ___
that my an - ger straight - way died. ___
they might just as well been closed. ___

And so it

was ___ that lat - er ___

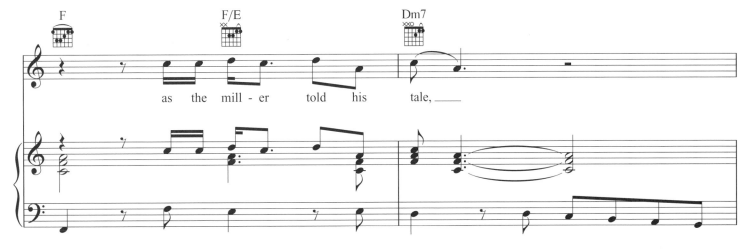

as the mill - er told his tale, ____

that her face at first just ghost - ly turned a

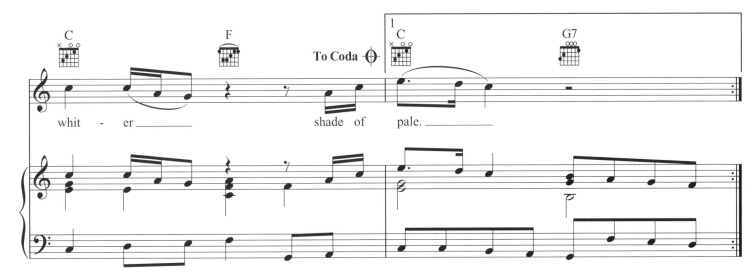

whit - er ____ shade of pale. ____

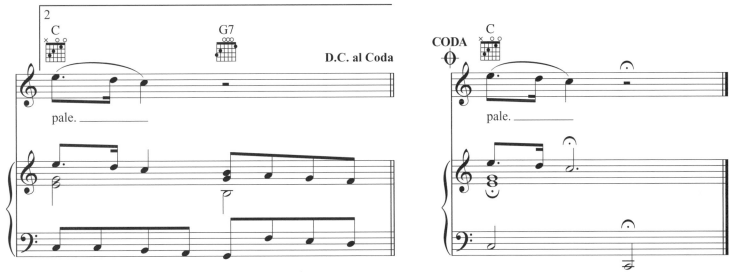

pale. ____ pale. ____

THE WRECK OF THE EDMUND FITZGERALD

Words and Music by
GORDON LIGHTFOOT

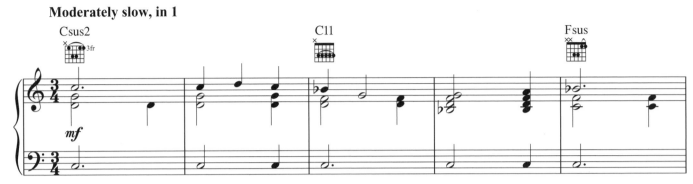

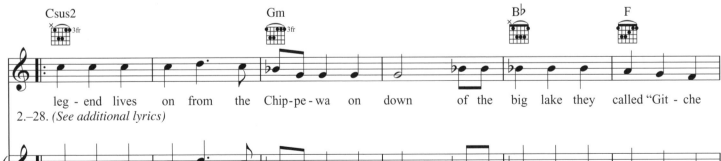

leg - end lives on from the Chip-pe - wa on down of the big lake they called "Git - che

2.–28. *(See additional lyrics)*

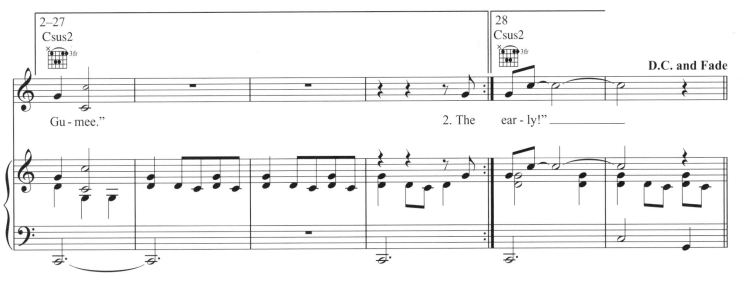

Gu - mee."   2. The   ear - ly!" _____

D.C. and Fade

Additional Lyrics

2. The lake, it is said, never gives up her dead
   When the skies of November turn gloomy.

3. With a load of iron ore twenty-six thousand tons more
   Than the Edmund Fitzgerald weighed empty.

4. That good ship and true was a bone to be chewed
   When the gales of November came early.

5. The ship was the pride of the American side
   Coming back from some mill in Wisconsin.

6. As the big freighters go it was bigger than most
   With a crew and a captain well seasoned.

7. Concluding some terms with a couple of steel firms
   When they left fully loaded for Cleveland.

8. And later that night when the ship's bell rang,
   Could it be the north wind they'd been feelin'?

9. The wind in the wires made a tattletale sound
   And a wave broke over the railing.

10. And ev'ry man knew as the captain did too
    'Twas the witch of November come stealin'.

11. The dawn came late and the breakfast had to wait
    When the gales of November came slashin'.

12. When afternoon came it was freezin' rain
    In the face of a hurricane west wind.

13. When suppertime came the old cook came on deck
    Sayin', "Fellas, it's too rough t'feed ya."

14. At seven P.M. a main hatchway caved in;
    He said, "Fellas, it's been good t'know ya!"

15. The captain wired in he had water comin' in
    And the good ship and crew was in peril.

16. And later that night when 'is lights went outta sight
    Came the wreck of the Edmund Fitzgerald.

17. Does anyone know where the love of God goes
    When the waves turn the minutes to hours?

18. The searchers all say they'd have made Whitefish Bay
    If they'd put fifteen more miles behind 'er.

19. They might have split up or they might have capsized;
    They might have broke deep and took water.

20. And all that remains is the faces and the names
    Of the wives and the sons and the daughters.

21. Lake Huron rolls, Superior sings
    In the rooms of her ice-water mansion.

22. Old Michigan steams like a young man's dreams;
    The islands and bays are for sportsmen,

23. And farther below Lake Ontario
    Takes in what Lake Erie can send her.

24. And the iron boats go as the mariners all know
    With the Gales of November remembered.

25. In a musty old hall in Detroit they prayed,
    In the "Maritime Sailors' Cathedral."

26. The church bell chimed 'til it rang twenty-nine times
    For each man on the Edmund Fitzgerald,

27. The legend lives on from the Chippewa on down
    Of the big lake they called "Gitche Gumee."

28. "Superior," they said, "never gives up her dead
    When the gales of November come early!"

THE BEST EVER
COLLECTION
ARRANGED FOR PIANO, VOICE AND GUITAR

100 of the Most Beautiful Piano Solos Ever
100 songs
00102787 ....$27.50

150 of the Most Beautiful Songs Ever
150 ballads
00360735 ....$27.00

150 More of the Most Beautiful Songs Ever
150 songs
00311318 ....$29.99

More of the Best Acoustic Rock Songs Ever
69 tunes
00311738 ....$19.95

Best Acoustic Rock Songs Ever
65 acoustic hits
00310984 ....$19.95

Best Big Band Songs Ever
68 big band hits
00359129 ....$17.99

Best Blues Songs Ever
73 blues tunes
00312874 ....$19.99

Best Broadway Songs Ever
83 songs
00309155 ....$24.99

More of the Best Broadway Songs Ever
82 songs
00311501 ....$22.95

Best Children's Songs Ever
102 songs
00310358 ....$22.99

Best Christmas Songs Ever
69 holiday favorites
00359130 ....$24.99

Best Classic Rock Songs Ever
64 hits
00310800 ....$22.99

Best Classical Music Ever
86 classical favorites
00310674 (Piano Solo) $19.95

The Best Country Rock Songs Ever
52 hits
00118881 ....$19.99

Best Country Songs Ever
78 classic country hits
00359135 ....$19.99

Best Disco Songs Ever
50 songs
00312565 ....$19.99

Best Dixieland Songs Ever
90 songs
00312326 ....$19.99

Best Early Rock 'n' Roll Songs Ever
74 songs
00310816 ....$19.95

Best Easy Listening Songs Ever
75 mellow favorites
00359193 ....$19.99

Best Gospel Songs Ever
80 gospel songs
00310503 ....$19.99

Best Hymns Ever
118 hymns
00310774 ....$18.99

Best Jazz Piano Solos Ever
80 songs
00312079 ....$19.99

Best Jazz Standards Ever
77 jazz hits
00311641 ....$19.95

More of the Best Jazz Standards Ever
74 beloved jazz hits
00311023 ....$19.95

Best Latin Songs Ever
67 songs
00310355 ....$19.99

Best Love Songs Ever
65 favorite love songs
00359198 ....$19.95

Best Movie Songs Ever
71 songs
00310063 ....$19.99

Best Praise & Worship Songs Ever
80 all-time favorites
00311057 ....$22.99

More of the Best Praise & Worship Songs Ever
76 songs
00311800 ....$24.99

Best R&B Songs Ever
66 songs
00310184 ....$19.95

Best Rock Songs Ever
63 songs
00490424 ....$18.95

Best Showtunes Ever
71 songs
00118782 ....$19.99

Best Songs Ever
72 must-own classics
00359224 ....$24.99

Best Soul Songs Ever
70 hits
00311427 ....$19.95

Best Standards Ever, Vol. 1 (A-L)
72 beautiful ballads
00359231 ....$17.95

Best Standards Ever, Vol. 2 (M-Z)
73 songs
00359232 ....$17.99

More of the Best Standards Ever, Vol. 1 (A-L)
76 all-time favorites
00310813 ....$17.95

More of the Best Standards Ever, Vol. 2 (M-Z)
75 stunning standards
00310814 ....$17.95

Best Torch Songs Ever
70 sad and sultry favorites
00311027 ....$19.95

Best Wedding Songs Ever
70 songs
00311096 ....$19.95

Prices, contents and availability subject to change without notice. Not all products available outside the U.S.A.

HAL•LEONARD® CORPORATION
7777 W. BLUEMOUND RD. P.O. BOX 13819 MILWAUKEE, WI 53213

Visit us online for complete songlists at
www.halleonard.com